Preliminary Assessment of Channel Stability and Bed-Material Transport in the Tillamook Bay Tributaries and Nehalem River Basin, Northwestern Oregon

By Krista L. Jones, Mackenzie K. Keith, Jim E. O'Connor, Joseph F. Mangano, and J. Rose Wallick

Prepared in cooperation with the U.S. Army Corps of Engineers and the Oregon Department of State Lands

Open-File Report 2012–1187

U.S. Department of the Interior
U.S. Geological Survey

U.S. Department of the Interior
KEN SALAZAR, Secretary

U.S. Geological Survey
Marcia K. McNutt, Director

U.S. Geological Survey, Reston, Virginia 2012

For product and ordering information:
World Wide Web: http://www.usgs.gov/pubprod
Telephone: 1-888-ASK-USGS

For more information on the USGS—the Federal source for science about the Earth,
its natural and living resources, natural hazards, and the environment:
World Wide Web: http://www.usgs.gov
Telephone: 1-888-ASK-USGS

Suggested citation:
Jones, K.L., Keith, M.K, O'Connor, J.E., Mangano, J.F., and Wallick, J.R., 2012, Preliminary assessment of
channel stability and bed-material transport in the Tillamook Bay tributaries and Nehalem River basin, northwestern Oregon: U.S. Geological Survey Open-File Report 2012–1187, 120 p.

Contents

Figures

Tables

Conversion Factors

Multiply	By	To obtain
Length		
centimeter (cm)	0.3937	inch (in.)
millimeter (mm)	0.03937	inch (in.)
meter (m)	3.281	foot (ft)
kilometer (km)	0.6214	mile (mi)
Area		
square meter (m^2)	10.76	square foot (ft^2)
square kilometer (km^2)	0.3861	square mile (mi^2)
Volume		
cubic meter (m^3)	0.0008107	acre-foot (acre-ft)
cubic meter (m^3)	35.31	cubic foot (ft^3)
cubic meter (m^3)	1.308	cubic yard (yd^3)
Flow rate		
cubic meter per second (m^3/s)	35.31	cubic foot per second (ft^3/s)
cubic meter per year (m^3/yr)	1.308	cubic yard per year (yd^3/yr)
meter per second (m/s)	3.281	foot per second (ft/s)
Mass		
kilogram (kg)	2.205	pound avoirdupois (lb)

Vertical coordinate information is referenced to the North American Vertical Datum of 1988 (NAVD 88).
Horizontal coordinate information is referenced to the North American Datum of 1983 (NAD 83).
Elevation, as used in this report, refers to distance above the vertical datum.

Preliminary Assessment of Channel Stability and Bed-Material Transport in the Tillamook Bay Tributaries and Nehalem River Basin, Northwestern Oregon

By Krista L. Jones, Mackenzie K. Keith, Jim E. O'Connor, Joseph F. Mangano, and J. Rose Wallick

Significant Findings

This report summarizes a preliminary study of bed-material transport, vertical and lateral channel changes, and existing datasets for the Tillamook (drainage area 156 square kilometers [km^2]), Trask (451 km^2), Wilson (500 km^2), Kilchis (169 km^2), Miami (94 km^2), and Nehalem (2,207 km^2) Rivers along the northwestern Oregon coast. This study, conducted in cooperation with the U.S. Army Corps of Engineers and Oregon Department of State Lands to inform permitting decisions regarding instream gravel mining, revealed that:

- Study areas along the six rivers can be divided into reaches based on tidal influence and topography. The fluvial (nontidal or dominated by riverine processes) reaches vary in length (2.4–9.3 kilometer [km]), gradient (0.0011–0.0075 meter of elevation change per meter of channel length [m/m]), and bed-material composition (a mixture of alluvium and intermittent bedrock outcrops to predominately alluvium). In fluvial reaches, unit bar area (square meter of bar area per meter of channel length [m^2/m]) as mapped from 2009 photographs ranged from 7.1 m^2/m on the Tillamook River to 27.9 m^2/m on the Miami River.

- In tidal reaches, all six rivers flow over alluvial deposits, but have varying gradients (0.0001–0.0013 m/m) and lengths affected by tide (1.3–24.6 km). The Miami River has the steepest and shortest tidal reach and the Nehalem River has the flattest and longest tidal reach. Bars in the tidal reaches are generally composed of sand and mud. Unit bar area was greatest in the Tidal Nehalem Reach, where extensive mud flats flank the lower channel.

- Background factors such as valley and channel confinement, basin geology, channel slope, and tidal extent control the spatial variation in the accumulation and texture of bed material. Presently, the Upper Fluvial Wilson and Miami Reaches and Fluvial Nehalem Reach have the greatest abundance of gravel bars, likely owing to local bed-material sources in combination with decreasing channel gradient and valley confinement.

- Natural and human-caused disturbances such as mass movements, logging, fire, channel modifications for navigation and flood control, and gravel mining also have varying effects on channel condition, bed-material transport, and distribution and area of bars throughout the study areas and over time.

- Existing datasets include at least 16 and 18 sets of aerial and orthophotographs that were taken of the study areas in the Tillamook Bay tributary basins and Nehalem River basin, respectively, from 1939 to 2011. These photographs are available for future assessments of long-term changes in channel condition, bar area, and vegetation establishment patterns. High resolution Light Detection And Ranging (LiDAR) surveys acquired in 2007–2009 could support future quantitative analyses of channel morphology and bed-material transport in all study areas.

- A review of deposited and mined gravel volumes reported for instream gravel mining sites shows that bed-material deposition tends to rebuild mined bar surfaces in most years. Mean annual deposition volumes on individual bars exceeded 3,000 cubic meters (m^3) on Donaldson Bar on the Wilson River, Dill Bar on the Kilchis River, and Plant and Winslow Bars on the Nehalem River. Cumulative reported volumes of bed-material deposition were greatest at Donaldson and Dill Bars, totaling over 25,000 m^3 per site from 2004 to 2011. Within this period, reported cumulative mined volumes were greatest for the Donaldson, Plant, and Winslow Bars, ranging from 24,470 to 33,940 m^3.

- Analysis of historical stage-streamflow data collected by the U.S. Geological Survey on the Wilson River near Tillamook (14301500) and Nehalem River near Foss (14301000) shows that these rivers have episodically aggraded and incised, mostly following high flow events, but they do not exhibit systematic, long-term trends in bed elevation.

- Multiple cross sections show that channels near bridge crossings in all six study areas are dynamic with many subject to incision and aggradation as well as lateral shifts in thalweg position and bank deposition and erosion.

- In fluvial reaches, unit bar area declined a net 5.3–83.6 percent from 1939 to 2009. The documented reduction in bar area may be attributable to several factors, including vegetation establishment and stabilization of formerly active bar surfaces, lateral channel changes and resulting alterations in sediment deposition and erosion patterns, and streamflow and/or tide differences between photo-

graphs. Other factors that may be associated with the observed reduction in bar area but not assessed in this reconnaissance level study include changes in the sediment and hydrology regimes of these rivers over the analysis period.

- In tidal reaches, unit bar area increased on the Tillamook and Nehalem Rivers (98.0 and 14.7 percent, respectively), but declined a net 24.2 to 83.1 percent in the other four tidal reaches. Net increases in bar area in the Tidal Tillamook and Nehalem Reaches were possibly attributable to tidal differences between the photographs as well as sediment deposition behind log booms and pile structures on the Tillamook River between 1939 and 1967.

- The armoring ratio (ratio of the median grain sizes of a bar's surface and subsurface layers) was 1.6 at Lower Waldron Bar on the Miami River, tentatively indicating a relative balance between transport capacity and sediment supply at this location. Armoring ratios, however, ranged from 2.4 to 5.5 at sites on the Trask, Wilson, Kilchis, and Nehalem Rivers; these coarse armor layers probably reflect limited bed-material supply at these sites.

- On the basis of mapping results, measured armoring ratios, and channel cross section surveys, preliminary conclusions are that the fluvial reaches on the Tillamook, Trask, Kilchis, and Nehalem Rivers are currently sediment supply-limited in terms of bed material—that is, the transport capacity of the channel generally exceeds the supply of bed material. The relation between transport capacity and sediment is more ambiguous for the fluvial reaches on the Wilson and Miami Rivers, but transport-limited conditions are likely for at least parts of these reaches. Some of these reaches have possibly evolved from sediment supply-limited to transport-limited over the last several decades in response to changing basin and climate conditions.

- Because of exceedingly low gradients, all the tidal reaches are transport-limited. Bed material in these reaches, however, is primarily sand and finer grain-size material and probably transported as suspended load from upstream reaches. These reaches will be most susceptible to watershed conditions affecting the supply and transport of fine sediment.

- Compared to basins on the southwestern Oregon coast, such as the Chetco and Rogue River basins, these six basins likely transport overall less gravel bed material. Although tentative in the absence of actual transport measurements, this conclusion is supported by the much lower area and frequency of bars and longer tidal reaches along all the north-coast rivers examined in this study.

- Previous studies suggest that the expansive and largely unvegetated bars visible in the 1939 photographs are primarily associated with voluminous sedimentation starting soon after the first Tillamook Burn fire in 1933. However, USGS studies of temporal bar trends in other Oregon coastal rivers unaffected by the Tillamook Burn show similar declines in bar area over approximately the same analysis period. In the Umpqua and Chetco River basins, historical declines in bar area are associated with long-term decreases in flood magnitude. Other factors may include changes in the type and volume of large wood and riparian vegetation. Further characterization of hydrology patterns in these basins and possible linkages with climate factors related to flood peaks, such as the Pacific Decadal Oscillation, could support inferences of expected future changes in vegetation establishment and channel planform and profile.

- More detailed investigations of bed-material transport rates and channel morphology would support assessments of lateral and vertical channel condition and longitudinal trends in bed material. Such assessments would be most practical for the fluvial study areas on the Wilson, Kilchis, Miami, and Nehalem Rivers and relevant to several ongoing management and ecological issues pertaining to sand and gravel transport. Tidal reaches may also be logical subjects for in-depth analysis where studies would be more relevant to the deposition and transport of fine sediment (and associated channel and riparian conditions and processes) rather than coarse bed material.

Introduction

This report summarizes a reconnaissance level study of channel condition and bed-material transport relevant to the permitting of instream gravel mining in six basins—the Tillamook, Trask, Wilson, Kilchis, Miami, and Nehalem River basins—on the northwestern Oregon coast (figs. 1 and 2). The Tillamook, Trask, Wilson, Kilchis, and Miami River basins are collectively referred to as the Tillamook Bay subbasins in this report. The study included a review of existing datasets (such as channel cross sections and instream gravel mining records), delineation of bars and wetted channels from aerial and orthophotographs spanning 1939–2009, and field observations and bed-material measurements made in October 2010. From these efforts, we identified key datasets and issues relevant to understanding channel condition, bed-material transport, and the potential effects of instream gravel mining on both; assessed vertical and lateral channel stability; and made preliminary conclusions regarding the relation between sediment supply and transport capacity for the six study areas. This reconnaissance level study is a "Phase I" assessment similar to those completed for the Umpqua River (O'Connor and others, 2009), Rogue River (Jones and others, 2012a), Coquille River (Jones and others, 2012b), and Hunter Creek (Jones and others, 2011) basins, in cooperation with the U.S. Army Corps of Engineers (hereafter Corps of Engineers) and the Oregon Department of State Lands to inform the permitting of instream gravel mining in Oregon.

Locations and Reporting Units

Locations within the six study areas (described below) are referenced to river kilometers (RKM). To develop this reference system, centerlines were digitized for the wetted channel of each river starting at locations indicated on figures 1 and 2 using orthoimagery acquired in 2009 by the U.S. Department of Agriculture's (USDA) National Agriculture Imagery Program (NAIP). Points were distributed at 0.2-km intervals along these centerlines, and the values increase in the upstream direction. After accounting for the conversion between river kilometers and river miles (RM), this reference system differs slightly from RM shown on recent U.S. Geological Survey (USGS) topographic quadrangle maps (1984–1986 for the Tillamook Bay subbasins; 1984–1985 for the Nehalem River). The discrepancies probably owe to factors such as slightly different starting points of the reference systems, recent changes in channel positions, and resolution at which they were mapped (figs. 1 and 2).

In this publication, we present all data collected and analyzed in this study as well as most data reported by other sources in metric (International System) units. Conversions to inch-pound (English) units are provided in the front matter of the report.

Study Basins

The Tillamook, Trask, Wilson, Kilchis, and Miami Rivers flow into Tillamook Bay near the towns of Tillamook and Garibaldi (fig. 1). In total, the five Tillamook Bay rivers have a drainage area of 1,369 km^2 and over 930 km of mapped streams (table 1). The Wilson and Trask River basins cover the largest areas (500 and 451 km^2, respectively) whereas the Tillamook and Kilchis Rivers encompass similar sized areas (156 and 169 km^2, respectively) and the Miami River the smallest area (94 km^2). The length of river affected by tide increases clockwise around the bay, with tidal river segments beginning at RKM 1.3 on the Miami River and RKM 10.2 on the Tillamook River (Oregon Department of State Lands, 2007). The five Tillamook Bay subbasins are within Tillamook, Washington, and Yamhill Counties. They are bordered by the Nehalem River basin to the north, Tualatin River basin to the east, Yamhill River basin to the southeast, and Nestucca River basin to the south.

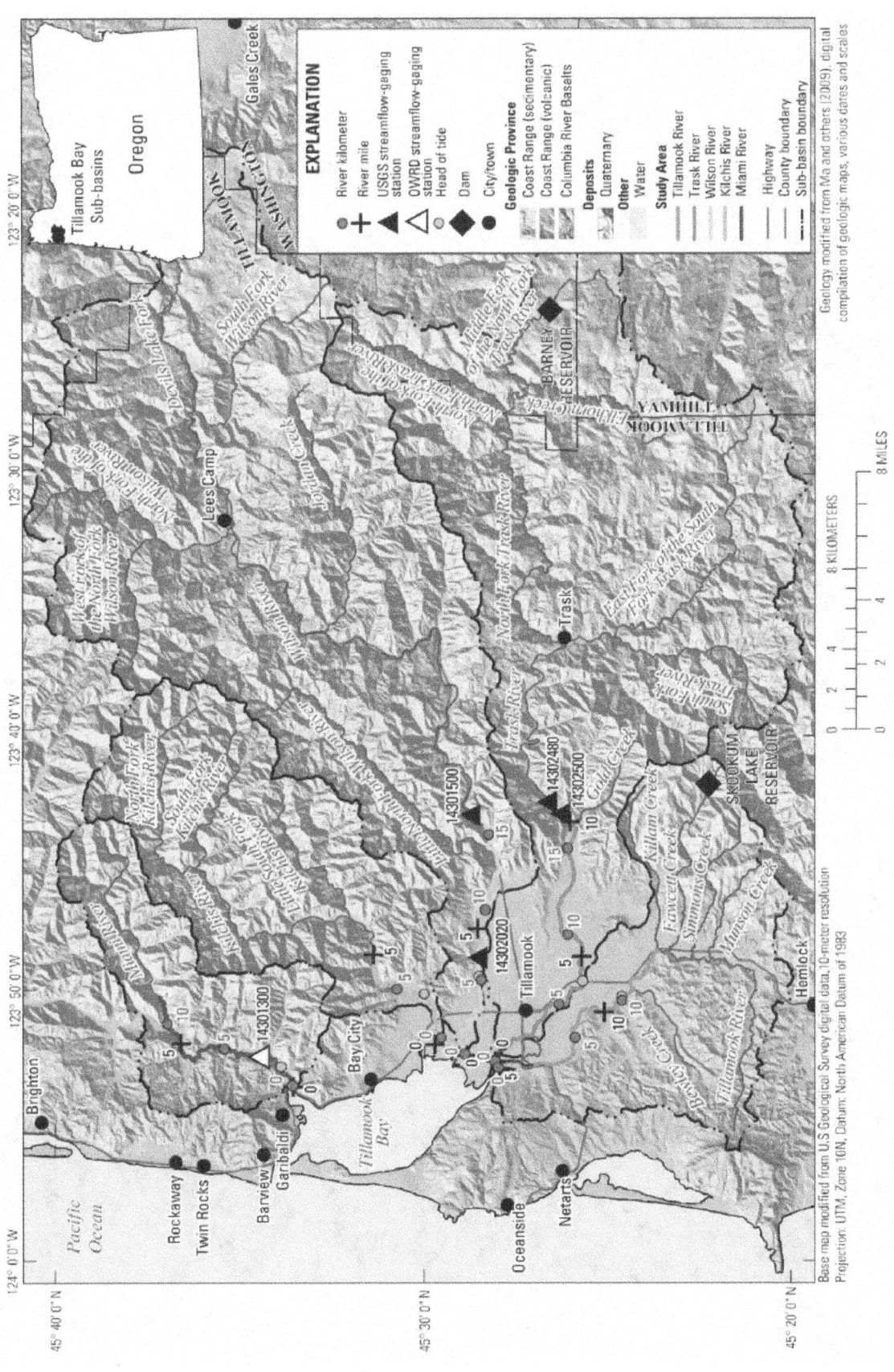

Figure 1. Map showing the stream network, basin and county boundaries, geologic provinces, study reaches, linear reference systems, streamflow-gaging stations, and other features in the Tillamook, Trask, Wilson, Kilchis, and Miami River basins, northwestern Oregon

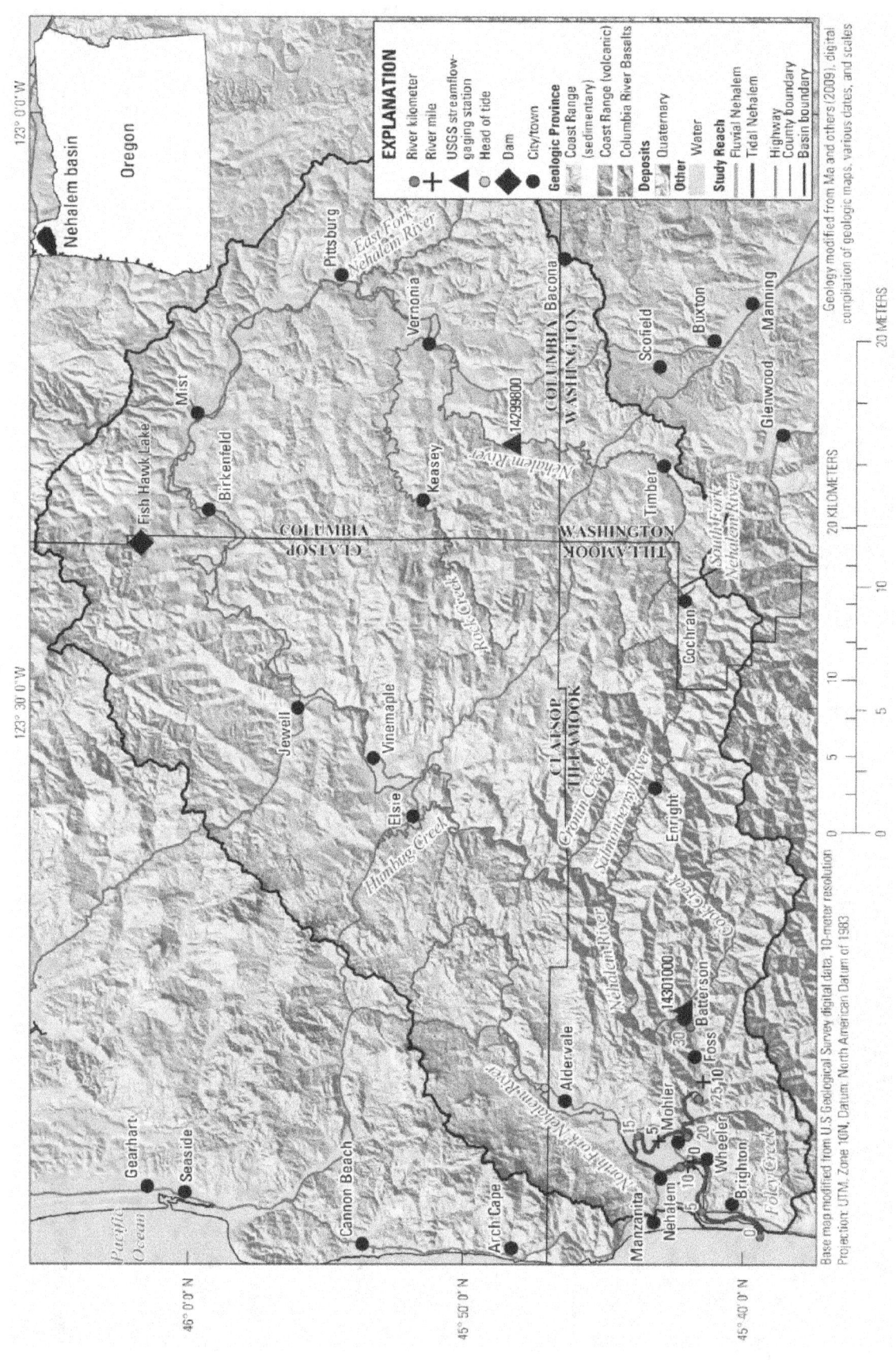

Figure 2. Map showing the stream network, basin and county boundaries, geologic provinces, study reaches, linear reference systems, streamflow-gaging stations, and other features in the Nehalem River basin, northwestern Oregon

6

To the north of the Tillamook Bay sub-basins, the larger Nehalem River (2,207 km^2) flows into Nehalem Bay near the towns of Nehalem and Brighton (fig. 2) and has nearly 1,500 km of mapped streams (table 1). Tide affects a substantially longer section (24.6 km) of the Nehalem River compared to the Tillamook Bay subbasins. The Nehalem River basin is bordered to the northwest by the Necanicum River basin, to the north and east by tributaries to the Columbia River, and to the south by the Tualatin, Wilson, Kilchis, and Miami River basins. The Nehalem River flows through Tillamook, Washington, Columbia, and Clatsop Counties.

Geomorphic and Geologic Setting

All six basins have rugged uplands, which abruptly transition downstream to lowland floodplains that make up relatively smaller portions of the basins (figs. 1 and 2). The steep uplands are chiefly underlain by Eocene volcanic and sedimentary rocks (Walker, 1991). These areas are extensively affected by mass movements, including shallow landslides, debris flows, and deeper earthflows and landslides (Tillamook Bay Taskforce and others, 1978; Johnson and Maser, 1999; Snyder and others, 2001; Snyder and others, 2003; Duck Creek Associates, 2008;

Reckendorf, 2008a). The valleys are mainly carved into the softer sedimentary rocks and are locally flanked by Quaternary alluvium as well as marine terraces and dunes near the coast.

Bedrock palisades on the Wilson River upstream of the study area.

Table 1. Drainage characteristics of the Tillamook Bay subbasins and Nehalem River basin, northwestern Oregon. Data determined at the mouth of the rivers.

[km^2, square kilometer; km, kilometer; RKM, river kilometer]

River basin	Attribute			
	[1]Drainage area (km^2)	[1]Mapped stream length (km)	[1]Drainage density (km/km^2)	[2]Head of tide (RKM)
Tillamook	156	132	0.8	10.2
Trask	451	328	0.7	7.0
Wilson	500	320	0.6	5.0
Kilchis	169	94	0.6	2.7
Miami	94	56	0.6	1.3
Nehalem	2,207	1,498	0.7	24.6

[1] Derived from StreamStats (*http://water.usgs.gov/osw/streamstats /oregon.html*) for the area upstream of RKM 0

[2] Derived from Oregon Department of State Lands (2007)

The proportions and distributions of geologic provinces, particularly the Coast Range sedimentary and volcanic subdivisions, differ between the six basins (table 2; figs 1 and 2). The Trask, Wilson, and Miami River basins are roughly 20 percent sedimentary rocks and 70 percent volcanic rocks. Both types of rocks are dispersed throughout the Trask and Wilson basins. In the Miami River basin, volcanic rocks dominate the headwaters and eastern portion of the lower basin, whereas sedimentary rocks encompass the western portion of the lower basin. The Tillamook and Nehalem River basins have more than half of their areas underlain by Coast Range sedimentary rocks, and 27 percent or less by volcanic rocks. The headwaters and mainstem of the Tillamook River drain sedimentary rocks, whereas its tributaries in the eastern portion of the basin drain volcanic rocks. In the Nehalem River basin, sedimentary rocks encompass the headwaters and majority of the mainstem, but volcanic rocks dominate the basin downstream of the town of Elsie and tributaries such as Cronin and Cook Creeks and the Salmonberry River. Unlike the others, the Kilchis River basin is 93 percent Coast Range volcanic rocks, with sedimentary rocks near the mouth making up only 3 percent of the basin's geology.

The distribution of volcanic and sedimentary rocks probably exerts substantial influence on the volume and distribution of bed material in these basins. Although both rock types likely contribute considerable bed material in high-relief headwater areas, ongoing analyses of downstream transport and particle attrition indicate that sedimentary rocks rapidly disaggregate into sand and silt, and thus are more likely to be transported as part of the suspended sediment load than as gravel-size bed material (Mangano and others, 2011; Wallick and others, 2011).

Upstream of the heads of tide, water-surface gradients are variable and locally steep in the headwaters of each basin (fig. 3A–F). Generally, water-surface gradients decline relatively smoothly (with the exception of small convex segments that may indicate slope discontinuities caused by mass movement-related sediment inputs) as the Trask, Wilson, Kilchis, and Miami Rivers approach the Tillamook Bay (fig. 3B–E).

Differences in bed-material transport rates associated with the varying geological environments may explain the different lengths of the rivers affected by tide (table 1; fig. 3A–F). The long, tidally affected reaches of the Tillamook, Trask, and Nehalem Rivers (7.0–24.6 km) indicate that coarse bed-material supply in these basins primarily underlain by sedimentary rocks is surpassed by Holocene sea-level rise, resulting in partly drowned river valleys near the present coast lines (Komar, 1997). In contrast, the shorter tidal reaches of the Wilson, Kilchis, and Miami Rivers are likely a consequence of relatively greater long-term supplies of bed material filling their valleys as sea level has risen over the last 10,000 years.

Table 2. Geologic province summary by percentage as generalized from Ma and others (2009) for the Tillamook Bay subbasins and Nehalem River basin, northwestern Oregon. Data determined at the mouth of the rivers.

| River basin | Geologic province | | | |
	Coast Range (sedimentary)	Coast Range (volcanic)	Columbia River basalts	Quaternary deposits
Tillamook	47.8	25.1	0.4	26.7
Trask	19.3	69.0	0	11.7
Wilson	22.4	70.8	0	6.8
Kilchis	2.8	93.1	0	4.1
Miami	18.9	71.7	0.8	8.6
Nehalem	63.7	27.1	4.3	4.9

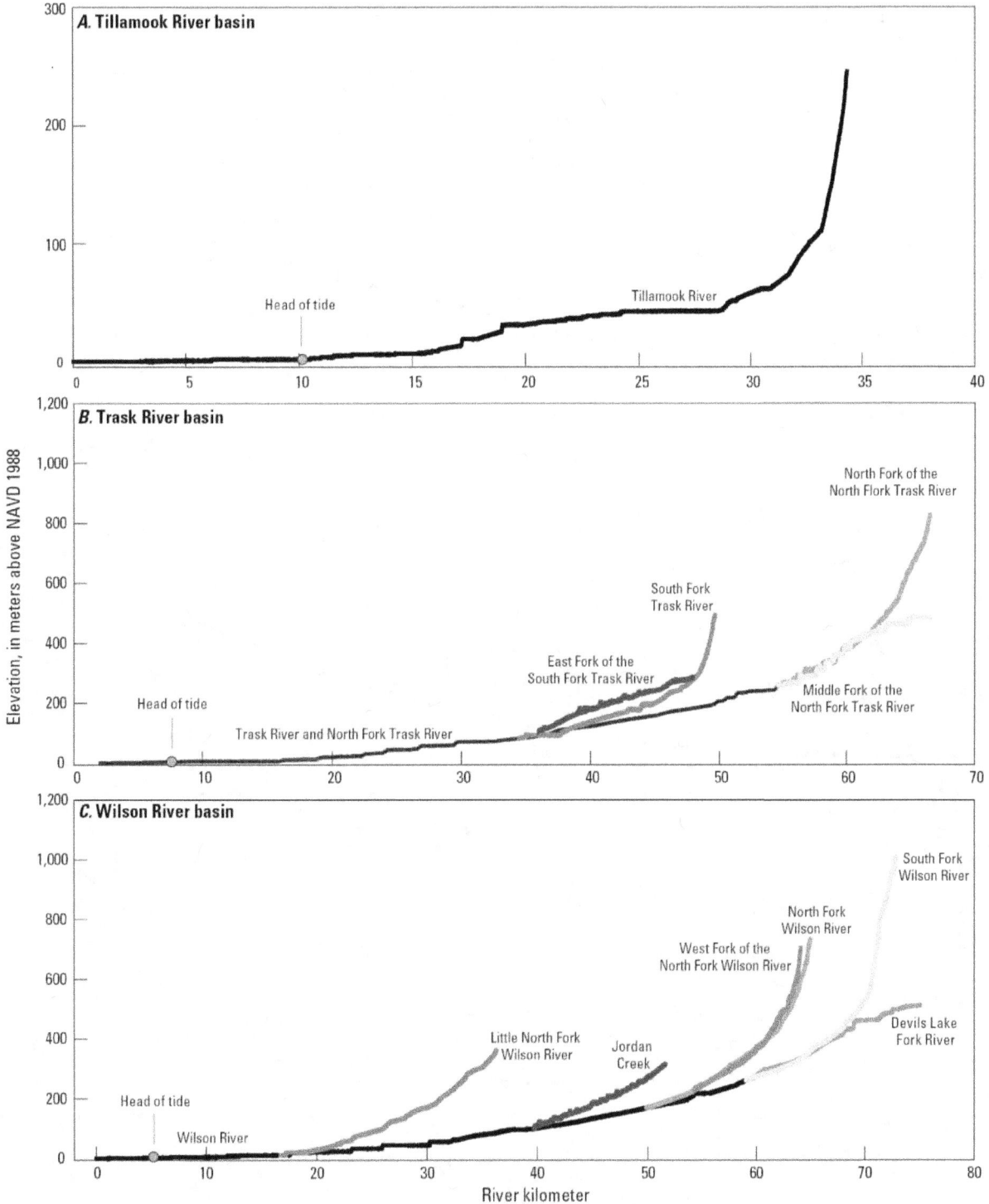

Figure 3. Diagrams showing the longitudinal profiles of the Tillamook, Trask, Wilson, Kilchis, Miami, and Nehalem River basins, northwestern Oregon. Profiles determined from the U.S. Geological Survey 10-m Digital Elevation Model along the channel centerlines

9

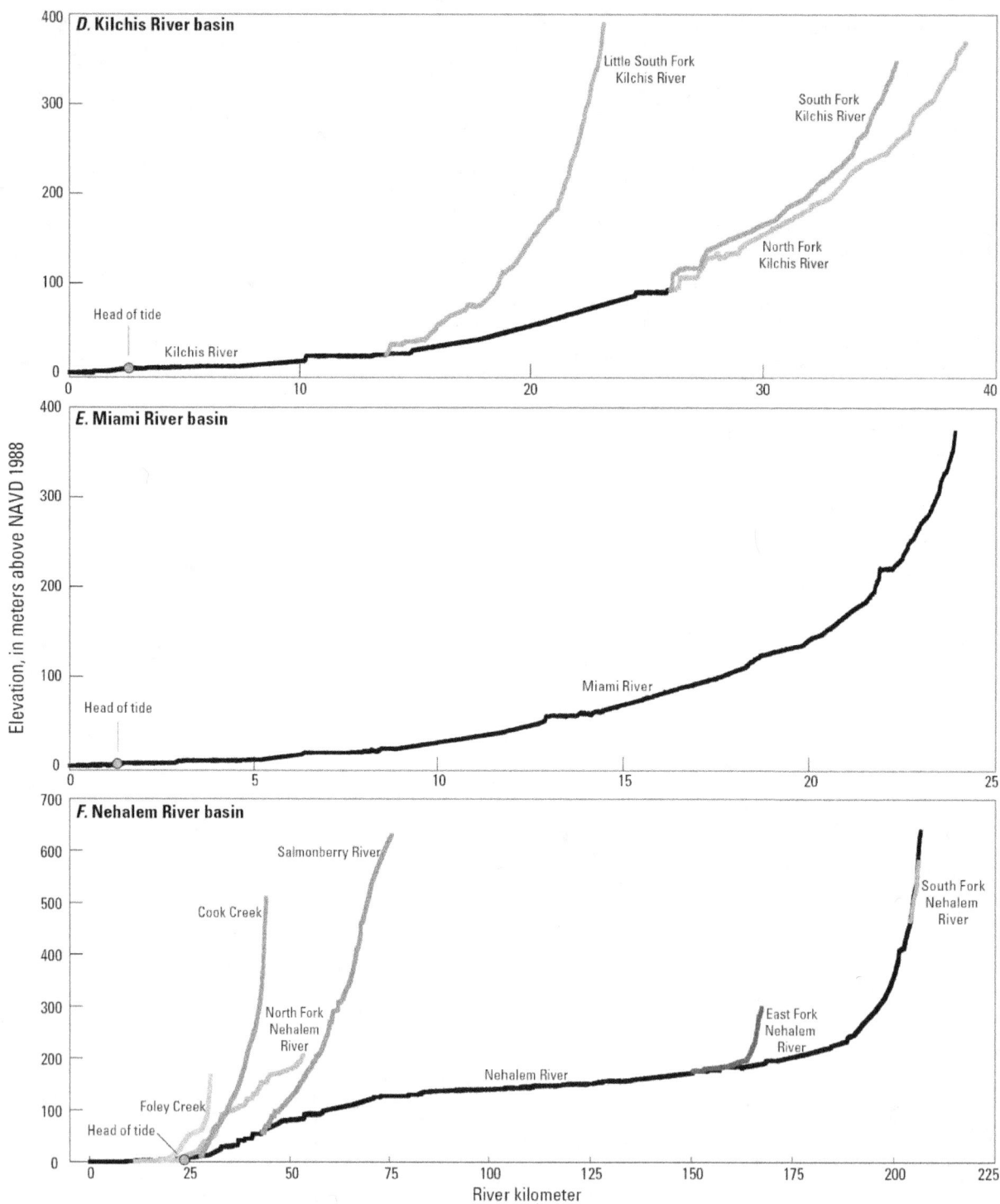

Figure 3 (continued). Diagrams showing the longitudinal profiles of the Tillamook, Trask, Wilson, Kilchis, Miami, and Nehalem River basins, northwestern Oregon. Profiles determined from the U.S. Geological Survey 10-m Digital Elevation Model along the channel centerlines.

Hydrology

Since the 1930s, the USGS has measured streamflow at stations in the Trask, Wilson, and Nehalem River basins (table 3). As of 2011, the USGS measures stage and streamflow on the Trask (Trask River above Cedar Creek, 14302480), Wilson (Wilson River near Tillamook, 14301500), and Nehalem (Nehalem River near Vernonia, 14299800; Nehalem River near Foss, 14301000) Rivers. Additionally, the Oregon Water Resources Department (OWRD) has measured stage and streamflow on the Miami River periodically since the 1970s (Miami River near Garibaldi, 14301300; *http://www.wrd.state.or.us/OWRD/SW/index.shtml*). Neither agency currently measures streamflow in the Tillamook and Kilchis River basins.

The hydrology of these rivers is driven by seasonal precipitation that falls predominately as rain from October to March. Mean annual precipitation ranges from 229 centimeters per year (cm/yr) near the town of Tillamook (Tillamook Bay National Estuary Project, 1998) to 241 cm/yr near Nehalem Bay to 508 cm/yr in the Salmonberry River basin (State Service Center for GIS [1996] as cited in Johnson and Maser [1999]). Mean annual streamflows range from 6.4 m^3/s on the Miami River to 75.0 m^3/s on the Nehalem River near Foss (table 3; fig. 4A–D). Mean January monthly flows are approximately 20–100 times those of mean August flows. Greater rainfall is most common from November to January in the Tillamook Bay subbasins (Tillamook Bay National Estuary Project, 1998) with flash flooding and mud flows frequent in the steep tributaries where thin soils cover bedrock (Coulton and others, 1996). Flooding is common in the lower mainstems of the Tillamook Bay subbasins because the capacity of the channels to convey floods has presumably been reduced (U.S. Army Corps of Engineers, 2005). Although rare, rain-on-snow events have triggered some floods in the basins, including those of 1955, 1964, and 1996 (Johnson and Maser, 1999; Snyder and others, 2003).

For select streamflow-gaging stations with 15 or more years of recent data collection, we identified peak flows from the gaging records because these flows in part drive bed-material transport. Peak flows reached 1,093 m^3/s on November 16, 2006, on the Wilson River, 730 m^3/s on February 8, 1996, on the Trask River, 220 m^3/s on November 12, 2008, on the Miami River, and 1,991 m^3/s on February 8, 1996, on the Nehalem River near Foss (table 3; fig. 5A–D). Since the December 1964 flood, the number of 10-year or greater recurrence-interval events on the Wilson River and 5-year or greater events on the Nehalem River has increased slightly. (The recurrence interval is the average frequency, in years, with which a flood of certain magnitude would be expected to occur. A 10-year recurrence interval flood, for example, has a 10 in 100, or 10 percent, chance of occurring in any particular year.) The ranking for the 1964 flood on the Trask River illustrates this shift in peak flow patterns; this flood on the Trask River was ranked as approximately a 90-year event in the 1960s, but is currently ranked as less than a 25-year event because of frequent floods in more recent years (Coulton and others, 1996). See Coulton and others (1996) and Johnson and Maser (1999) for summaries of historical peak floods in the Tillamook Bay area and Nehalem River basin, respectively.

Table 3. Summary of streamflow-gaging station information for the Trask, Wilson, Miami, and Nehalem Rivers, northwestern Oregon. Data from U.S. Geological Survey (2011) and Oregon Water Resources Department (2011).

[~, approximately; km, kilometer; RKM, river kilometer; km², square kilometer; WY, water year; m³/s, cubic meter per second; --, data not available]

River	Station name	Station ID	Study reach	Location	Nearest bridge	Drainage area (km²)	Period of record	Mean annual flow (m³/s)	Mean January flow (m³/s)	Mean August flow (m³/s)	Peak flow (m³/s)	Date of peak flow event
Trask	Trask River above Cedar Creek, near Tillamook[1]	14302480	--	~1.8 km above study area	~6.4 km downstream	404	4/1996–present	27.6	64.0	3.1	637.0	11/25/1999
	Trask River near Tillamook	14302500	--	~0.9 km above study area	5.4 km downstream	376	7/1931–36/1972	27.4	62.0	3.0	730.5	[2]2/8/1996
Wilson	Wilson River near Tillamook	14301500	--	~0.1 km above study area[3]	1.2 km downstream	417	10/1914–19/1915; 8/1916–11/1916; 7/1931–present	[4]33.3	72.4	3.0	1,092.9	11/6/2006
	Wilson River at Sollie Smith Bridge at Tillamook[5]	14302020	Lower Fluvial Wilson	RKM 6.3	At station	490	7/2008–present	--	--	--	Only stage data available	11/12/2008
Miami	Miami River near Garibaldi	14301300	Tidal Miami	RKM 2.7	At station	73	10/1973–9/1995; 10/2008–present	6.5	13.7	0.8	220.0	11/12/2008
Nehalem	Nehalem River near Vernonia	14299800	--	~140 km above study area	At station	181	7/2001–present	6.4	19.9	0.2	498.4	12/3/2007
	Nehalem River near Foss	14301000	--	~0.4 km above study area	2.6 km upstream	1,728	10/1939–present	75.0	176.7	4.2	1,990.7	2/8/1996

1 Streamflow measurements are made at Long Prairie Road Bridge, RKM 11.6 (~6.4 km downstream of the current gage location). USGS (2011) calculates the gage's drainage area at the discharge measurement location. Drainage area at the gage is 373 km² as measured from StreamStats.

2 Flow was estimated based on flood marks

3 Location of gage has changed over time

4 Mean annual flow reported for water years 1932–2010

5 Gage heights only; no streamflow data collected at this station

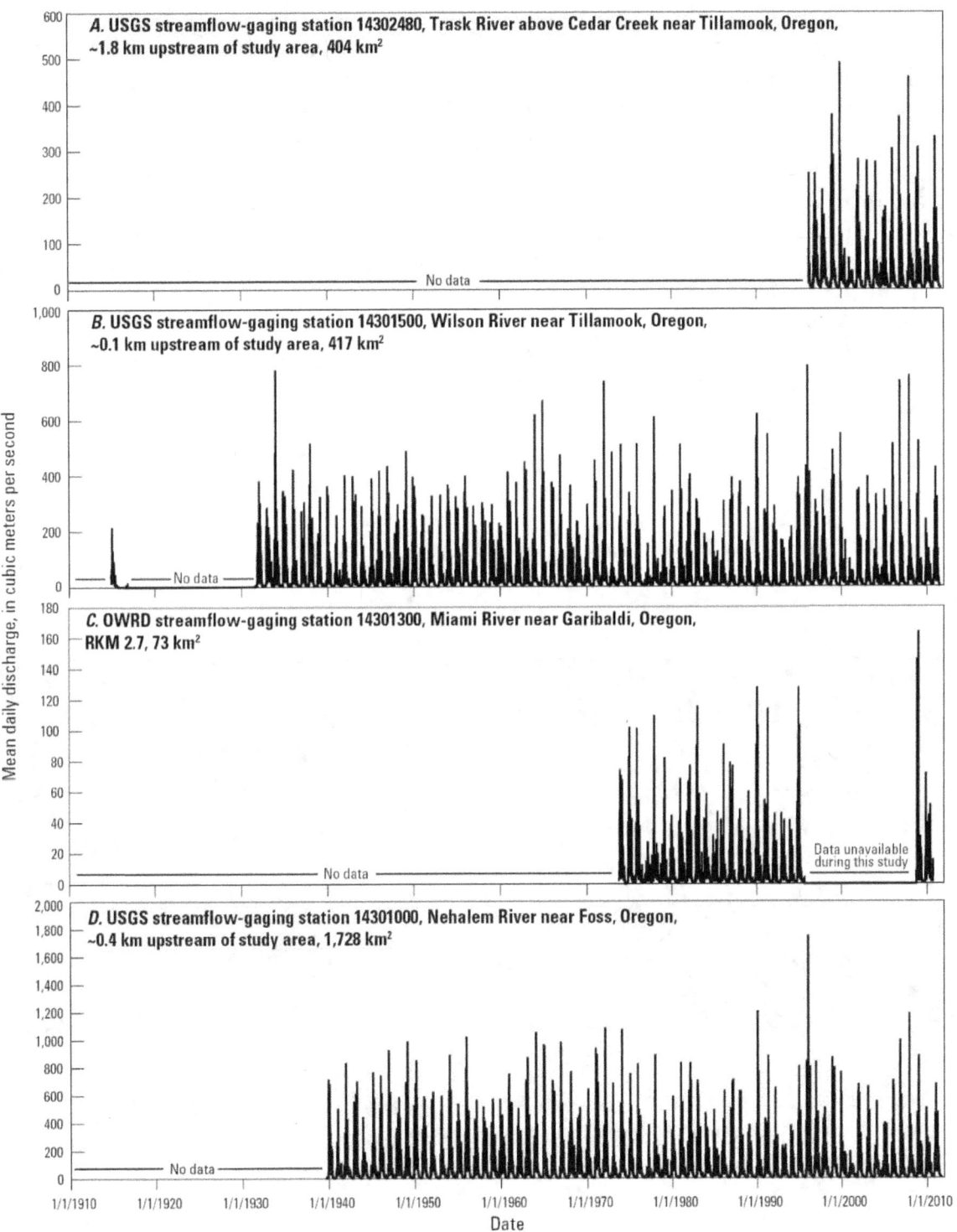

Figure 4. Graphs showing mean daily streamflow for U.S. Geological Survey and Oregon Water Resource Department streamflow-gaging stations on the (A) Trask River above Cedar Creek near Tillamook, Oregon (14302480), (B) Wilson River near Tillamook, Oregon (14301500), (C) Miami River near Garibaldi, Oregon (14301300), and (D) Nehalem River near Foss, Oregon (14301000), northwestern Oregon. [km, kilometer; km², square kilometer; RKM, river kilometer]

Streamflow alterations in the study basins include water withdrawals for agricultural, municipal, and domestic uses primarily in the floodplains of the Tillamook Bay subbasins and Nehalem River basin and near several towns along the Nehalem River (figs. 1 and 2). Additionally, small dams are in the headwaters of the Trask and Tillamook Rivers and on Fishhawk Creek, a tributary to the Nehalem River. The dam forming Skookum Lake Reservoir on Fawcett Creek, a tributary to the Tillamook River, was built in 1965 to provide the city of Tillamook with municipal drinking water (City of Tillamook, 2011). At the Barney Reservoir on the Middle Fork of the North Fork Trask River, water is diverted to the headwaters of the Tualatin River (U.S. Geological Survey, 2011) for use by the cities of Beaverton, Hillsboro, and Forest Grove. Fishhawk Lake is a private recreational lake on Fishhawk Creek north of the town of Birkenfeld. Historically, several small dams that no longer exist were operated for hydropower, fire control, and logging activities throughout the Nehalem River basin (Johnson and Maser, 1999). Effects of existing dams on overall bed-material flux are likely limited because these dams are small and affect 5 percent or less of these basins.

A flood on December 3, 2007, undermined bridge piers and railroad tracks adjacent to the Salmonberry River near its confluence with the Nehalem River (Oregon Department of Forestry).

Bridge pier blocking large wood on the North Fork Trask River near its confluence with the South Fork Trask River.

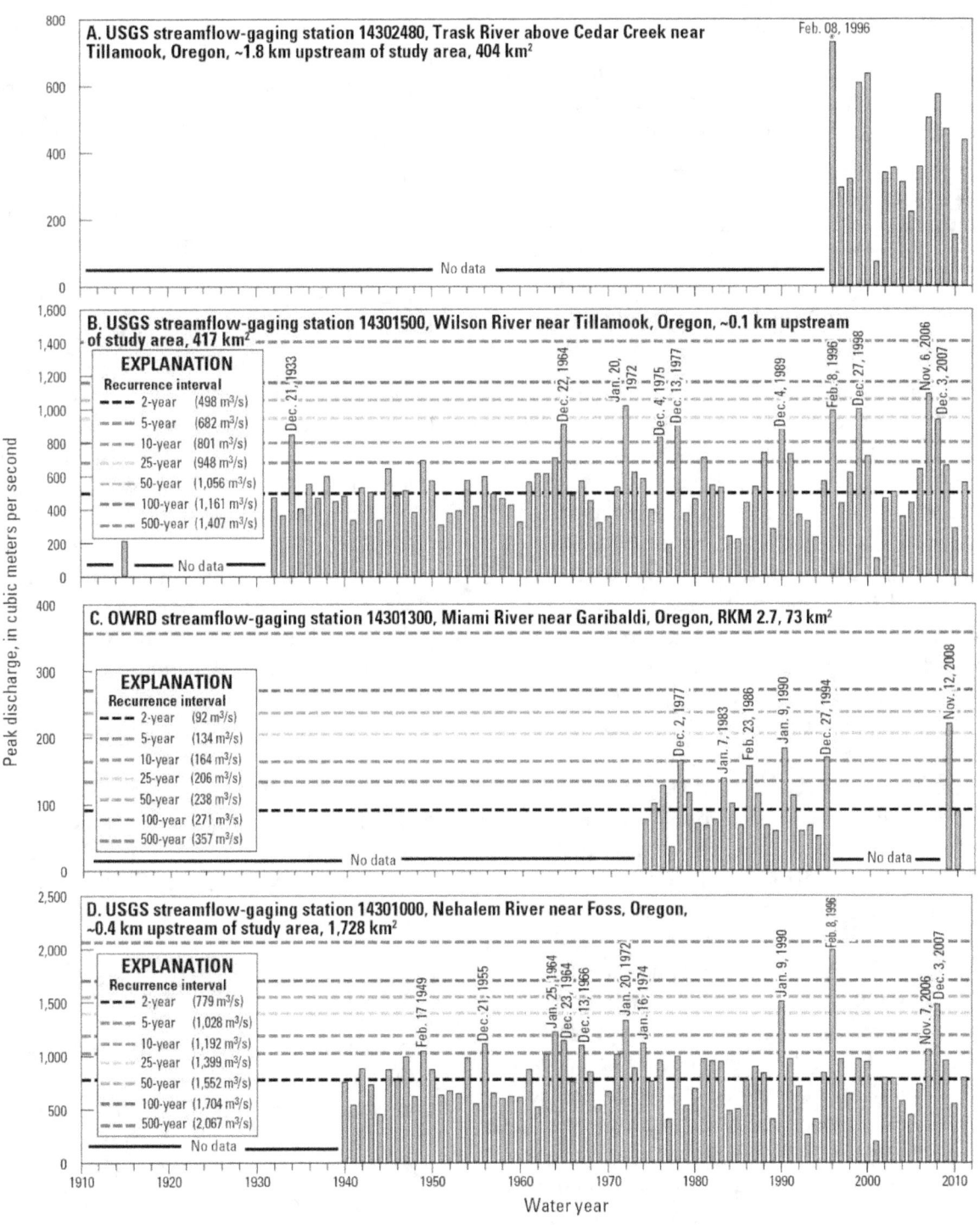

Figure 5. Graphs showing annual peak streamflow for U.S. Geological Survey and Oregon Water Resource Department streamflow-gaging stations on the (A) Trask River above Cedar Creek near Tillamook, Oregon (14302480), (B) Wilson River near Tillamook, Oregon (14301500), (C) Miami River near Garibaldi, Oregon (14301300), and (D) Nehalem River near Foss, Oregon (14301000), northwestern Oregon. Reported flow recurrence intervals from Cooper (2005). [km, kilometer; km², square kilometer; m³/s, cubic meter per second; RKM, river kilometer; * above peak in "A" (Trask River) is from field measurement]

15

Historical Channel Descriptions

Historical observations of river channels are useful counterpoints for comparing present channel conditions. Although most historical accounts describe conditions within the bays and in relation to navigation and trade development, some describe general channel characteristics, channel planform changes, and transport of sediment and large wood in the rivers. Coulton and others (1996) describe historical changes in Tillamook Bay.

Early accounts by the Corps of Engineers described the region's suitability for future land uses. In 1886, Lieutenant Edward Burr noted that, "There are large quantities of spruce, fir, and cedar timber on the streams tributary to the bay, and the winter freshets on these streams fit them for the driving of logs" (U.S. Congress, 1889). In 1888, Captain Charles F. Powell reported, "The rivers are mountain streams in the upper part of their course and tidal sloughs in the lower portion. The best country, grazing and farming, of the region is on these rivers and around the head of the bay; higher up the rivers are timber lands" (U.S. Congress, 1889). Powell added, "Tillamook River is by far the best stream for navigation, but its banks are low and over-flowed for miles, affording at no place on its navigable part, it is judged, a suitable landing, nor a convenient and accessible point for the trade of the settled country. Neither is such a point found along the north or south channels of the bay on account of the little room at the foot of the steep bluffs there and the absence of ordinarily practicable land routes to the settled country" (U.S. Congress, 1889). These historical observations indicate overbank flooding on the Tillamook River, seasonal high flows on the bay's tributaries, and future distributions of land uses owing to the mountainous uplands and limited floodplain lands.

Coulton and others (1996) summarized historical accounts of channel width, bed-material composition, and channel planform changes for the Tillamook Bay rivers, from which the fol-lowing observations were extracted. The Tillamook River was described as a "river one hundred dred yards [approximately 90 m] wide, has no falls, and no difficult rapids" in an 1830 publication (Holman, 1910). Later in 1857, Samuel D. Snowden, a General Land Office (GLO) surveyor, described the Kilchis River as "3 feet [approximately 0.9 m] deep, gravel bottom" near RKM 12.6 (Township 1 North, Range 9 West section line) (General Land Office, 1856-57). Downstream at approximately RKM 6.5 (the intersection of the north boundary of Township 1 South, Range 9 West, Section 5), Snowden noted the "[f]ast current, gravelly bottom, 100 links [66 ft or 20 m] wide" channel of the Kilchis River (General Land Office, 1856-57). As summarized by Coulton and others (1996), Henry Meldrum, another GLO surveyor, revisited this location in 1884 and recorded that "[t]he Kilchis River has changed its bed at this point, about 3.50 chains [230 ft or 70 m] north of [the] old channel which has filled with gravel, sand, [and other material]." Coulton and others (1996) also reported the Wilson River channel migrated at about river mile 5 (RKM 8.2) between the GLO surveys of the 1850s and 1939 aerial photographs. These descriptions are comparable with current conditions, particularly the planform changes on the Kilchis and Wilson Rivers (described later in this report).

Some historical accounts noted by Coulton and others (1996) document sediment transport in the Tillamook Bay rivers and along the Oregon coast. The Corps of Engineers reported in 1902 and 1907 that "a considerable quantity of gravel, sand, and mud is annually deposited in the [Tillamook] bay and channels by tributary streams" (Gilkey, 1974). In 1896, Assistant Engineer David B. Ogden noted some difficulty driving piles approximately 3.7 m into the streambed for the dikes at the Wilson River mouth owing to sand and gravel (U.S. Army Corps of Engineers, 1896). On the Oregon coast north of the Nehalem River, during the winter 1805–1806, explorer William Clark chronicled the occurrence of landslides where "fifty or a hundred acres at a time give way and a great proportion of an instant precipitated into the ocean" (Bancroft, 1884), illustrating the likely contributions of landslides to sediment fluxes in Oregon coastal rivers.

Likewise, GLO surveyors and the Corps of Engineers described the occurrence and transport of large wood in the Tillamook region, as summarized by Coulton and others (1996). Surveyors noted in 1857 that "…the Tillamook River is navigable from section 7 to the ocean—and would be so for small steamboats if cleared of drift" (General Land Office, 1856–57). The Wilson River had jams over 200 m long (General Land Office, 1856–57). The GLO surveyed the Kilchis River "to a point where the river becomes shallow and obstructed by drift [and] it was thought useless to meander [survey] it any further up" (General Land Office, 1856–57). Later, the Corps of Engineers (1895) noted, "[t]he first mouth [of the Trask River], locally known as the North Fork, has become clogged up so with timber jams as to divert most of the water into the South Fork. It is proposed to remedy the evil by building a dike across the head of the South Fork and removing the jams from the North Fork" (U.S. Army Corps of Engineers, 1895). The following year, the Corps of Engineers reported that, "Now that the South Fork has been diverted, the jams in the North Fork [or mainstem Trask channel near mouth] should be removed, banks trimmed, and sunken logs removed to permit it to carry the flood waters without flooding the farm lands" (U.S. Army Corps of Engineers, 1897). Summarizing the accumulation of wood in Tillamook Bay, the Corps of Engineers noted, "One of the most serious troubles with this bay is caused by the large number of snags and fallen trees that are carried in on floods, and which eventually sink on the shoals and become buried in the same" (U.S. Army Corps of Engineers, 1897).

We found fewer historical accounts for the Nehalem River. Of these, two accounts highlight the Nehalem River's potential for transporting timber (owing likely to its steep gradient and high winter flows) above the head of tide. In 1884, J. L. Barnard traveled down the Nehalem River to assess logging prospects. Barnard reported, "[he] found only one piece of slab-wood lodged in the bed of the river from Browse's Mill [approximately 161 km from the mouth of the Nehalem River] to tide-water, with one lodgement of driftwood on top of a rock about 20 feet [6.1 m] high in the middle of the river, left there during some freshet, showing that it is a beautiful stream to run logs down, for 100 miles [160 km] or more, to tide-water, furnishing an almost inexhaustible supply of timber" (as cited in Farnell, 1981). In 1889, J.S. Polhemus of the Corps of Engineers reported, "For 20 miles at least above the head of tide to the Middle Nehalem [a settlement near the three Fish Hawk Creeks, or between the towns of Birkenfeld and Jewell; fig. 2], the river flows as a rapid stream over a rocky bottom between steep hills all covered with fine timber. It is not navigable, but I have been informed by old settlers, that it offers good facilities for driving logs for 70 or 80 miles, being particularly free from drift and other obstructions" (U.S. Congress, 1890).

Other historical accounts of the Nehalem River document sediment transport. In 1889, Gwynn A. Lyell noted, "The [Nehalem] river was surveyed from the entrance to the islands above Kinney's cannery [near Wheeler, Oregon]. The channel at the islands is obstructed by gravel bars formed by accumulated drift. Above the islands the banks of the river are low and the width contracted deeper water than that below the islands" (U.S. Congress, 1890). Lyell also reported that "[t]he inner shore of the river opposite the entrance, and up to Fishery Point, is composed of sand, gravel, and cobble stones" (U.S. Congress, 1890).

Settlement and Land Ownership Patterns

The Tillamook and Nehalem tribes inhabited the basins prior to Euro-American settlement (Coulton and others, 1996; Tillamook Bay National Estuary Project, 1998; Johnson and Maser, 1999). John Meares and other explorers came to the Tillamook Bay area in the 1770s–1780s (Coulton and others, 1996), nearly 80 years before Euro-American settlers came to "fish, farm, and raise milk cows on the rich coastal plain" of the Tillamook Bay in 1851 (Wells, 1999). Many settlers built farms in the Kilchis and Wilson River valleys (Coulton and others, 1996). The Nehalem basin had its first Euro-American settler nearly 17 years later in 1866 and its towns of Wheeler and Nehalem established in 1868 (Johnson and Maser, 1999). Basin land use initially focused on farming, dairies, and fishing and later included forestry (Coulton and others, 1996; Johnson and Maser, 1999).

Land use patterns vary some among the basins (table 4) (Oregon Natural Heritage Program, 1999). Approximately 58–89 percent of the Trask, Wilson, Kilchis, and Miami River basins are managed largely as the Tillamook State Forest by the State of Oregon. The State managed Tillamook and Clatsop State Forests make up nearly a third of the Nehalem River basin. Most of these lands were transferred to the Oregon State Board of Forestry after the Tillamook Burn (Coulton and others, 1996; Johnson and Maser, 1999). Private lands account for 98 and 68 percent of the Tillamook and Nehalem River basins, respectively, with a large proportion managed for timber in the Nehalem River basin (Johnson and Maser, 1999). Federal and county holdings are less than 5 percent of these basins. State managed lands dominate the headwaters and upper portions of the Tillamook Bay subbasins, whereas private lands used for residential, agriculture, and other purposes dominate the lowlands. In the Nehalem basin, State managed lands are in the basin's headwaters to approximately the town of Timber, on south-flowing tributaries entering the mainstem between the towns of Birkenfeld and Jewell, lands draining to the mainstem from approximately Cronin to Foley Creeks, and most of the Cook Creek and Salmonberry River basins (fig. 2). Agriculture and other developed lands are near the towns of Vernonia, Mist, Birkenfeld, Jewell, Vinemaple, and Mohler. These land use distributions in combination with geology and valley topography likely have considerable influence on bed-material dynamics (as discussed below).

Table 4. Summary of land ownership for the Tillamook Bay subbasins and Nehalem River basin, northwestern Oregon.

[%, percent]

River basin	Land ownership (%)			
	Federal	State	County	Private
Tillamook	1.0	0.8	0	98.2
Trask	4.8	62.1	0	33.0
Wilson	1.2	88.6	0.2	10.1
Kilchis	1.5	84.2	2.6	11.7
Miami	0	57.8	0	42.2
Nehalem	0.9	30.8	0	68.3

Determined from Oregon Natural Heritage Program (1999)

Natural and Anthropogenic Disturbances Affecting Bed-Material Dynamics

Several natural and human-related disturbances have had substantial effects on sediment yield and transport and channel morphology in the Tillamook Bay subbasins and Nehalem River basin. Logging, channel alterations for navigation, flood control, and gravel mining are some human activities that can affect channel and bed-material conditions. Fire and mass movements are natural processes affecting sediment yield and transport, but both processes have likely been affected by human activities. Although streambank erosion is another natural process that is influenced by human actions, it was outside the scope of this study because it primarily increases fine sediment inputs rather than bed-material inputs.

Bank erosion on the Wilson River, 1922 (Oregon State University Archives, 1238972454917)

Mass Movements

Mass movements and debris flows are probably the primary mechanisms that introduce bed material from hillslopes into the Tillamook Bay rivers and Nehalem River. Alluvial reworking of debris fans and accumulated terrace gravels further contributes bed material to the channels. In general, the steep headwater gradients, weathered sedimentary and volcanic rocks, and episodically intense rains promote abundant landslides and debris flows (Tillamook Bay Taskforce and others, 1978; Johnson and Maser, 1999; Snyder and others, 2001, Snyder and others, 2003; Duck Creek Associates, 2008; Reckendorf, 2008a). For example, the Oregon Department of Geology and Mineral Industries (DOGAMI, 1973) reported that "Throughout the Tillamook drainage at the height of the [January 1972] flooding, many small creeks, some too small to be shown on a map, turned into rivers of flowing mud, rocks and wood debris."

Mass movements also sometimes briefly dam the rivers. For instance, the Wilson River was dammed completely by a debris flow stretching over 120 m across the channel on January 31, 1965 (Levesque, 1980) and a landslide that moved over 383,000 m^3 of material on April 4, 1991 (Burns, 1998; Preiffer and others, 1998). During field reconnaissance, we visited a debris flow site near RKM 30.7 that probably resulted from the storm on December 2–3, 2007, and appears to contribute sediment and wood in mainstem Nehalem River. The volume and character of sediment delivered to streams may vary with the specific delivery process, geology, and disturbance factors. In particular, coarse bed material delivered from volcanic rocks may be a more considerable source of bed material because of these rocks have much greater resistance to abrasion than sedimentary rocks (Mangano and others, 2011). As described below, the frequency and character of mass movements can be affected by natural and human related disturbances.

Logging and Related Transportation Activities

Timber harvests can have many effects on terrestrial and aquatic ecosystems, including reducing vegetation cover and increasing surface water and sediment run-off to nearby rivers. Settlers initially harvested forests in the valleys and riparian areas of these six basins to establish fields and dairy pastures and for local construction needs (Coulton and others, 1996; Johnson and Maser, 1999). By the beginning of the 20th century, industrial logging was widespread throughout the basins. In the Tillamook area, logging peaked in 1952, when salvage logging operations removed 609,624 board feet from the Tillamook Burn (Snyder and others, 2003; Andrews and Kutara, 2005). In the Nehalem River basin, timber harvests peaked during the 1920–1940s, with the last old growth forests harvested in 1945 (Johnson and Maser, 1999). Harvests continue in these basins, and may increase in coming years as forests replanted after the Tillamook Burn reach harvestable ages (Snyder and others, 2003) and trees are harvested and thinned to combat Swiss Needle Cast, a forest pathogen infecting the region's Douglas fir stands (Follansbee and Stark, 1998b; Johnson and Maser, 1999; Snyder and others, 2003; Jenkins and others, 2005).

Transportation of timber can also affect the hydrology and sediment fluxes of nearby rivers. Log drives (the floating of logs during naturally occurring flood events; fig. 6A–B) and splash damming (log drives coupled with managed and repeated dam releases) were early transportation methods. Log drives occurred on all six rivers (table 5) and several tributaries (Farnell, 1980, 1981; Miller, 2010). The longest log drives were on the Nehalem River and ran approximately 140 km from the East Fork Nehalem River to the bay (Farnell, 1981). Later, splash dams were constructed on Bewley Creek (a tributary to the Tillamook River), North Fork Nehalem River, and Humbug Creek (a tributary to the Nehalem River; Farnell, 1980, 1981; Miller, 2010). Millions of logs were floated down the Nehalem River and tributaries, such as the North Fork Nehalem River, Humbug Creek, and Salmonberry River (Farnell, 1981). Log drives and splash damming may have increased flood frequency and magnitude, sediment fluxes, and streambed scouring (possibly to bedrock in some locations). For example, floods caused by splash damming probably exceeded 100-year flood events in headwater areas, and equaled 100-year flood events in downstream areas in basins south of the Tillamook basin (Phelps, 2011). As suggested for the Coquille basin (Benner, 1991), riparian vegetation and instream wood and boulders were probably removed to maximize log transport ef-

ficiency; such changes may have increased sediment fluxes and bank instability in these rivers.

Timber transport shifted from log runs and splash dams in the 1870s–1920s (table 5) to railroads in the early 1900s and to trucks in the 1940s (Coulton and others, 1996; R2 Resource Consultants, Inc., 2005). Recent forest road estimates include approximately 1,840 km of roads on Oregon Department of Forestry (ODF) lands in the Tillamook Bay subbasins (Snyder and others, 2001) and over 1,910 km of forest roads in the Nehalem River basin (Portland State University [2000] as cited in R2 Resource Consultants, Inc. [2005]). Roads on steep slopes in conjunction with timber harvests can increase the magnitude and frequency of mass movements (Swanson and Dyrness, 1975; Beschta, 1978; Amaranthus and others, 1985; Harden and others, 1995), particularly in regions naturally prone to mass movements like the Coast Range. As described by Coulton and others (1996), roads and culvert failures are likely substantial contributors to mass wasting and sediment inputs in the Tillamook Bay subbasins. Roads are also cited as "the principal cause of human-induced landslides in the forests" of the Tillamook Bay subbasins (Tillamook Bay National Estuary Project, 1998).

Table 5. Time periods of log drives and splash damming in the Tillamook Bay subbasins and Nehalem River basin, northwestern Oregon. [Source: Farnell (1980,1981)]

[~, approximately]

Activity	River/Creek	Time period
Log drive	Tillamook	1887–1915
	Trask	1879, 1890–1915
	Wilson	1893–1908
	Kilchis	1872–1915
	Miami	1900–1920
	Nehalem	1901–1926
Splash damming	Bewley	1892–1915
	North Fork Nehalem	~1923–1926
	Humbug	1916–1923

Nehalem River along the Pacific Railway & Navigation Company, 1910 (Oregon State University, 1238951456889).

Several studies reinforce the abundance of road related landslides on forestlands in these basins. In 1978, 240 natural landslides and 4,440 human related landslides were reported in the Tillamook Bay subbasins, with the number of landslides greatest in the Trask and Wilson River basins and lowest in the Tillamook River basin (Benoit, 1978). Reported landslides are likely lowest in the Tillamook basin where the effects of the Tillamook Burn and subsequent salvage logging were minimal. In the Kilchis River basin, 57 landslides were documented after the storms of 1995–1996, primarily near forest roads in use since 1972 (Mills, 1997). Additionally, over half of the ODF roads in the Tillamook Bay subbasins likely "pose a moderate or high risk of contributing sediment to a stream if a road-related landslide was to occur" with high-risk sites occurring about every 2 miles along ODF roads (Snyder and others, 2001). In the Upper Nehalem River basin, R2 Resource Consultants, Inc. (2005) reported that the highest landslide density coincided with roads.

Fire

Before and after Euro-American settlement, fires burned the Tillamook Bay subbasins and Nehalem River basin, reducing vegetation cover and soil moisture and episodically increasing sediment fluxes to nearby rivers. Native American tribes regularly burned the valleys and upland prairies in late fall to improve hunting, resource gathering, and visibility (Morris, 1934; Coulton and others, 1996). In approximately 1800 and prior to Euro-American settlement, a large fire occurred south of the town of Mist in the Nehalem River basin (Johnson and Maser, 1999). The Great Fire of 1845 was started by settlers on the western edge of the Willamette Valley and then crossed the Coast Range, affecting approximately 6,070 km^2 from Tillamook to Newport (Morris, 1934; Coulton and others, 1996). An 1868 fire moved south from Clatsop County, burning the higher elevations of the Coast Range (Coulton and others, 1996) and likely portions of the Nehalem River basin and

Tillamook Bay subbasins. Notes and maps from a timber cruise in 1908 indicated prior fires in most of the Trask, Wilson, and Kilchis valleys, particularly near the mainstems and major wagon roads (Coulton and others, 1996).

More recently, the Tillamook Burn, a series of several fires between 1933 and 1951, and the Salmonberry Fire on the Nehalem and Salmonberry Rivers in 1945 destroyed a total of 1,436 km^2 and over 13 million board feet of timber in the Trask, Wilson, Kilchis, Miami, and Nehalem River basins (Oregon State Department of Forestry, 1983). Historical photographs illustrate the effects of these fires and subsequent replanting efforts (fig. 7A–C). During the first fire, the caretaker at the Wilson River streamflow-gaging station noted, "During August there occurred the most disastrous fire in Oregon in many years, perhaps in history. The fire covered heavy stands of timber over almost the entire Wilson River watershed, burning down nearly to the gaging station. It reached a climax of intensity on Aug. 25–26 forcing the gage reader to leave his home. Shortly afterwards, gentle showers enabled fighters to place the fire under control" (from records for 14301500 housed at the USGS Oregon Water Science Center). These 1933–1951 fires repeatedly burned some areas in the Trask, Wilson, Miami, and Salmonberry River basins. Sediment from these affected lands was eroded and delivered to the rivers until reforestation efforts from 1949 to 1970 reduced erosion rates (Coulton and others, 1996). Today, most of lands affected by the Tillamook Burn and Salmonberry Fire are managed as the Tillamook and Clatsop State Forests.

Figure 6. Historical photographs showing log drives on the (A) Nehalem River circa 1915 [Oregon State University Archives, LLID 1238951456889] and (B) Trask River (date unknown) [Oregon Historical Society bb009090]. The Oregon State University Archives and Oregon Historical Society granted permission to use these photographs.

Figure 7. Historical photographs of the Tillamook Burn: (A) the Wolf Creek subbasin of the Salmonberry River basin in 1932 [Tillamook County Pioneer Museum], (B) a burned riparian corridor along the Wilson River [Oregon Historical Society bb009089], and (C) students planting trees as part of the Tillamook Burn reforestation effort [Oregon Department of Forestry]. The Tillamook County Pioneer Museum, Oregon Historical Society, and Oregon Department of Forestry granted permission to use these photographs.

Channel Alterations for Navigation and Flood Control

Before highways, waterways connected this region with nearby markets. The Corps of Engineers constructed and maintained jetties at the Tillamook Bay entrance since approximately 1914 (Willingham, 1983; Coulton and others, 1996), and completed two jetties at the Nehalem River mouth in 1918 (Willingham, 1983). As noted by Coulton and others (1996), the Corps of Engineers regularly dredged littoral sands from the Tillamook Bay's entrance and main naviga-

tion channel from the late 1880s to the mid-1970s (U.S. Army Corps of Engineers, 1975). On average, nearly 24,000 m^3 per year (a total of approximately 1.2 million m^3) was removed and disposed of offshore from 1929 to 1979 (Tillamook Bay National Estuary Project, 1998). Farther upstream, the Corps of Engineers maintained a navigation channel to the town of Tillamook from approximately 1890 to the 1920s (Farnell, 1980; Tillamook Bay National Estuary Project, 1998). Also, emergency dredging to reduce flooding during the winter of 1971–1972 removed over 82,570 m^3 from the mouths of the

Wilson and Trask Rivers and disposed of that material on their deltas (Follansbee and Stark, 1998a). On the Nehalem River, Federal entities dredged approximately 9,500 m^3 of sand from the bay during 1932–1933 (Ferdun, 2010). The Corps of Engineers, however, does not presently dredge the Nehalem River because of the absence of a Federal navigation channel (Katharine Groth, U.S. Army Corps of Engineers, written commun., 2010).

Upstream, Federal entities and local diking districts built levees and dikes for channel maintenance and flood prevention starting in the early 1900s in the Tillamook Bay area and Nehalem basin (Coulton and others, 1996; Ferdun, 2010). As described above, the Corps of Engineers built dikes, such as those near the Trask River mouth in 1896–1897 and on the historical Wilson River channel in 1900–1901 to reduce the amount of large wood and sediment blocking the channels and prevent flooding. Additionally, the Corps of Engineers "constructed dikes to redirect and direct water in an attempt to reduce the deposition of gravel and sand in the navigation channel" (Coulton and others, 1996). In the 1920s, a dike was built to direct flow and logs to the sawmill near Wheeler on the Nehalem River (Johnson and Maser, 1999). Many of the historical levees and dikes in the lowland and tidal channels of the Tillamook Bay were constructed directly on both river banks (Phillip Williams & Associates, 2002). During the 20th and early 21st centuries, flood control structures in the Tillamook and Nehalem areas have undergone frequent repairs and modifications (Coulton and others, 1996; Jenkins and others, 2005; U.S. Army Corps of Engineers, 2005; Ferdun, 2010).

An inventory of levees and dikes in tidal areas along the Oregon coast (Oregon Coastal Management Program, 2011) indicates that floodplain modifications (or levees, dikes, and naturally formed levees reinforced with nonerodible materials) border over 70 percent of the mainstem in the Tidal Tillamook, Trask, and Wilson Reaches and approximately 30 percent of the mainstem in the Tidal Kilchis, Miami, and Nehalem Reaches (table 6). This inventory also included some modifications along the channels in the Fluvial Trask and Kilchis Reaches and the Lower Fluvial Reaches on the Wilson and Miami Rivers. These levees, dikes, and other bank protection features have probably affected hydrology and sediment fluxes, reduced channel migration, locally increased channel scour, and increased sediment deposition in downstream areas.

Large wood also has been removed from these river systems. As described in Coulton and others (1996), the Corps and Engineers and the Port of Tillamook removed over 9,300 snags from the Tillamook Bay channels during 1890–1920 to improve navigation (Benner and Sedell, 1987). Wood was mainly removed from areas near the mouth of the Tillamook River to the town of Tillamook and the lower Trask channels (Coulton and others, 1996). Upstream, wood jams were documented on all Tillamook Bay rivers (as described previously) and were so prevalent on the Wilson River that log jams were often broken up using dynamite at river mile 16, approximately 1.6 km upstream of the Wilson River study area (Coulton and others, 1996). Judging from the well documented activities on the Coquille River (Benner, 1991), many wood jams were likely removed during the period of log drives and splash dam operations. After the Tillamook Burn, wood removal (or "stream cleaning") occurred until the 1960s and early 1970s to improve fish passage in the Wilson River, upper Miami River and several tributaries, and the upper and lower Nehalem River and several of its tributaries (Johnson and Maser, 1999; Jenkins and others, 2005; R2 Resource Consultants, 2005; Duck Creek Associates, 2008). Reductions in large wood possibly contributed to simplification of channel morphology and instream habitats and likely affected channel processes, including rates of bank erosion and sediment storage.

Table 6. Summary of floodplain modifications in the study areas of the Tillamook Bay sub-basins and Nehalem River basin, northwestern Oregon. Data derived from the Oregon Coastal Management Program (2011).

River	Reach	Wetted channel perimeter (meters)[1]	Estimated length of floodplain modifications (meters)	Channel bordered by floodplain modifications (percent)	Figure in this report
Tillamook	Fluvial	8,140	0	0	9
	Tidal	20,670	15,830	77	9
Trask	Fluvial	19,240	1,100	6	10
	Tidal	14,280	10,170	71	10
Wilson	Upper Fluvial	5,690	0	0	11
	Lower Fluvial	16,040	5,560	35	11
	Tidal	10,190	7,860	77	11
Kilchis	Fluvial	10,760	400	4	12
	Tidal	5,420	1,810	33	12
Miami	Upper Fluvial	4,850	0	0	13
	Lower Fluvial	16,240	1,680	10	13
	Tidal	2,770	960	34	13
Nehalem	Fluvial	15,320	0	0	14
	Tidal	59,500	16,670	28	15

[1] Total bank length for each reach is approximated using wetted channel perimeter.

Gravel Mining

Instream gravel mining can potentially lead to lowering of the channel bed, changes in cross sections, increased turbidity, armoring of bar surfaces, and reductions in downstream bed-material fluxes (Kondolf, 1994). These geomorphic changes may correspond to changes in the frequency and geometry of pools and riffles, scouring of salmon redds, filling of interstitial spaces (spaces between sand grains or gravel) with fine sediment, and declines in macroinvertebrates (Kondolf and others, 2002). Other biological effects may include dewatering of salmon redds built on mined bar surfaces during higher flows. Bed material has been mined from the Wilson and the Trask Rivers since at least the early 1900s to support local construction needs and build levees (Coulton and others, 1996) and from the Kilchis River since at least the 1940s (Follansbee and Stark, 1998a). Gravel was also mined from the Miami River near Peterson and Stuart Creeks in the 1960s–1970s (Jenkins and others, 2005) and the mainstem Nehalem River to build Highway 26 (Johnson and Maser, 1999; R2 Resource Consultants, 2005). Reports from 1991 indicated that over 44,000 m^3 of gravel were removed annually from the Trask, Wilson, Kilchis, and Miami Rivers and nearby Nestucca River (Tillamook County, 2000).

Owing to possible adverse effects of instream gravel mining on local chum salmon populations, the Tillamook Gravel Mediated Agreement was developed in 1992 to halt commercial instream gravel mining above the head of tide on the Trask, Wilson, Kilchis, and Miami Rivers by October 1, 1997 (Tillamook County, 2000). After this termination date, instream gravel mining was only permitted to prevent bank erosion and for noncommercial purposes (Tillamook County, 2000), with the exception of existing commercial gravel mining permits (Robert Lobdell, Oregon Department of State Lands, oral commun., 2012). After October 1997, Tillamook County (2000) noted the building of gravel bars (partly in association with sedimentation during the February 1996 flood) and severe bank erosion opposite of gravel bars by the winter of 1998–1999. These concerns resulted in modifications to the 1992 agreement, including a pilot project to reduce bank erosion opposite of Bush (Trask, RKM 12.2), Tannler (Wilson, RKM 6.6), Upper Landolt (Kilchis, RKM 5.3), and Gomes (Kilchis, RKM 4.8) Bars. These modifications also clarified that gravel mining in tidal reaches was excluded from this agreement since Federal, State and local laws and requirements address it.

As of 2011, active instream mining permits are located on the Trask, Wilson, Kilchis, Miami, and Nehalem Rivers with annual limit removal limits ranging from 2,000 to 11,000 m^3 per site (table 7; Judy Linton, U.S. Army Corps of Engineers, written commun., 2010; Robert Lobdell, Oregon Department of State Lands, written commun., 2011). A permitted mining site on the South Fork Nehalem River with an annual mining limit of 11,470 m^3 was not included in this study because it is located in the upper portion of the basin, where narrow canyon walls preclude geomorphic mapping from photographs. Dill Bar on the Kilchis River was excluded from the mapping because it is 1.1 km upstream of the Kilchis River study area, but was included in the compilation of reported deposited and mined gravel volumes. All ongoing mining sites are above the head of tide (see maps of study reaches below). Refer to the "Gravel-Operator Information and Surveys" section for more details.

Like instream gravel mining, floodplain mining can also affect channel condition and bed-material transport. The most recent USGS topographic quadrangles from 1984 to 1986 (which are based on aerial photographs from 1980) denote gravel mining sites on the Trask River floodplain. Although not specifically assessed in this study, the active channel near floodplain mining sites is commonly channelized, levied, and armored to prevent avulsions (channel excursions) into floodplain excavations, which can result in a diversion of the river into the mine pit (pit capture) and channel incision (Kondolf and others, 2002).

Table 7. Ongoing instream gravel mining permits in the Tillamook Bay subbasins and Nehalem River basin, northwestern Oregon. Data from Judy Linton (U.S. Army Corps of Engineers, written commun., 2010) and Robert Lobdell (Oregon Department of State Lands, written commun., 2011).

[RKM, river kilometer; km, kilometer]

River	Bar	Approximate locations	Permitted limit on annual mining volume (cubic meters)
Trask	Bush	RKM 12.2	4,330
Wilson	Donaldson	RKM 10.4	6,000
	Barker	RKM 6.9	2,100
Kilchis	Dill	~0.1 km upstream	5,500
	Gomes	RKM 4.8	3,000
Miami	Waldron	RKM 4.8	2,000
Nehalem	Plant	RKM 25.8	[1]11,000
	Winslow	RKM 24.8	
South Fork Nehalem	Unknown	Near the town of Cochran	11,000

[1]Limit is combined for Plant and Winslow Bars

Study Areas and Reaches

For the purposes of this study, we identified 14 study reaches encompassing the major alluvial portions of 6 river systems, including the lowermost 14.1 km of the Tillamook River, 16.3 km of the Trask River, 15.2 km of the Wilson River, 7.8 km of the Kilchis River, 11.6 km of the Miami River, and 31.4 km of the Nehalem River (figs. 1 and 2). These mainstem corridors contain most of the alluvial deposits and historical and ongoing instream gravel mining sites within the basins. The 6 study areas were subdivided into 12 reaches based primarily on tidal extent and topography.

Tillamook River

The Tillamook River begins east of the Cape Lookout State Park and flows eastward for 9.5 km and then northward for 6.7 km, gaining tributaries that drain Coast Range sedimentary rocks and Quaternary deposits to the west but also Coast Range volcanic rocks to the east (fig. 1). Larger tributaries like Munson (8.3 km^2), Simmons (11.0 km^2), Fawcett (16.2 km^2), and Killam (15.4 km^2) Creeks draining Coast Range volcanic rocks to the east probably provide most of the bed material to the Fluvial Tillamook Reach. The Tillamook River study area begins downstream of Killam Creek at RKM 14.1 (fig. 8). From here, the Tillamook River generally continues northwestward for 14.1 km, augmented by several small tributaries like Bewley (RKM 11.1; 15.8 km^2), Sutton (RKM 8.7; 6.5 km^2), Beaver (RKM 8.0; 13.7 km^2), Anderson (RKM 7.2; 6.5 km^2), and Esther (RKM 1.5; 3.4 km^2) Creeks. The South Branch Trask River connects the Tillamook and Trask Rivers at RKM 1.8. The study area for the Tillamook River was divided at the head of tide (table 8) into the Fluvial Tillamook (RKM 14.1–10.2) and Tidal Tillamook (RKM 10.2–0) Reaches. Upstream of the study area, the Tillamook River contains a few, small gravel bars. No permits for ongoing instream gravel mining exist along the Tillamook River.

In the Fluvial Tillamook Reach (RKM 14.1–10.2), the Tillamook River has a drainage area that increases from 89 km^2 near its upstream boundary to 110 km^2 at the head of tide and a concomitant increase in floodplain width from 50 to 720 m (table 8; fig. 8). The channel is largely unconfined, but flows against valley walls to the southwest near RKM 14.1, 12.9–12.5, and 11.1–10.8 in addition to Highway 101 on the east bank near RKM 11.8–11.6. The gradient of the Fluvial Tillamook Reach is 0.0022 m/m (table 8; fig. 9). The active channel, encompassing the wetted channel area and flanking gravel bars, ranges in width from 17 to 27 m, and contains elongated lateral and point bars (up to 5,160 m^2 in 2009 photographs) composed of gravel and finer grained sediments. The channel flows over cobble and fine grained alluvial deposits within this reach.

The head of tide is at about RKM 10.2 (table 1), and marks the transition to the Tidal Tillamook Reach, where the channel continues to flow over alluvial deposits and against western valley walls in several locations, such as near RKM 8.8, 7.9–7.6, 5.8, and 2.8–1.8 (table 8; fig. 8). In this reach, gradient declines to 0.0002 m/m (table 8; fig. 9) and bars are scarce except for near RKM 0 where large (up to 119,610 m^2) bars line the channel. The width of the active channel ranges from 15 to 137 m and the width of the floodplain ranges from 720 to 4,300 m, reaching its greatest width at the downstream end of the reach where the Tillamook and Trask Rivers share the floodplain. The drainage area of the Tillamook River is 156 km^2 at RKM 0. A noncomprehensive inventory of levees and dikes in tidal areas along the Oregon coast (Oregon Coastal Management Program, 2011) shows that almost the entirety of the Tillamook River from RKM 8.8 to 0 has either been diked or reinforced along its natural levees except for a short segment near RKM 2.2 (table 6; fig. 8). On current USGS quadrangle maps, roads near RKM 10.2–8.8 border the Tillamook River. Piling remnants likely installed to concentrate streamflows and

Table 8. Summary of characteristics for study reaches on the Tillamook, Trask, Wilson, Kilchis, Miami, and Nehalem Rivers, northwestern Oregon.

[m/m, meter change in elevation per meter of channel length; km², square kilometers; m, meter; RKM, river kilometer; Hwy, highway; LiDAR, Light Detection And Ranging]

River	Reach	Channel description	Reach gradient[2] (m/m)	Drainage area (km²)	Active channel width (m)	Floodplain description	Background sediment drivers	River corridor modifications and disturbances
Tillamook	Fluvial; RKM 14.1–10.2	Largely unconfined channel flows on alluvium and periodically against valley wall on west bank; lateral and point bars throughout reach	0.0022	89–110	17–27	Progressively widening floodplain; width 50–720 m	Inputs from tributaries and other upstream sources such as eroded bank material	Bordered by Hwy 101 from RKM 11.1 to 10.8; log drives and splash dams
	Tidal; RKM 10.2–0	Tidally affected channel flows on alluvium and periodically against valley wall on west bank; fewer and smaller bars	0.0002	110–156	15–137	Wide floodplain; width 1,500–4,300 m and shared with Trask River	Low-gradient promotes deposition of bed and suspended loads from upstream sources	Confined by levees and dikes in lower 8.8 km; pile structures and log boom remnants in channel; log drives and splash dams
Trask	Fluvial; RKM 16.3–7.0	Channel flows on alluvium; confined in upper 2 km; flows between north and south valley walls; lateral, medial, and point bars throughout reach	0.0016	378–425	28–56	Narrow valley in upper 2 km that progressively widens; width 100–1,530 m	Inputs from tributaries and other upstream sources such as eroded bank material, debris flows, and landslides	Intermittently confined by levees and dikes from RKM 10.6 to 7.0; historical and ongoing gravel mining; floodplain mining of unknown status; log drives
	Tidal; RKM 7.0–0	Tidally affected channel on alluvium; sparse lateral and point bars	0.0001	425–451	26–66	Wide floodplain; width 1,500–4,300 m and shared with Tillamook River	Low-gradient promotes deposition of bed and suspended loads from upstream sources	Entire reach confined by levees and dikes; log drives

Table 8. Summary of characteristics for study reaches on the Tillamook, Trask, Wilson, Kilchis, Miami, and Nehalem Rivers, northwestern Oregon. —continued

[m/m, meter change in elevation per meter of channel length; km², square kilometers; m, meter; RKM, river kilometer; Hwy, highway; LiDAR, Light Detection And Ranging]

River	Reach	Channel description	Reach gradient² (m/m)	Drainage area (km²)	Active channel width (m)	Floodplain description	Background sediment drivers	River corridor modifications and disturbances
Wilson	Upper Fluvial; RKM 15.2–12.6	Largely confined channel flows on alluvium plus intermittent bedrock in and along channel; lateral and point bars throughout reach	0.0017	417–474	42–66	Narrow valley that peaks in width at Little North Fork Wilson River confluence; width 110–150 m	Inputs from tributaries and other upstream sources such as eroded bank material, debris flows, and landslides	Log drives
	Lower Fluvial; RKM 12.6–5.0	Channel flows on alluvium and periodically against valley walls along north and south banks; lateral and point bars throughout reach	0.0011	474–492	50–58	Progressively widening to head of tide; width 150–2,200 m	Inputs from tributaries and other upstream sources such as eroded bank material, debris flows, and landslides	Intermittently confined by levees and dikes (RKM 12.4–5.0) and roads (RKM 6.3–5.0); historical and ongoing gravel mining; log drives
	Tidal; RKM 5.0–0	Tidally affected channel on alluvium; sparse lateral, point, and medial bars in upper ~1.8 km	0.0002	492–500	30–42	Wide floodplain; width 2,200–3,000 m	Low-gradient promotes deposition of bed and suspended loads from upstream sources	Confined by levees and dikes (RKM 5.0–0) and roads (RKM 5.0–4.8, 2.8–2.2, 1.7–0.2); log drives
Kilchis	Fluvial; RKM 7.8–2.7	Channel flows on alluvium; flows through narrow valley and periodically against valley walls along south and east banks; medial, lateral, and point bars throughout reach	0.0015	149–162	27–42	Progressively widening to head of tide; width 110–1,040 m	Inputs from tributaries and other upstream sources such as eroded bank material, debris flows, and landslides	Confined by levees and dikes (RKM 4.0–3.7); historical and ongoing instream gravel mining; log drives

Table 8. Summary of characteristics for study reaches on the Tillamook, Trask, Wilson, Kilchis, Miami, and Nehalem Rivers, northwestern Oregon. —continued

[m/m, meter change in elevation per meter of channel length; km², square kilometers; m, meter; RKM, river kilometer; Hwy, highway; LiDAR, Light Detection And Ranging]

River	Reach	Channel description	Reach gradient² (m/m)	Drainage area (km²)	Active channel width (m)	Floodplain description	Background sediment drivers	River corridor modifications and disturbances
Kilchis (cont.)	Tidal: RKM 2.7–0	Tidally affected channel on alluvium; larger lateral and point bars in upper ~1 km; flows periodically against valley wall along east bank	0.0007	162–169	23–42	Wide floodplain; width 800–2,500 m	Low-gradient promotes deposition of bed and suspended loads from upstream sources	Confined by levees and dikes (RKM 2.0–0) and roads (such as near RKM 1.5–0.8); log drives
Miami	Upper Fluvial: RKM 11.6–9.2	Channel flowing on alluvium through narrow valley; alternates between valley walls; large alternating, channel flanking bars	0.0075	32–45	32–41	Narrow floodplain; width 150–170 m	Inputs from tributaries and other upstream sources such as eroded bank material, debris flows, and landslides	Potential log drives
	Lower Fluvial: RKM 9.2–1.3	Channel flowing on alluvium; alternates against valley walls; medial, lateral, and point bars throughout reach with bars larger and more numerous downstream of tributaries and where mainstem crosses floodplain	0.0030	45–86	18–32	Progressively widening floodplain that narrows briefly at RKM 8.8, 8.1, 7.4, 3.6; width 170–390 m	Inputs from tributaries and other upstream sources such as eroded bank material, debris flows, and landslides	No levees on quads, but natural or anthropogenic levee evident in LiDAR from RKM 5.6 to 5.4 and 3.6 to 2.2; bermed, ditched or riprapped (RKM 3.2–1.3); historical and ongoing instream gravel mining; log drives
	Tidal: RKM 1.3–0	Tidally affected channel on alluvium; flows against northwest valley wall; sparse lateral and point bars	0.0013	86–93	15–20	Narrower floodplain than other rivers; width 390–520 m	Low-gradient promotes deposition of bed and suspended loads from upstream sources	Bermed, ditched, or riprapped (RKM 1.3–1.2) and leveed (RKM 0.6–0); log drives

Table 8. Summary of characteristics for study reaches on the Tillamook, Trask, Wilson, Kilchis, Miami, and Nehalem Rivers, northwestern Oregon. —continued

[m/m, meter change in elevation per meter of channel length; km²: square kilometers; m, meter; RKM, river kilometer; Hwy, highway; LiDAR, Light Detection And Ranging]

River	Reach	Channel description	Reach gradient² (m/m)	Drainage area (km²)	Active channel width (m)	Floodplain description	Background sediment drivers	River corridor modifications and disturbances
Nehalem	Fluvial; RKM 31.4–24.6	Channel flows mostly on alluvium with some bedrock on margins and in channel such as near RKM 31.2, 30.8, 30.2; confined by valley from RKM 31.4–29.6 and unconfined from RKM 29.6–24.6; flows periodically against valley walls; point, medial, and lateral bars throughout reach that increase in area in lower 1.6 km	0.0013	1,821–1,847	54–254	Narrow floodplain from RKM 31.4–29.6; widens then toward head of tide; width 170–490 m	Inputs from tributaries and other upstream sources such as eroded bank material, debris flows, and landslides	Historical and ongoing instream gravel mining; log drives and splash dams
	Tidal; RKM 24.6–0	Tidally affected channel on alluvium with confined and unconfined segments; flows against valley wall at RKM 24.4–22.6; bars present in upper 5.8 km; large tidal flats and islands near mouth	0.0001	1,847–2,207	47–2,190	Confined near RKM 24.6–18.8, RKM 9.8 (Dean Point), and RKM 4.6 (Fishery Point) to mouth; width 340 to 4,720 m	Low-gradient promotes deposition of bed and suspended loads from upstream sources	Leveed, diked, or riprapped along channel (RKM 24–23.1, 20.2–19.6,18.8–9.0) and intermittently throughout Nehalem Bay; jetties at the mouth of bay; historical dredging; log drives and splash dams

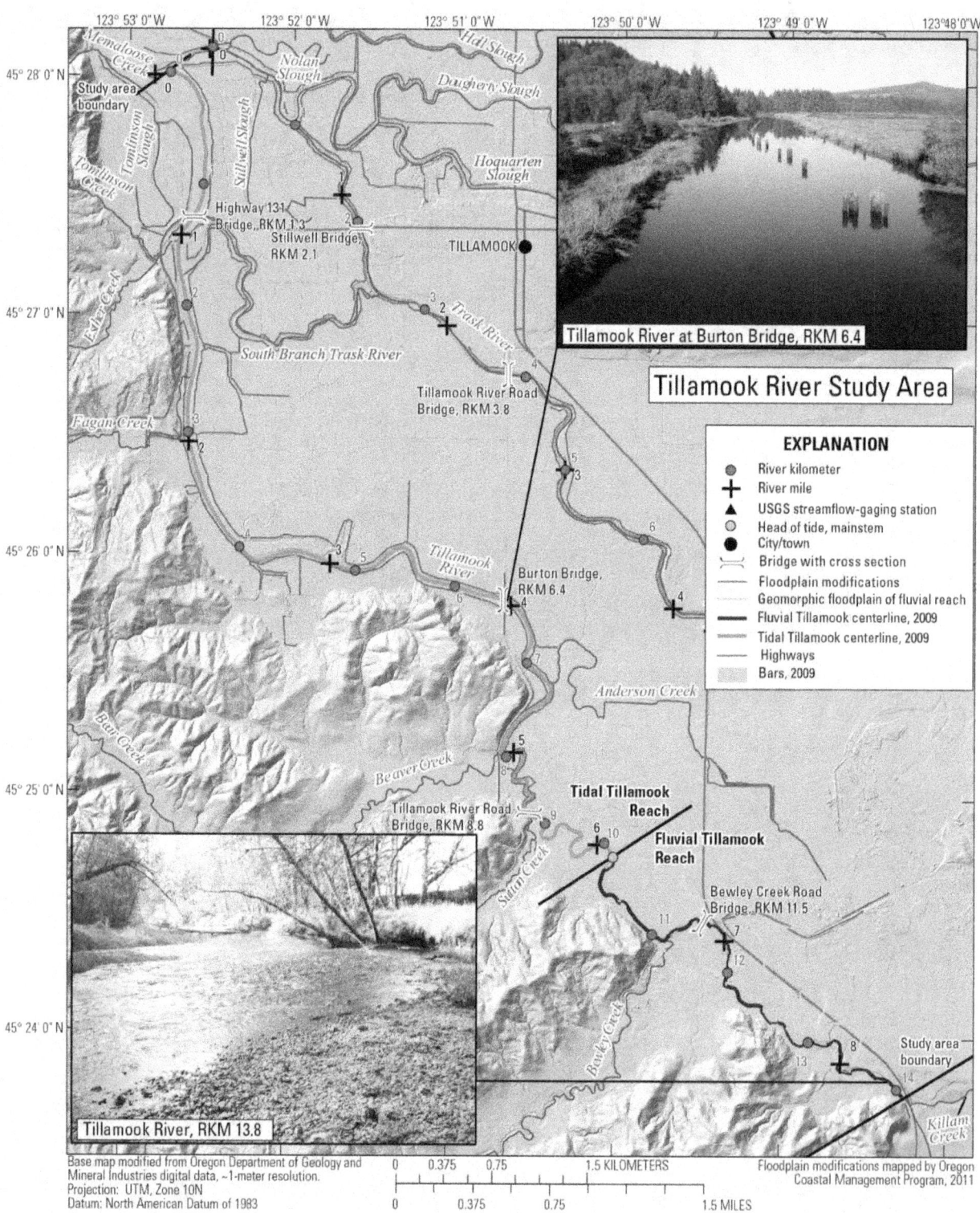

Figure 8. Map showing key locations, bars, and channel centerline delineated from 2009 orthophotographs and field reconnaissance photographs of the Tillamook River study area, northwestern Oregon. Floodplain modifications identified in the map include dikes, levees, and naturally formed levees reinforced with nonerodible materials (source: Oregon Coastal Management Program, 2011).

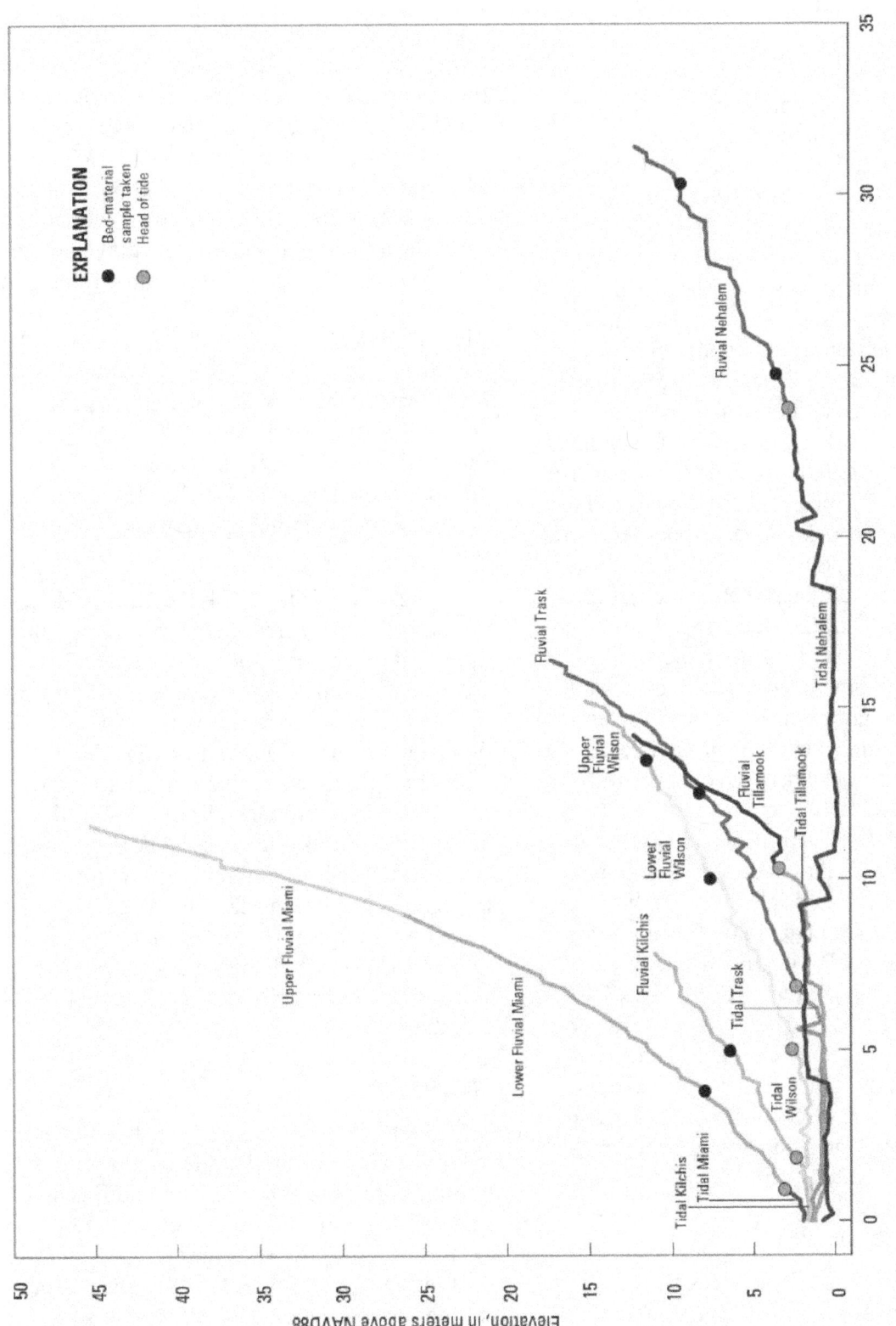

Figure 9. Diagram showing longitudinal profiles for the study reaches on the Tillamook, Trask, Wilson, Kilchis, Miami, and Nehalem River basins, northwestern Oregon. Profiles derived from 1-m Light Detection And Ranging (LiDAR) topographic surveys acquired from 2007 to 2009 along channel centerlines. Profile steps in the tidal reaches probably reflect LiDAR acquisition at different tide stages.

transport logs are present in this reach (fig. 8) and likely affect fine sediment deposition.

Trask River

The headwaters and most of the Trask River flow through the Tillamook State Forest. The mainstem begins at the confluence of the North and South Forks of the Trask River (20.7 and 135.4 km^2, respectively) and generally flows westward for approximately 30.7 km toward Tillamook Bay and the town of Tillamook (fig. 1). In the upper watershed, the mainstem flows over bedrock, such as near the confluence of the North and South Forks of the Trask River, and through a bedrock canyon near the town of Trask. The South Fork Trask River contributes gravel to the mainstem, as evidenced by a gravel delta at its mouth. The channel of the North Fork Trask River has bedrock and large boulders at its confluence with the South Fork Trask River, indicating that less bed material emanates from this tributary. Upstream of the study area, bed-material sediment is present along the Trask River, primarily as a thin veneer over bedrock and boulders, at high amplitude bends, or as lateral and point bar features near the confluence of Samson Creek and the Trask River. The study area begins at RKM 16.3, upstream of Gold Creek (RKM 16.2; 17.3 km^2), which contributes some bed material to the mainstem, based upon deposits evident in the aerial and orthophotographs from 1939, 2005, and 2009. Within the study area, the Trask River gains Hanenkrat (RKM 15.5; 1.2 km^2), Green (RKM 12.2; 3.4 km^2), and Mill (RKM 8.7; 12.3 km^2) Creeks and the tidal Dougherty (RKM 1.0) and Hoquarten (RKM 1.0) Sloughs (fig. 10). The South Branch Trask River (RKM 2.6) connects the Trask and Tillamook Rivers. The study area for the Trask River was divided into the Fluvial Trask (RKM 16.3–7.0) and Tidal Trask (RKM 7.0–0) Reaches at the head of tide (table 8).

In the Fluvial Trask Reach (RKM 16.3–7.0), the drainage area of the Trask River ranges from 378 to 425 km^2 (table 8; fig. 10). The valley is narrow (approximately100 m wide) in the upper 2 km of this reach, but then progressively increases to 1,530 m in width at the head of tide. Likewise, the width of the active channel ranges from 28 to 56 m wide. Downstream of the confined, upper 2 km, the Trask River crosses the floodplain multiple times after flowing against the floodplain boundary near RKM 13.2, 11.8–11.4 and 9.2. The Trask River has a gradient of 0.0016 m/m (table 8; fig. 9), flows over alluvial deposits, and contains lateral, medial, and point bars (up to 21,840 m^2 in 2009) throughout this reach. Levees intermittently border the Trask River from RKM 10.6 to 7.0 (table 6; fig. 10) (Oregon Coastal Management Program, 2011). Key locations in this reach include the active instream gravel mining site at RKM 12.2 (Bush Bar) and floodplain mining sites of unknown status are denoted near RKM 14.8, 13.4, and 12.8 on USGS topographic quadrangles produced from 1984 to 1986.

Within the Tidal Trask Reach (RKM 7.0–0), the Trask River decreases in gradient to 0.0001 m/m as it enters the wide coastal plain shared with the Tillamook River (approximately 1,500–4,300 m wide; table 8; fig. 10). At RKM 0, the drainage area of the Trask River is 451 km^2. The width of the active channel ranges from 26 to 66 m in this tidally influenced reach. Here, the Trask River flows over alluvial deposits, but contains fewer lateral and point bars (up to 8,970 m^2 in 2009) relative to the Fluvial Trask Reach. As shown in figure 10, levees including natural to man-made dikes discontinuously line the Trask River from RKM 7.0 to 2.6 and at RKM 0.8 (table 6).

Wilson River

The mainstem Wilson River begins east of the town of Lees Camp at the confluence of the South Fork of the Wilson River and Devils Lake Fork, which drain 41.3 and 68.6 km^2, respectively (fig. 1). The Wilson River then continues in a southwestward direction for 38.5 km gaining tributaries such as the North Fork Wilson River (69.9 km^2), Cedar (24.5 km^2), Jordan (64.4 km^2), and Fall (11.9 km^2) Creeks before its confluence

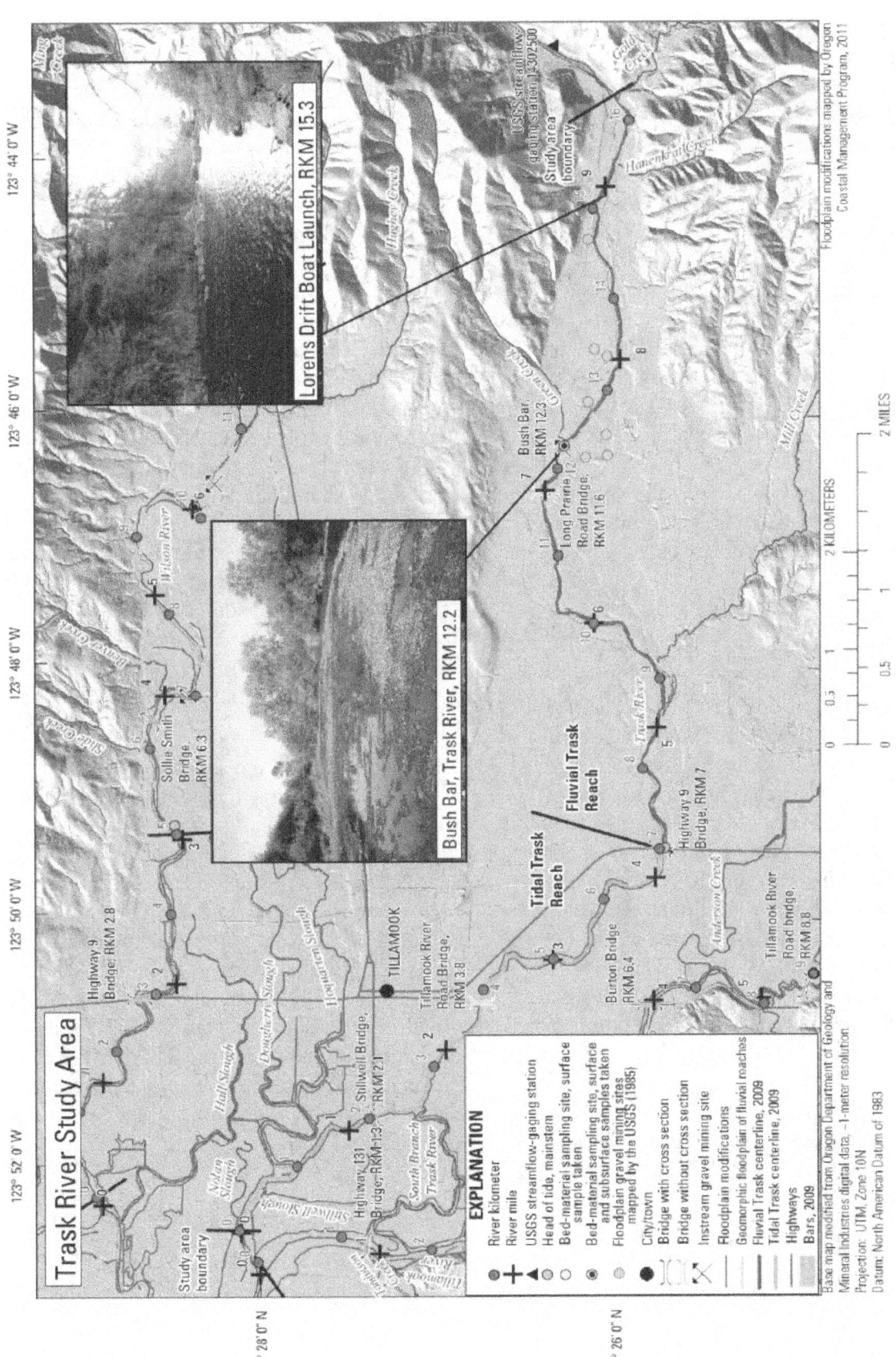

Figure 10. Map showing key locations, bars, and channel centerline delineated from 2009 orthophotographs and field reconnaissance photographs in the Trask River study area, northwestern Oregon. Floodplain modifications identified in the map include dikes, levees, and naturally formed levees reinforced with nonerodible materials (source: Oregon Coastal Management Program, 2011).

with the Little North Fork Wilson River (RKM 13.9; 51.1 km^2). The Wilson River then continues westward for approximately 13.6 km toward the Tillamook Bay. Like the Trask River, the headwaters, forks, and mainstem of the Wilson River upstream of RKM 11.6 are chiefly within the Tillamook State Forest. The Wilson River study area begins at RKM 15.2, upstream of the confluence of the Wilson and Little North Fork Wilson River (fig. 11). Tributaries like the Little North Fork Wilson River deliver bed material to the mainstem as indicated by gravel deposits and overbank deposition at its mouth (fig. 11). Upstream of the study area, the Wilson River intermittently flows through some wider sections containing large gravel bars (such as the 3 km long segment near Sylvan Creek) and confined gorges and basalt palisades and over bedrock outcrops that provide lateral and vertical channel stability.

The study area on the Wilson River was divided into three reaches—the Upper Fluvial Wilson (RKM 15.2–12.6), Lower Fluvial Wilson (RKM 12.6–5.0), and Tidal Wilson (RKM 5.0–0) Reaches (table 8; fig. 11). The fluvial section of the Wilson River was divided into the Upper and Lower Fluvial Reaches because the river is confined from RKM 15.2 to 12.6 and has a much wider floodplain from RKM 12.6 to 5.0. In the Upper Fluvial Wilson Reach (RKM 15.2–12.6), the Wilson River flows over alluvial deposits as well as intermittent bedrock outcrops in and along the channel (table 8; fig. 11). Here, the Wilson River has a gradient of 0.0017 m/m (table 8; fig. 9), and contains lateral and point bars (up to 14,930 m^2 in 2009) throughout the reach. The channel is confined by a narrow (approximately 110 m wide) valley that increases in width (150 m) at the confluence of the Wilson and Little North Fork Wilson Rivers (RKM 13.9; fig. 11), and has an active channel 42–66 m wide. The drainage area of the Wilson River ranges from 417 to 474 km^2 in this reach. No instream gravel mining permits are active in this reach.

In contrast, the channel in the Lower Fluvial Wilson Reach (RKM 12.6–5) flows predominately over alluvial deposits and through a valley that increases from 150 to 2,200 m in width toward the head of tide (table 8; fig. 11). The relatively lower gradient (0.0011 m/m; fig. 9) channel flows against valley walls to the south at RKM 12.4–12.2 and to the north at RKM 12.0–11.6, 9.6–8.2, and 6.2, and ranges from 50 to 58 m in active width. Bar deposits (up to 16,830 m^2 in 2009) are most abundant in the upper 4.4 km of this reach. The Wilson River is bordered by levees intermittently along RKM 12.6–7.0 and almost continually along RKM 7.0–5.0 (table 6; fig. 11) and by roads (such as along RKM 6.3–5.0) on current USGS quadrangles. The drainage area of the Wilson River is 492 km^2 at the downstream boundary of the Lower Fluvial Wilson Reach. Instream gravel mining sites are active at Donaldson (RKM 10.4) and Barker (RKM 6.9) Bars. Stinson and Stinson (1998) noted also instream gravel mining at Widmer (RKM 12.2) and Tannler (RKM 6.6) Bars (see the Gravel-Operator Information and Surveys section below).

Downstream in the Tidal Wilson Reach, the channel continues to flow over alluvial deposits, but declines in gradient to 0.0002 m/m (table 8; figs. 9 and 11). Sparse lateral, point, and medial bars (up to 1,010 m^2 in 2009) are primarily in the reach's upper 1.8 km. Near the Tillamook Bay, the width of the valley increases to 3,000 m and the river has a total drainage area of 500 km^2 at RKM 0. The active channel ranges from 30 to 42 m wide. Roads shown on current USGS quadrangles border the river near RKM 5.0–4.8, 2.8–2.2, and 1.7–0.2, whereas levees are present along one or both banks for most of the reach (table 6; fig. 11).

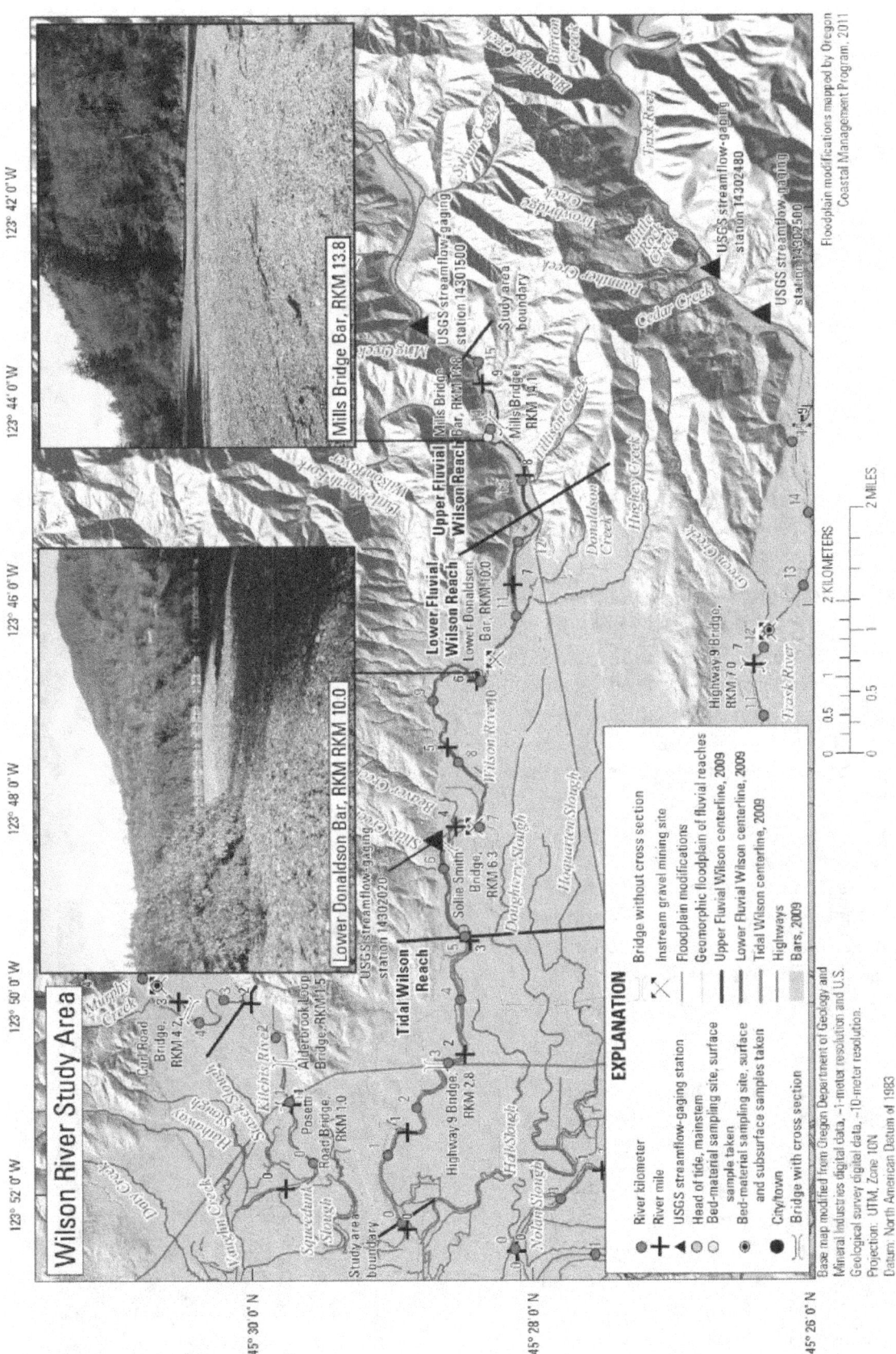

Figure 11. Map showing key locations, bars, and channel centerline delineated from 2009 orthophotographs and field reconnaissance photographs in the Wilson River study area, northwestern Oregon. Floodplain modifications identified in the map include dikes, levees, and naturally formed levees reinforced with nonerodible materials (source: Oregon Coastal Management Program, 2011).

Kilchis River

Much of the Kilchis River basin upstream of RKM 9.2 is within the Tillamook State Forest. The North and South Forks of the Kilchis River (41.4 and 26.6 km^2, respectively) drain opposite flanks of Sawtooth Ridge, and form the mainstem at their confluence (fig. 1). The mainstem then flows in southwestward for 4.5 km to Tilton Creek (4.2 km^2) and then continues generally southward for 6.8 km to the Little South Fork Kilchis River (30.9 km^2). In its final 10.1 km to the Tillamook Bay, the Kilchis River flows southwestward, and gains several tributaries, such as Clear Creek (RKM 9.2; 11.7 km^2). The study area, beginning at RKM 7.8 and approximately 1.2 km downstream of Clear Creek, was subdivided into two reaches at the head of tide (Fluvial Kilchis, RKM 7.8–2.7; Tidal Kilchis, RKM 2.7–0; table 8; fig. 12).

Outside the study area, the channel flows over bedrock in several locations like near the confluence of the North and South Forks of the Kilchis River, but contains intermittent lateral and point bars downstream of the confluence of the North and South Forks of the Kilchis River. Stream barbs were installed in the channel in the late 1990s to reduce bank erosion at Bruck Bar (approximately 2.3 km downstream of the North-South Forks of the Kilchis River confluence), but were not included in the Oregon Coastal Management Program (2011) dataset which primarily focused on tidal areas. Gravel was mined historically at Bruck Bar (Stinson and Stinson, 1998), and is actively mined at Dill Bar (approximately 0.1 km upstream of the study area; Judy Linton, U.S. Army Corps of Engineers, written commun., 2010; Robert Lobdell, Oregon Department of State Lands, written commun., 2011).

Throughout the Fluvial Kilchis Reach (RKM 7.8–2.7), the Kilchis River flows over gravel and other alluvial deposits and contains lateral, medial, and point bars (up to 5,050 m^2 in 2009; table 8; fig. 12). The channel has a gradient of 0.0015 m/m (table 8; fig. 9), and flows through a confined valley (approximately 110 m wide) and against valley walls to the south along RKM 7.8–6.4. At RKM 6.0, the Kilchis River is restricted by the valley wall to the west and a road to the east. In this confined reach, the active channel is 27 to 42 m wide. Downstream of RKM 6.0, the valley progressively widens to 1,040 m near the head of tide. The drainage area of the Kilchis River ranges from 149 to 162 km^2 in this reach. Between RKM 4.0 and 3.7, the levees constrain the Kilchis River (table 6; fig. 12). Active instream gravel mining occurs at Gomes (RKM 4.8) Bar whereas historical mining sites were present throughout the reach (see the Gravel-Operator Information and Surveys section below).

In the Tidal Kilchis Reach (RKM 2.7–0), the river continues to flow over alluvial deposits that are mostly sand and gravel, but declines in gradient to 0.0007 m/m (fig. 9), and contains larger lateral and point bars (up to 12,670 m^2 in 2009) in the reach's upper 1 km (table 8; fig. 12). Although the channel flows through a wide (800–2,500 m) valley, it flows against valley walls to the east at RKM 2.6 and to the south at RKM 1.9–1.6. The active channel ranges from 23 to 42 m wide. Current USGS quadrangles show roads near RKM 1.5–0.8 whereas levees border the Kilchis River from RKM 2.0–0 (table 6; fig. 12). The drainage area of the Kilchis River at RKM 0 is 169 km^2.

Measurement transect at Bruck Bar.

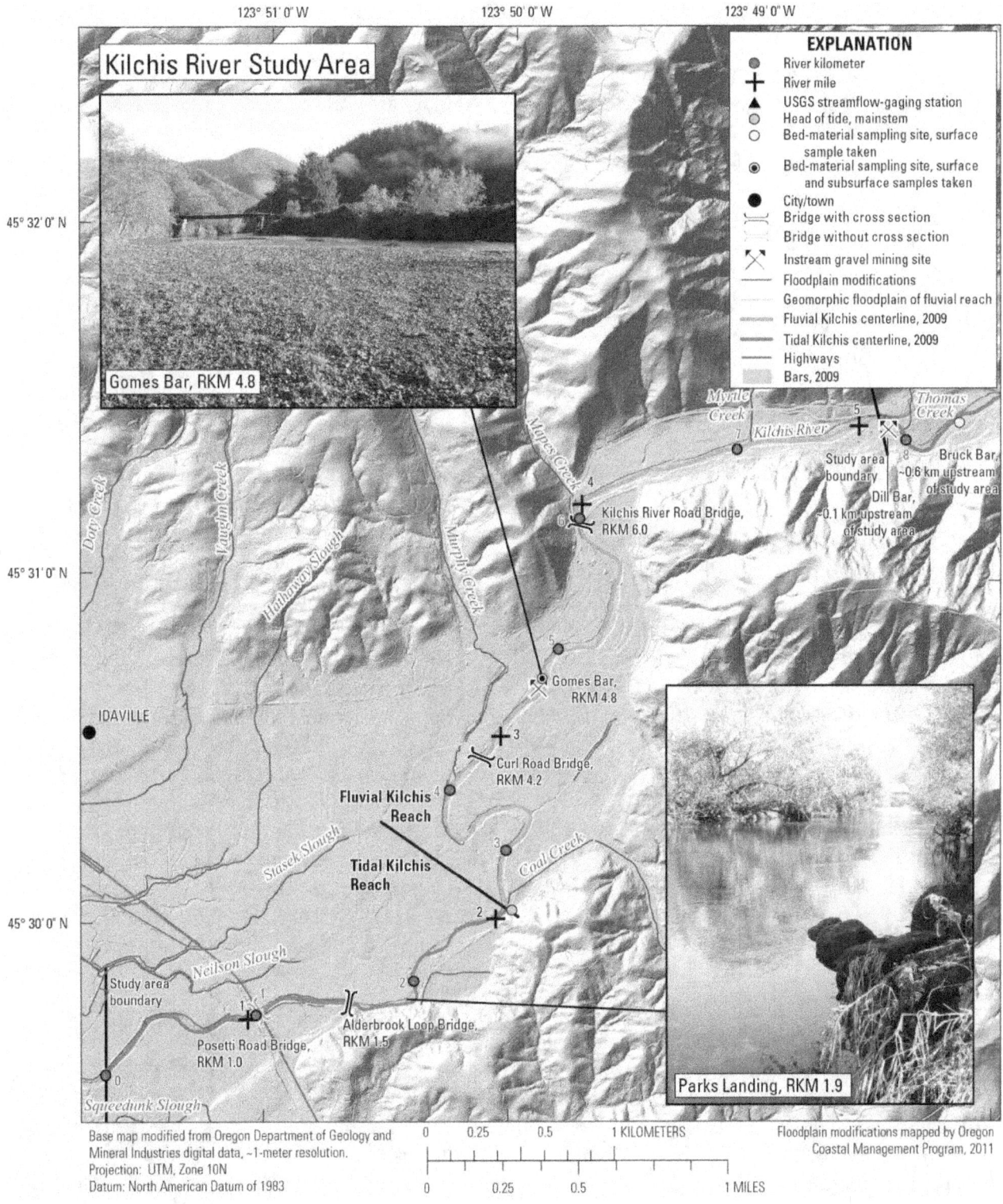

Figure 12. Map showing key locations, bars, and channel centerline delineated from 2009 orthophotographs and field reconnaissance photographs in the Kilchis River study area, northwestern Oregon. Floodplain modifications identified in the map include dikes, levees, and naturally formed levees reinforced with nonerodible materials (source: Oregon Coastal Management Program, 2011).

Miami River

The Miami River begins in the Tillamook State Forest and flows southwestward for approximately 24.5 km to the north end of the Tillamook Bay near town of Garibaldi (fig. 1). The study area on the Miami River begins at RKM 11.6, approximately 2.3 km upstream of the Miami River and Prouty Creek confluence. Within the study area, the Miami River is supplemented by Stuart (RKM 9.5, 3.0 km^2), Prouty (RKM 9.3; 3.1 km^2), Peterson (RKM 7.2, 7.1 km^2), and Moss (RKM 2.2, 11.6 km^2) Creeks (fig. 13). The Miami River study area was divided into three reaches—the Upper Fluvial Miami (RKM 11.6–9.2), Lower Fluvial Miami (RKM 9.2–1.3), and Tidal Miami (RKM 1.3–0) Reaches (table 8; fig. 13).

Flowing on alluvial deposits through a narrow valley (150–170 m wide), the Miami River in the Upper Fluvial Reach (RKM 11.6–9.2) contains large (up to 11,840 m^2 in 2009) alternating, channel flanking bars (table 8; fig. 13). Field observations from the October 2010 reconnaissance trip indicate that large wood may contribute to bar formation in this reach. This channel has the highest gradient in this study (0.0075 m/m; fig. 9) and ranges from 32 to 41 m in active channel width. The channel swings between valley walls to the south (RKM 11.6, 11.3, 10.4, and 10.1), north (RKM 11, and 10.8), and west (RKM 9.8, 9.6, and 9.3–9.2). The basin area of the Miami River ranges from 32 to 45 km^2 in this reach.

In the Lower Fluvial Reach (RKM 9.2–1.3), the Miami River continues to flow on alluvial deposits and has medial, lateral, and point bars that are larger and more numerous downstream of tributaries and where the mainstem crosses the floodplain (table 8; fig. 13). The bars in this reach are generally smaller (up to 5,790 m^2 in 2009) than those in the Upper Fluvial Reach. Here, channel gradient declines to 0.0030 m/m (fig. 9). The width of the floodplain increases from 170 to 390 m, but narrows locally at RKM 8.8, 8.1, 7.4, and 3.6. The river continues to al-ternate between valley walls, flowing against them to the north (RKM 9.2–8.6 and 1.5), south (RKM 8.1), west (RKM 7.2, 6.8, and 6.1–5.5) and east (RKM 6.5–6.4, 4.8, 4.4, and 3.7). The active channel varies from 18 to 32 m in width. The Miami River has a drainage area of 86 km^2 at the reach's downstream boundary. Although no roads are shown along the river on current USGS quadrangles, natural or anthropogenic levees are evident in the 2008 LiDAR survey between RKM 5.6–5.4 and 3.6–2.2 (fig. 13). The east bank has been intermittently bermed, ditched, or riprapped between RKM 3.2–1.2 (table 6; fig. 13). Gravel is actively mined at Waldron Bar (Judy Linton, U.S. Army Corps of Engineers, written commun., 2010; Robert Lobdell, Oregon Department of State Lands, written commun., 2011). Historically, at least four other sites were mined for gravel (see the Gravel-Operator Information and Surveys section below).

In the Tidal Miami Reach (RKM 1.3–0), the shortest and steepest tidal reach in this study (table 1; fig. 9), the Miami River flows on alluvial deposits, against the northwest valley wall from RKM 1.2 to 1.0, and through a narrower floodplain (390–520 m wide) relative to the other five rivers (table 8; fig. 13). Here, the river contains fewer lateral and point bars (up to 1,530 m^2 in 2009) relative to its upstream reaches. The active channel ranges from 15 to 20 m in width. Levees are present from RKM 0.6 to 0 (table 6; fig. 13). The total drainage area of the Miami River is 93 km^2.

Large wood jams trapping sediment above the Miami River study area.

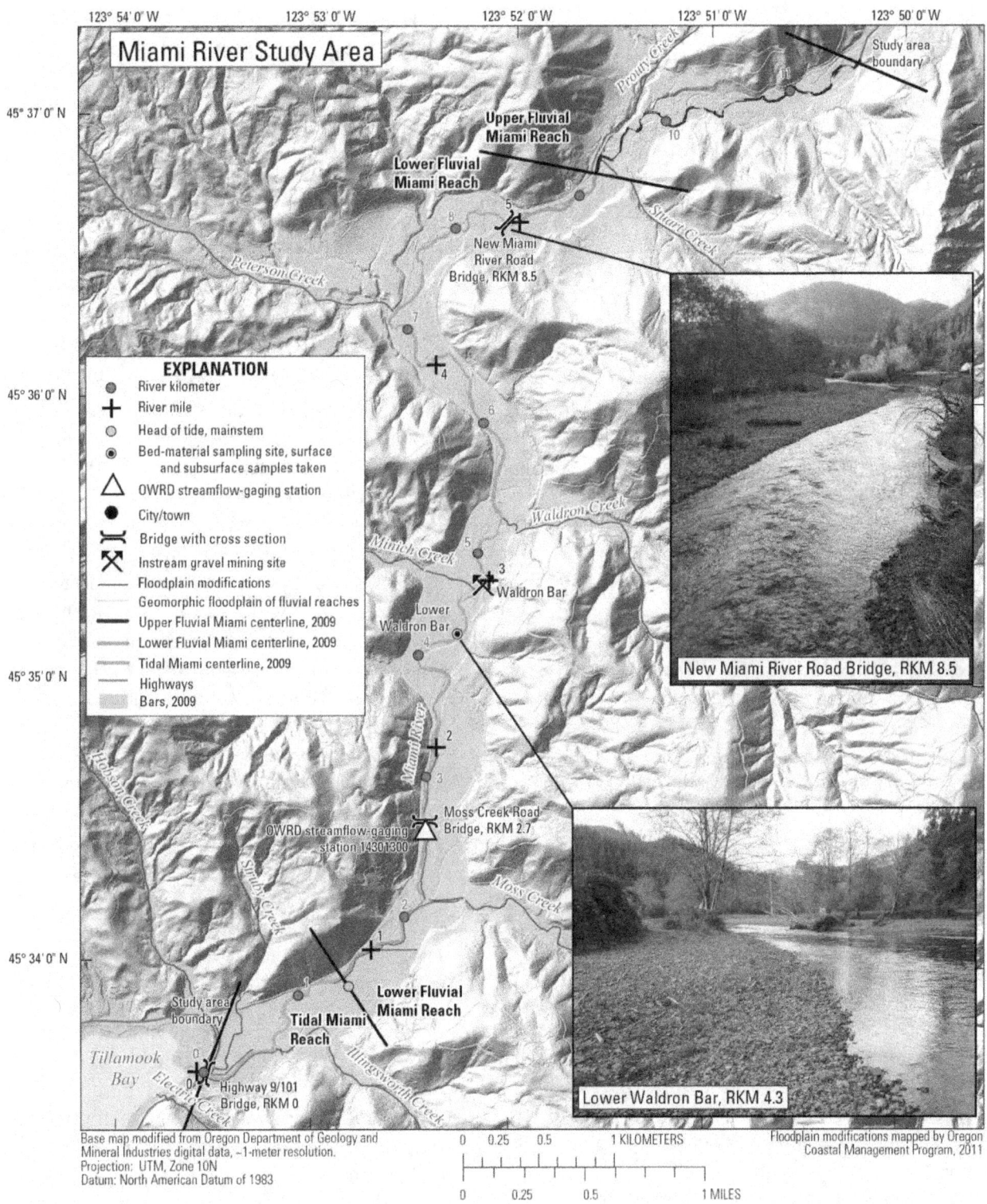

Figure 13. Map showing key locations, bars, and channel centerline delineated from 2009 orthophotographs and field reconnaissance photographs in the Miami River study area, northwestern Oregon. Floodplain modifications identified in the map include dikes, levees, and naturally formed levees reinforced with nonerodible materials (source: Oregon Coastal Management Program, 2011).

Nehalem River

The headwaters of the Nehalem River begin in the Tillamook and Clatsop State Forests near Giveout Mountain (827 m). The mainstem flows southeast a short distance before it is joined by the South Fork Nehalem River (3.2 km^2; fig. 2) and then continues northeastward for 53 km to the East Fork Nehalem River (83.4 km^2), acquiring Lousignont (27.3 km^2), Wolf (43.7 km^2), Clear (33.2 km^2), Beaver (32.8 km^2), Rock (161.9 km^2), and Pebble (56.2 km^2) Creeks. From the East Fork Nehalem River to Salmonberry River (183.9 km^2), the mainstem cuts a counter clockwise path for 99 km through the Coast Range, picking up Crooked (32.6 km^2), Fishhawk (60.3 km^2), Deep (58.8 km^2), Beneke (129.1 km^2), Humbug (75.0 km^2), and Cronin (33.1 km^2) Creeks. The river then flows west for 11 km to Fall Creek and then south for 4 km gaining Lost Creek (19.9 km^2) and Cook Creek (76.3 km^2). The confluence of the Nehalem River and Cook Creek marks the beginning of the Nehalem River study area. Within the study area, the Nehalem River continues west for 10 km to Foley Creek (RKM 21.9; 44.0 km^2) and then north for 8 km until its confluence with the southwestward flowing North Fork Nehalem River (RKM 13.5; 250.5 km^2). The mainstem then continues for 6 km until it reaches the Pacific Ocean near the town of Brighton. The study area was divided into two reaches—the Fluvial Nehalem (RKM 31.4–24.6; fig. 14) and Tidal Nehalem Reaches (RKM 24.6–0; fig. 15).

The Nehalem River in the Fluvial Reach (RKM 31.4–24.6) flows predominantly over alluvial deposits as well as locally on bedrock in and along the channel in the upper part of the reach (table 8; fig. 14). With a gradient of 0.0013 m/m (fig. 9), the channel has lateral, medial, and point bars (up to 18,880 m^2 in 2009), but their area is greatest in the reach's lower 1.6 km. The channel is relatively confined by its narrow (170 m wide) valley from RKM 31.4–29.6. Downstream of RKM 29.6, the floodplain progressively widens to 490 m toward the head of tide. The channel flows against valleys walls to the south

(RKM 29.2, 28.4–27.6, 26.5–26.2), north (RKM 25.8–25.4), and west (RKM 25.0–24.8), and has an active width that ranges from 54 to 254 m. The drainage area of the Nehalem River increases from 1,821 to 1,847 km^2 in the Fluvial Nehalem Reach. Levees flank the channel near RKM 27.2–26.2 (table 6; fig. 14). Gravel mining permits are active for Plant and Winslow Bars at RKM 25.8 and 24.8, respectively (Judy Linton, U.S. Army Corps of Engineers, written commun., 2010; Robert Lobdell, Oregon Department of State Lands, written commun., 2011).

In the Tidal Nehalem Reach (RKM 24.6–0), the river flows over alluvial deposits and through unconfined and confined segments (table 8; fig. 15). The low gradient channel (0.0001 m/m; fig. 9) is confined from RKM 24.6 to 18.8, at Dean Point (RKM 9.8), and from Fishery Point (RKM 4.6) to the mouth. The Nehalem River also flows against a valley wall to the northeast near RKM 24.4–22.6. The width of the floodplain throughout this reach ranges from 340 to 4,720 m. A few small bars (up to 0.09 km^2 in 2009) flank the channel in the upper section of this reach, whereas large tidal flats and islands (up to 4.7 km^2 in 2009) occur in the Nehalem Bay. On the current USGS quadrangles, roads may constrain a few small segments (such as near RKM 17.6–17.4, 17.0–16.2, 15.2–14, and 10.8–9.6). Riprap and human-made dikes and natural levees are near RKM 24.0–23.1, 20.2–19.6, and 18.8–9.0 and within the Nehalem Bay (table 6; fig. 15).

Approach and Key Findings

For this study, we reviewed existing datasets and studies relevant to channel condition and bed-material transport in the Tillamook Bay sub-basins and Nehalem River basin, applied reconnaissance-level geographic information system (GIS) analyses, and made field observations and particle size measurements in October 2010. The objectives of these efforts were to (1) identify existing datasets that would support more detailed analyses of bed-material transport and channel condition, (2) summarize reported

Figure 14. Map showing key locations, bars, and channel centerline delineated from 2009 orthophotographs and field reconnaissance photographs in the Fluvial Reach of the Nehalem River, northwestern Oregon. Floodplain modifications identified in the map include dikes, levees, and naturally formed levees reinforced with nonerodible materials (source: Oregon Coastal Management Program, 2011).

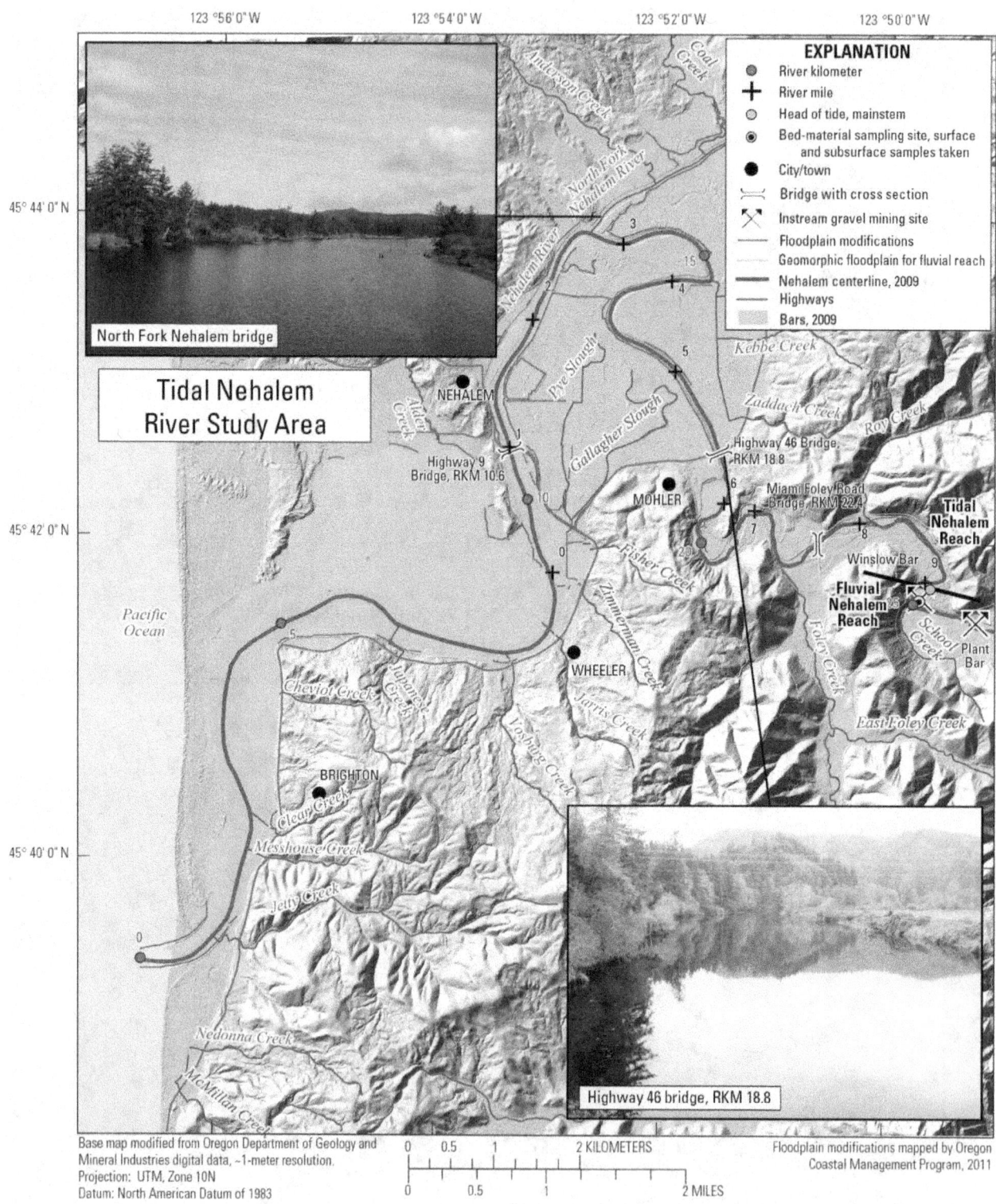

Figure 15. Map showing key locations, bars, and channel centerline delineated from 2009 orthophotographs and field reconnaissance photographs in the Tidal Reach of the Nehalem River, northwestern Oregon. Floodplain modifications identified in the map include dikes, levees, and naturally formed levees reinforced with nonerodible materials (source: Oregon Coastal Management Program, 2011).

44

volumes of mined and deposited material at instream gravel mining sites, (3) characterize broad-scale bar and channel patterns using aerial and orthophotographs spanning 1939–2009, (4) identify locations where the channels may be aggrading, incising, prone to migration, or stable, and (5) assess the transport capacity and sediment supply relation for each reach. Overall, this study provides a preliminary review of channel condition and bed-material transport in these rivers, and identifies outstanding issues relevant to the permitting of instream gravel mining that may be addressed by future studies. The following sections summarize each of the major activities and key findings.

Review of Existing Datasets

We assessed the availability of spatial datasets for the Tillamook Bay subbasins and Nehalem River basin that could be used to evaluate channel condition and bed-material transport. This search focused primarily on aerial and orthophotographs, but included other geospatial datasets, such as LiDAR topographic data, geologic maps, General Land Office (GLO) surveys, and navigation surveys.

Aerial and Orthophotographs

We reviewed aerial and orthophotography coverages of the Tillamook Bay subbasins and Nehalem River basin available from the U.S. Army Corps of Engineers' Aerial Photograph Library (Portland, Oregon) and the University of Oregon Map and Aerial Photography Library (Eugene, Oregon) as well as digital orthophotographs available from public, online sources. Other potential sources of photographs not investigated for this review include the Bureau of Land Management, National Archives, county government collections, and private timber companies.

The entire study areas in the Tillamook Bay subbasins and Nehalem River basin were photographed at least 12 and 15 times, respectively, between 1939 and 2011 (table 9; table 10). Several additional sets of aerial photographs provide nearly complete coverage of the study areas (tables 9 and 10). Of the Tillamook Bay subbasins, study areas along the Tillamook, Trask, and Wilson Rivers were photographed most frequently (table 9). Of the two Nehalem River reaches, the Tidal Nehalem Reach was photographed more frequently (table 10). At least 16 photograph sets in table 9 and 18 sets of photograph sets in table 10 provide comprehensive coverage of all or most of the study areas and were taken at scales of 1:24,000 or greater. These sets would be suitable for use in future studies assessing long-term changes in channel attributes, bar frequency and area, and vegetative cover throughout the study areas.

For bar and channel delineations in the six study areas, we used aerial photographs taken in 1939 and 1967 and orthophotographs taken in 2005 and 2009 (tables 9 and 10, described below). At the time of this study, the 2009 photographs were the most recent and were chosen to represent relatively recent bar and channel conditions throughout the study areas. The 1939, 1967, and 2005 photographs were selected so we could compare data between this and completed studies in the Chetco (Wallick and others, 2010), Umpqua (Wallick and others, 2011), Rogue (Jones and others, 2012a), and Coquille (Jones and others, 2012b) River basins and Hunter Creek basin (Jones and others, 2011). The 1939 photographs are the earliest photographs of the study areas (table 9; table 10) and the 1967 photographs provide coverage of the study areas following the December 22, 1964 flood, which exceeded a 10-year flood event on the Wilson, Miami, and Nehalem Rivers (fig. 5B–D).

Table 9. Aerial photographs with coverage of the Tillamook Bay subbasins, northwestern Oregon.

[Aerial photographs shown in **bold** were used to delineate bar and channel features in this study. --, data unavailable; USACE, U.S. Army Corps of Engineers; UO, University of Oregon Map and Aerial Photography Library; RKM, river kilometer; USC&GS, U.S. Coast and Geodetic Survey; ODF, Oregon Department of Forestry; USDA, U.S. Department of Agriculture; WAC, Western Aerial Contractor; ODR, Oregon Department of Revenue; AM; Aerial Mapping; USGS, U.S. Geological Survey; m, meter]

Full coverage of study area(s)	Partial coverage of study area(s)	Year	Collection month/day	Scale	Collection entity	Repository
All	--	**1939**	**5/8, 5/12, 7/20**	**1:10,200**	**USACE**	**USACE**[1]
--	Miami, RKM 5-0	1944	5/3	1:30,000		USACE
Trask, Kilchis	Partial coverage of Tilla-mook, Wilson, and Miami	1945	--	1:6,000	USACE	UO
Tillamook	Wilson, RKM 9-0; Trask, RKM 14-0	1946	8/9	1:10,000	USC&GS	USACE
All except Tilla-mook	--	1951	--	1:12,000	ODF	UO
Tillamook; Trask; Wilson	--	1952	5/17; 5/22	1:25,000	USC&GS	USACE
All	--	1954	--	1:12,000	USDA; ODF	UO
--	Tillamook, RKM 11-0; Trask, RKM 6-0; Wilson, RKM 5.5-0; Kilchis, 2.5-0; Miami, RKM 5-0	1955	8/26-27	1:9,600	USACE	USACE
Tillamook; Kilchis	Trask, RKM 10-0; Wilson, RKM 9-0	1962	3/13	1:14,700	USACE	USACE
--	Trask, RKM~2-0; Wilson, RKM ~3-0; Miami, RKM 10-0	1964	8/20	1:22,000	USACE	USACE
All	--	1965	4/26	1:12,000	USACE	USACE
--	Miami, RKM 10-0	1966	8/17	1:30,000	USACE	USACE
All	--	**1967**	2/19	**1:20,000**	**USDA**	**UO**
All	--	1969	7/18	1:48,000	WAC	USACE
All	--	1970	--	1:12,000	ODF	UO
--	Tillamook, RKM 14-0; Trask, RKM 7.5-0; Wilson, RKM 4-0	1972	7/3	1:30,000	Delano	USACE
Tillamook; Trask; Wilson	--	1974	--	1:12,000	ODR	UO
Tillamook	Trask, RKM 9-0; Wilson, RKM 10-0; Kilchis, RKM 2-0	1978	3/2	1:12,000	Aerial Mapping	USACE
Tillamook	Trask, RKM 9-0; Wilson, RKM 11-0; Kilchis, RKM 7.5-0	1978	10/2	1:24,000	WAC	USACE
Tillamook	Trask, RKM 14-0; Wilson, RKM 15-0; Kilchis, RKM 7.5-0	1978	10/12-13	1:24,000	AM	USACE

Table 9. Aerial photographs with coverage of the Tillamook Bay subbasins, northwestern Oregon.—continued

[Aerial photographs shown in **bold** were used to delineate bar and channel features in this study. --, data unavailable; USACE, U.S. Army Corps of Engineers; UO, University of Oregon Map and Aerial Photography Library; RKM, river kilometer; USC&GS, U.S. Coast and Geodetic Survey; ODF, Oregon Department of Forestry; USDA, U.S. Department of Agriculture; WAC, Western Aerial Contractor; ODR, Oregon Department of Revenue; AM; Aerial Mapping; USGS, U.S. Geological Survey; m, meter]

Full coverage of study area(s)	Partial coverage of study area(s)	Year	Collection month/day	Scale	Collection entity	Repository
--	Tillamook, RKM 11–0; Trask, RKM 8–0; Wilson, RKM 8.5–0	1980	7/7	1:12,000	AM	USACE
Tillamook; Kilchis; Miami	Trask, RKM 11–0; Wilson, RKM 11–0	1982	3/23–24	1:48,000	WAC	USACE
All	--	1982	--	1:80,000	USGS	UO
Tillamook; Trask; Wilson	--	1986	7/11	1:48,000	WAC	USACE
All except Miami	Miami, RKM 4–0	1989	10/31	1:24,000	Bergman	USACE
All	--	1994	5/30; 7/18; 9/4; 6/27	1:24,000	USGS	USGS, UO
--	Tillamook, RKM 11–0; Trask, RKM 6–0; Wilson, RKM 5.5–0; Kilchis, RKM 2.5–0; Miami, RKM 5–0	1999	9/29	1:6,000	Earth Data	USACE
Kilchis	Trask, RKM 2–0; Wilson, RKM 8–0	2000	5/24	1:6,000	Bergman	USACE
All except Trask	Trask, RKM 16–0	2000	9/12	1:6,000	Bergman	USACE
All	--	2000	7/30; 8/8; 8/16–17; 8/22	1:24,000	USGS	USGS
Tillamook; Trask; Wilson	--	2001	5/11; 5/20	1:24,000	WAC	USACE
All	--	**2005**	**7/17; 7/19– 20**	**1 pixel = 0.5 m**	**USDA**	**USGS**
All	--	**2009**	**6/23; 6/27**	**1 pixel = 1 m**	**USDA**	**USGS**
All	--	2011	7/2; 7/5	1 pixel = 1 m	USDA	USDA

[1] Limited coverage of the study area available from UO

Donaldson Bar on the Wilson River.

Table 10. List of aerial photographs with coverage of the Nehalem River, northwestern Oregon.

[--, data not available; USACE, U.S. Army Corps of Engineers; UO, University of Oregon Map Library; RKM, river kilometer; ODF, Oregon Department of Forestry; USGS, U.S. Geological Survey; USDA, U.S. Department of Agriculture; ODR, Oregon Department of Revenue; WAC, Western Aerial Contractor; AM; Aerial Mapping; m, meter]

Full coverage of reach(es)	Partial coverage of reach(es)	Year	Collection month/day	Scale	Collection entity	Repository
All	--	1939	5/8; 5/12	1:10,200	USACE	USACE, UO
Fluvial Nehalem	Tidal Nehalem, RKM 24.6–8.2	1951	--	1:12,000	ODF	UO
All	--	1953	--	1:37,400	USGS	UO
--	Tidal Nehalem, RKM 8.2–0	1954	--	1:20,000	USDA	UO
Fluvial Nehalem	Tidal Nehalem, RKM 24.6–8.2	1954-55	--	1:12,000	ODF	UO
All	--	1960	--	1:12,000	ODR	UO
--	Tidal Nehalem, RKM 13–0	1962	3/13	1:12,000	USACE	USACE
--	Tidal Nehalem, RKM 14–0	1963	5/28	1:18,000; 1:16,200	USACE	USACE
--	Tidal Nehalem, RKM 17–0	1964	8/20	1:22,000	USACE	USACE
Tidal Nehalem	Fluvial Nehalem, RKM 29-24.6	1965	4/26	1:12,000	USACE	USACE
--	Tidal Nehalem, RKM 24–0	1965	7/13–14; 7/23	1:24,000	USACE	USACE
--	Tidal Nehalem, RKM 11–0	1966	8/17	1:30,000	USACE	USACE
All	--	1967	2/19	1:20,000	USDA	UO
	Tidal Nehalem, RKM 23.5–0	1969	7/18	1:48,000	WAC	USACE
All	--	1970	--	1:12,000	ODF	UO
--	Tidal Nehalem, RKM 18–0	1972	7/3	1:12,000	Delano	USACE
--	Tidal Nehalem, ~RKM 22.6–0	1974	--	1:12,000	ODR	UO
--	Tidal Nehalem, ~RKM 8–0	1977	10/17	1:36,000	WAC	USACE
--	Tidal Nehalem, ~RKM 8–0	1977	12/26	1:24,000	WAC	USACE
Tidal Nehalem	Fluvial Nehalem, RKM 25–24.6	1978	3/2	1:12,000	AM	USACE
--	Tidal Nehalem, RKM 23–0	1978	10/2	1:24,000	WAC	USACE
--	Tidal Nehalem, RKM 22.5–0	1978	10/12	1:24,000	AM	USACE
--	Tidal Nehalem, ~RKM 8–0	1980	4/2	1:24,000	WAC	USACE
Tidal Nehalem	Fluvial Nehalem, RKM 25–24.6	1980	7/7	1:12,000	AM	USACE
All	--	1980	--	1:24,000	USGS	UO
All	--	1982	3/24	1:48,000	WAC	USACE
--	Tidal Nehalem, RKM 21-0	1983	9/28	1:48,000	WAC	USACE
All	--	1986	6/11	1:48,000	WAC	USACE
All	--	1989	10/31	1:24,000	Bergman	USACE
All	--	1994	5/30; 7/18; 8/30; 9/4	1:24,000	USGS	UO, USGS

Table 10. List of aerial photographs with coverage of the Nehalem River, northwestern Oregon.—continued

[--, data not available; USACE, U.S. Army Corps of Engineers; UO, University of Oregon Map Library; RKM, river kilometer; ODF, Oregon Department of Forestry; USGS, U.S. Geological Survey; USDA, U.S. Department of Agriculture; ODR, Oregon Department of Revenue; WAC, Western Aerial Contractor; AM; Aerial Mapping; m, meter]

Full coverage of reach(es)	Partial coverage of reach(es)	Year	Collection month/day	Scale	Collection entity	Repository
All	--	2000	7/30; 8/8; 8/22	1:24,000	USGS	USGS
All	--	2001	5/11	1:24,000	WAC	USACE
All	--	**2005**	**07/17; 8/3**	**1 pixel = 0.5 m**	**USDA**	**USGS**
All	--	**2009**	**6/27**	**1 pixel = 1 m**	**USDA**	**USGS**
All	--	2011	7/2; 7/5	1 pixel = 1 m	USDA	USDA

Confluence of Cook Creek and the Nehalem River.

Historical Maps and Survey Data

We reviewed historical maps and survey data that are available from several sources for the six study areas. The purpose of this review was to identify datasets with information on channel condition, bar distribution and area, and channel morphology and bed elevations that could support assessments of channel change in future studies. For the Tillamook Bay subbasins, we focused on our study areas; see Coulton and others (1996) for datasets relevant to the Tillamook Bay.

The GLO conducted the earliest surveys of the six study areas from 1857 to 1858 and 1858 to 1884, respectively (table 11). The main purpose of these surveys was to establish the Township, Range and Section lines of the Public Land Survey System (PLSS) (Atwood, 2008). Along the lower sections of the Tillamook, Trask, Wilson, and Kilchis Rivers and entire Nehalem River study area, channel edges were surveyed (a process typically described as "meandering"), thereby providing an accurate planview depiction of channel geometry at the time of the survey. Future reviews of the GLO maps and accompanying surveyor notes would help determine if surveyors recorded channel and vegetation descriptions that would be useful for assessing historical changes in channel morphology or bed-material transport. Existing GLO reconstructions have focused primarily vegetation communities, swamps, and marshes in the Tillamook Bay area (Coulton and others, 1996) and saltwater marshes and freshwater wetlands in the lower Nehalem River (Christy, 2004).

Other datasets include nautical charts showing bathymetry for multiple times for the lower Nehalem, Tillamook, and Trask Rivers by the National Ocean Survey (table 11). The USGS surveyed the position and profile of the Wilson and Trask Rivers in 1953 and Nehalem River in 1936 (table 11). The Oregon Department of Geology and Mineral Industries (DOGAMI) is the source for recent, high-resolution (1-m) LiDAR data as well as maps of the major geologic units

and geomorphic divisions for the study areas (table 11). Maps of the Nehalem River's shoreline from 1954 and estuary habitats from 1978 are also available (table 11). Other datasets that may be useful for assessing longitudinal profile changes (but not included in table 11) are flood insurance maps and data from the Federal Emergency Management Agency and Corps of Engineers.

Previous Hydrologic and Geomorphic Studies

For the Tillamook Bay subbasins, issues related to sedimentation, flooding, water quality, aquatic habitat, and instream gravel mining have motivated several studies of hydrology and geomorphology. The number and scope of these studies contrasts with the Nehalem River basin for which we found no such studies. Based on our literature review, the only available studies for the Nehalem River basin are two general watershed studies (Johnson and Maser, 1999; R2 Resource Consultants, 2005).

Relevant studies of river geomorphology in the Tillamook Bay subbasins include (1) a basin erosion and sediment study by the Tillamook Bay Task Force and others (1978), (2) an environmental history of the estuary and surrounding watersheds by Coulton and others (1996), (3) an analysis of the effects of gravel bar mining on the Wilson, Kilchis, and Miami Rivers by Stinson and Stinson (1998), and (4) a geomorphic analysis of Tillamook Bay rivers by Pearson (2002). Additional sources include watershed assessments and analyses for the Trask (Follansbee and Stark, 1998b; Snyder and others, 2003), Wilson (Duck Creek Associates, 2008), Kilchis (Follansbee and Stark, 1998a), and Miami (Snyder and others, 2001; Jenkins and others, 2005) River basins as well as several reports on bar gravel mining in the Tillamook area, such as those by Reckendorf (2006, 2008a,b). Key findings from these studies will be noted in relation to the findings of our analyses presented in subsequent report sections.

Table 11. List of existing datasets reviewed for the Tillamook Bay subbasins and Nehalem River basin, northwestern Oregon.

[BLM, Bureau of Land Management; RKM, river kilometer; NOS, National Ocean Survey; NOAA, National Oceanic and Atmospheric Administration; USGS, U.S. Geological Survey; NA, not available; OCA, Oregon Coastal Atlas; ODFW, Oregon Department of Fish and Wildlife; OSU, Oregon State University; LiDAR, Light Detection and Ranging; m, meter; DOGAMI, Oregon Department of Geology and Mineral Industries; Oregon GEO, Oregon Geospatial Enterprise Office]

Dataset	Study Area(s)	Scale	Date(s)	Source	Depository	Description
General Land Office (GLO) survey	Tillamook, Trask, Wilson, Kilchis, and Miami	~1:31,680	1857–87	GLO maps	BLM[1]	Earliest surveys conducted between 1857 and 1858; meander surveys conducted in 1858 for Tillamook (RKM 6.4–0), Trask (RKM 3.3–0), Wilson (RKM 3–0), and Kilchis (RKM 1.6–0) Rivers; surveys not meandered for Miami River; maps show plan view of channels and surrounding lands; limited details on river features
	Nehalem	~1:31,680	1858–84	GLO maps	BLM[1]	Earliest surveys conducted in 1858; meander surveys conducted in 1858, 1873, 1882 and 1884 for the entire study area on the Nehalem River (RKM 31.4–0); maps show planview of channel and surrounding lands; limited details on river features
Nautical chart	Nehalem	1:20,000	Multiple years[2]	NOS	NOAA[3]	Bathymetric map of ~RKM 9.5–0 of the Nehalem River in 1891 and 1947 and ~RKM 13.4–0 in subsequent years
	Tillamook, Trask	1:20,000	Multiple years[4]	NOS	NOAA[3]	Bathymetric map of Tillamook (~RKM 1.6–0 in 1928 and 1948; ~RKM 3–0 in subsequent years) and Trask (~RKM 2–0) Rivers
Plan and profile	Nehalem	1:24,000	1936	USGS	USGS	Contour map of Nehalem River from ~RKM 31.4–18.8; includes profiles; published in 1939
	Trask, Wilson	1:24,000	1953	USGS	USGS	Contour map of Trask (RKM 16.3–11.7) and Wilson (RKM 20.7–10.2) Rivers; includes profiles
Shoreline map	Nehalem	1:5,000	1954	NOS	OCA[5]	Vectorized Nehalem River shoreline from 1954 and ~RKM 21–0.4
Estuary habitat map	Tillamook, Trask, Miami	NA	1978	ODFW	OSU[6]	Map of estuary categorized by tidal inundation, habitat type, vegetation, and sediment for Tillamook (~RKM 1.4–0), Trask (~RKM 1.8–0), and Miami (RKM 0.4–0) Rivers
	Nehalem	NA	1978	ODFW	OSU[6]	Map of estuary categorized by tidal inundation, habitat type, vegetation, and sediment for ~RKM 21.4–0
LiDAR	Tillamook, Trask, Wilson, Kilchis, and Miami	~1 m	2007–09	DOGAMI	DOGAMI[7]	High resolution topographic survey of all study areas
	Nehalem	~1 m	2009	DOGAMI	DOGAMI[7]	High resolution topographic survey of entire study area
Geologic map	All study areas	1:12,000 to 1:500,000	2009	DOGAMI	Oregon GEO[8]	Digital compilation of geologic maps in Oregon (Ma and others, 2009); complete coverage of all study areas

Table 11 footnotes

[1] BLM: http://www.blm.gov/or/landrecords/survey/ySrvy1.php

[2] 1860, 1947, 1970, 1973, 1978, 1982, 1990, 2006; other years likely

[3] NOAA: *http://historicalcharts.noaa.gov/; http://www.charts.noaa.gov/OnLineViewer/PacificCoastViewerTable.shtml*

[4] Such as 1969, 1971, 1973, 1975, 1977, 1979, 1984, 1990, 2006; other years likely

[5] OCA: *http://www.coastalatlas.net/index.php?option=com_custompages&e=3&Itemid=68*

[6] OSU library: *http://oregondigital.org/digcol/index.php*

[7] DOGAMI Oregon LiDAR Consortium: *http://www.oregongeology.org/sub/projects/olc/*

[8] Oregon Geospatial Enterprise Office: *http://www.oregon.gov/DAS/EISPD/GEO/sdlibrary.shtml*

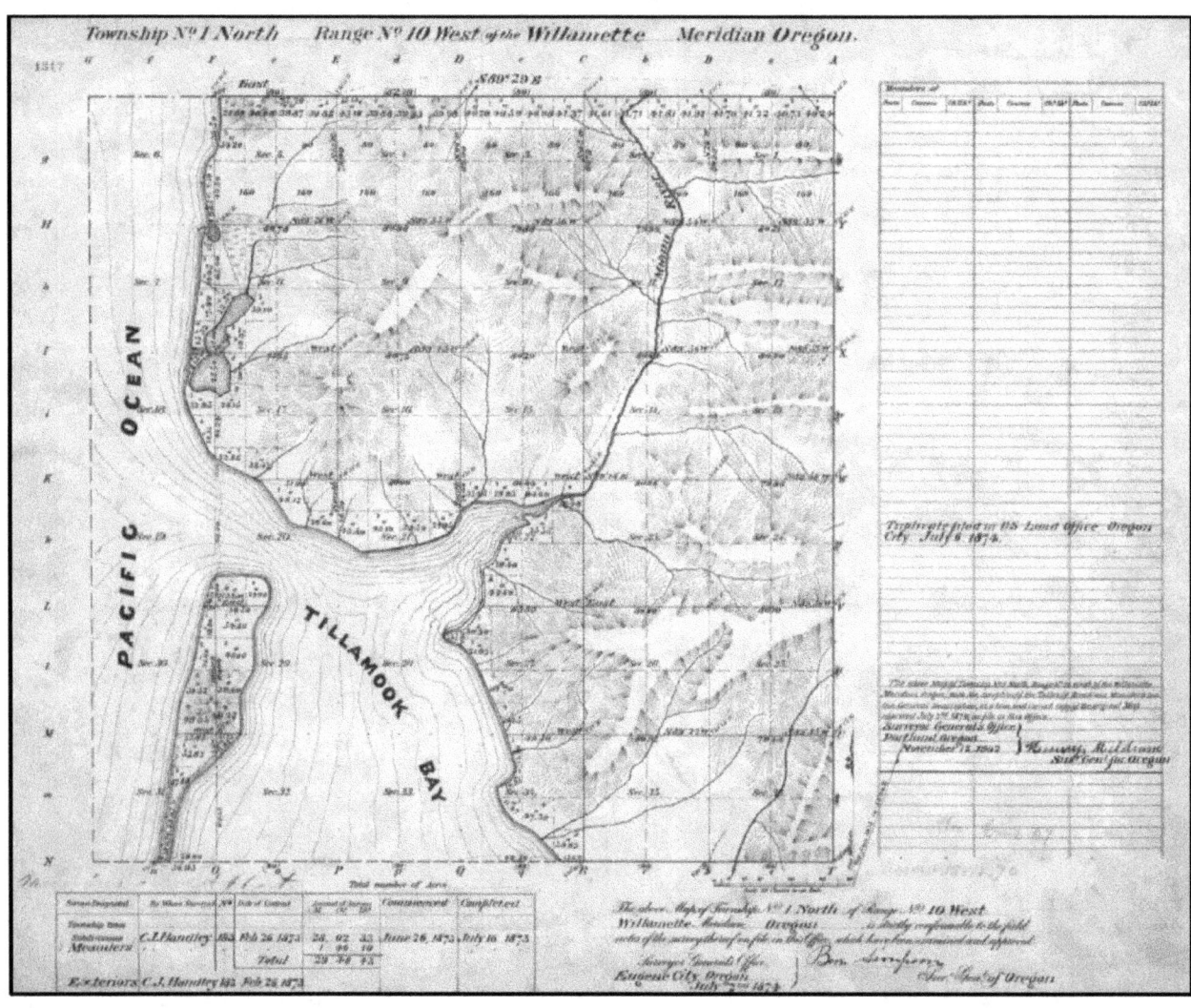

General Land Office map of the Tillamook Bay, circa 1874 (Courtesy of the Bureau of Land Management).

Gravel-Operator Information and Surveys

In August 2011, we reviewed permit files at the Oregon Department of State Lands to obtain estimates of deposited and mined volumes of bed-material reported for the active instream gravel mining sites in the Tillamook Bay sub-basins and Nehalem River basin. Coastwide Ready-Mix provided copies of surveys taken in 2009 at Donaldson, Barker, Dill, and Gomes Bars (Dennis Johnson, Coastwide Ready-Mix, written commun., 2010) and Mohler Sand and Gravel, LLC provided copies of surveys taken in 2010 at Plant Bar (Brian Mohler, Mohler Sand and Gravel, LCC, written commun., 2010). From the permit files and surveys, we derived partial estimates of deposited and mined gravel volumes, primarily from repeat topographic surveys, for eight instream gravel-mining sites (table 12; figs. 10–14). Stinson and Stinson (1998) also compiled deposited and mined gravel volumes for mined and unmined sites from 1993 to 1997 (tables 12 and 13). Because these data compilations are incomplete, actual volumes of mined and deposited bed material were probably greater than reported here.

Although the compilations are incomplete, some patterns emerge from the available measurements. From 1993 to 1997, operators reported removal of 40,040 m^3 and 71,910 m^3 of gravel from the Wilson and Kilchis Rivers, respectively, whereas 6,160 m^3 of gravel were taken from the Miami River for the same period (table 13). From 2004 to 2011, the reported cumulative volumes of bed-material deposition were also greatest for the Wilson and Kilchis Rivers, where deposition volumes totaled over 25,000 m^3 at Donaldson and Dill Bars, respectively (table 12). Mean annual volumes of deposition on individual bars exceeded 3,000 m^3 for Donaldson and Dill Bars and both bars on the Nehalem River. From 2003 to 2011, reported cumulative mined volumes per site was greatest for Donaldson, Plant, and Winslow Bars, ranging from 24,470 to 33,940 m^3 (table 12). For most years and sites with volumes of deposited and mined sediment, bar deposition matched or exceeded mined volumes (fig. 16A–I). The greatest surveyed deposition volume, 8,950 m^3 on Donaldson Bar on the Wilson River, followed a flood on November 6, 2006 that exceeded a 50-year event (fig. 5B), which is consistent with the relation between discharge and deposition volumes noted for other rivers on the Oregon coast (Wallick and others, 2010; Jones and others, 2011; Wallick and others, 2011; Jones and others, 2012a, b).

Although the limited dataset hinders comparison of decadal trends in bed-material recruitment, deposition volumes from 1995, as reported by Stinson and Stinson (1998), were comparable to deposition volumes reported from 2003 to 2010 for Dill and Gomes Bars on the Kilchis River and Waldron Bar on the Miami River (table 12). Because gravel mining likely creates preferential depositional areas on mined bar surfaces, deposition estimates at individual, mined bars cannot be reliably extrapolated to assess overall deposition rates for all bars along these rivers, but they do provide evidence of minimum annual bed-material flux rates (Wallick and others, 2012).

Table 12. Partial compilation of deposited and mined gravel volumes from 2003 to 2011 reported for instream mining sites along the Trask, Wilson, Kilchis, Miami, and Nehalem Rivers, northwestern Oregon.

[Original data reported in cubic yards. Reported annual values were converted to cubic meters, and rounded to the nearest 10. Mean and cumulative values based on rounded annual values. Mean values calculated using sum and number of rounded annual estimates owing to data gaps. m^3, cubic meter; RKM, river kilometer; ~, approximately; Dep, deposited volume; Mined, mined volume; --, data gap; data compiled from permits files housed at Oregon Department of State Lands (accessed August 2011)]

River	Trask		Wilson				Kilchis				Miami		Nehalem			
Reach	Fluvial		Lower Fluvial				Fluvial				Lower Fluvial		Fluvial			
Bar	Bush		Donaldson		Barker		Dill		Gomes		Waldron		Plant		Winslow	
RKM	12.2		10.4		6.9		~0.1 km upstream of study area		4.8		4.8		25.8		24.8	
Bar change	Dep	Mined	Dep	Mined	Dep	Mined	Dep	Mined	Dep	Mined	Dep	Mined	Dep	Mined	Dep	Mined
2003	--	--	--	4,790	--	--	--	--	--	2,120	--	--	--	2,330	--	0
2004	--	--	--	0	2,580	1,780	3,480	3,430	1,150	--	--	--	--	860	--	5,240
2005	--	910	4,950[A]	2,320	1,020	1,090	4,720	3,680	--	--	1,240	1,160	--	3,960	--	4,290
2006	--	2,780	4,260	3,960	1,100	1,640	4,160	3,160	4,140	2,190	2,380	1,010	--	7,860	--	6,810
2007	--	2,680	8,950	5,660	1,290	810	3,070	2,010	1,430	1,350	1,380	1,310	--	7,140	--	6,750
2008	--	2,690	3,060	2,980	1,890	900	1,880	1,840	880	830	--	--	--	4,650	6,420	3,250
2009	--	1,150	4,780	4,760	1,550	1,540	4190[B]	4,150	1,100[B]	1,090	--	0	6,350	5,610	8,410	4,840
2010	--	NR[C]	--	0	--	0	--	0	--	0	--	0	4,820	1,530	--	0[B]
2011	--	--	4,160[A]	--	--	--	3,890[A]	--	--	--	--	--	--	--	--	--
Mean annual volume by site[D]	--	2,040	3,770	4,080	1,570	1,290	3,170	3,050	1,740	1,520	1,670	1,160	5,590	4,240	7,420	5,200
Cumulative volumes by site	--	10,210	30,160	24,470	9,430	7,760	25,390	18,270	8,700	7,580	5,000	3,480	11,170	33,940	14,830	31,180
Cumulative volumes by river	--	10,210	39,590	32,230			34,090	25,850			5,000	3,480	26,000	65,120		

[A] Deposition estimate is cumulative for year indicated and previous year

[B] Operator provided information on 2010 mining activities

[C] Mined volume not included in permit file; field observations indicate mining

[D] Mean values calculated using number of estimates listed in table

Table 13. Partial compilation of deposited and mined gravel volumes from 1993 to 1997 at active and historical instream gravel mining reported in Stinson and Stinson (1998).

[Locations approximated using drawings in report. Original data reported in cubic yards. Reported annual values were converted to cubic meters, and rounded to the nearest 10. Cumulative values for each river basin based on rounded annual values. RKM, river kilometer; C, control site; M, mining site; Dep, deposited volume; Mined, mined vol-ume; --, data gap; ~, approximately; km, kilometer; NA, unavailable]

River	Bar	Site Type	Approximate location	Estimate type	Volume measured by Stinson and Stinson (1998)				Volume estimated by operator and reported in Stinson and Stinson (1998)					Total mined volume per river basin reported by operator
					1993	1994	1995	1996	1993	1994	1995	1996	1997	
Wilson	Jacob	C	RKM 12.4	Dep	--	--	--	--	--	--	--	--	--	40,040
				Mined	800	270	--	--	490	380	--	--	--	
	Widmer	M	RKM 12.2	Dep	--	--	--	--	--	--	--	--	--	
				Mined	--	--	--	--	--	--	--	--	3,290	
	Upper Donaldson[1]	C	RKM 10.4	Dep	3,080	--	--	--	--	--	--	--	--	
				Mined	--	--	--	--	2,490	2,980	2,700	10,470	6,290	
	Lower Donaldson	M	RKM 10.0	Dep	1,500	--	--	--	--	--	--	--	--	
				Mined	--	--	--	--	1,700	--	--	--	--	
	Barker[2]	M	RKM 6.9	Dep	790	--	--	--	--	--	--	--	--	
				Mined	--	--	--	--	800	550	1,180	1,450	--	
	Tannler	M	RKM 6.6	Dep	540	--	--	--	--	--	--	--	--	
				Mined	--	--	470	--	870	930	710	1,530	1,230	
Kilchis	Bruck	M	~0.6 km above study area	Dep	3,240	--	--	--	--	--	--	--	--	71,910
				Mined	--	--	4,420	NA	2,230	1,840	4,290	--	4,260	
	Bay City[3]	M	~0.1 km above study area	Dep	--	--	5,300	--	--	--	--	--	--	
				Mined	1,400	940	5,430	--	1,090	1,430	4,820	8,450	3,170	
	Lower Bay City	M	RKM 7.8	Dep	--	--	--	--	--	--	--	--	--	
				Mined	--	250	--	--	--	--	--	--	--	
	Darby	M	RKM 6.8	Dep	--	--	610	--	--	--	--	--	--	
				Mined	100	270	550	--	270	330	780	710	470	
	Crusher	M	RKM 5.8	Dep	--	--	420	--	--	--	--	--	--	
				Mined	--	300	490	NA	--	--	780	--	2,980	
	Upper Landolt	M	RKM 5.3	Dep	--	--	2,010	--	--	--	--	--	--	
				Mined	430	460	830	--	760	930	970	5,860	950	

Table 13. Partial compilation of deposited and mined gravel volumes from 1993 to 1997 at active and historical instream gravel mining reported in Stinson and Stinson (1998).—continued

[Locations approximated using drawings in report. Original data reported in cubic yards. Reported annual values were converted to cubic meters, and rounded to the nearest 10. Cumulative values for each river basin based on rounded annual values. RKM, river kilometer; C, control site; M, mining site; Dep, deposited volume; Mined, mined vol-ume; ~, approximately; km, kilometer; --, data gap; NA, unavailable]

River	Bar	Site Type	Approximate location	Estimate type	Volume measured by Stinson and Stinson (1998)				Volume estimated by operator and reported in Stinson and Stinson (1998)					Total mined volume per river basin reported by operator
					1993	1994	1995	1996	1993	1994	1995	1996	1997	
Kilchis (cont.)	Lower Landolt[4]	M	RKM 4.8	Dep	--	1,680	2,190	--	--	--	--	--	--	
				Mined	--	--	2,060	--	360	1,360	2,330	--	870	
	Curl	C	RKM 4.4	Dep	--	--	50	--	--	--	--	--	--	
				Mined	--	--	--	NA	--	--	--	--	--	
	Bosch	C	RKM 4.1	Dep	--	--	--	--	--	--	--	--	--	
				Mined	--	--	--	NA	--	--	--	--	--	
	Averill	M	RKM 2.9	Dep	820	1,780	6,120	--	--	--	--	--	--	
				Mined	--	--	6,380	--	1,610	2,970	6,500	6,380	2,160	
Miami	Wald	C	RKM 6.1	Dep	--	--	--	--	--	--	--	--	--	
				Mined	--	NA	--	--	NA	NA	NA	NA	NA	6,160
	Upper Waldron[5]	M	RKM 4.8	Dep	--	480	770	--	--	--	--	--	--	
				Mined	--	--	--	--	--	--	--	4,590	900	
	Middle Waldron	M	RKM 4.6	Dep	--	600	310	--	--	--	--	--	--	
				Mined	--	--	--	--	--	--	--	--	--	
	Lower Waldron	M	RKM 4.4	Dep	--	210	280	--	--	--	--	--	--	
				Mined	--	--	--	--	--	--	--	--	670	
	Filosi	M	RKM 2.3	Dep	100	--	750	--	--	--	--	--	--	
				Mined	--	50	560	--	--	--	--	--	--	

[1] Ongoing mining site under the name Donaldson Bar

[2] Ongoing mining site

[3] Ongoing mining site under the name Dill Bar

[4] Ongoing mining site under the name Gomes Bar

[5] Ongoing mining site under the name Waldron Bar

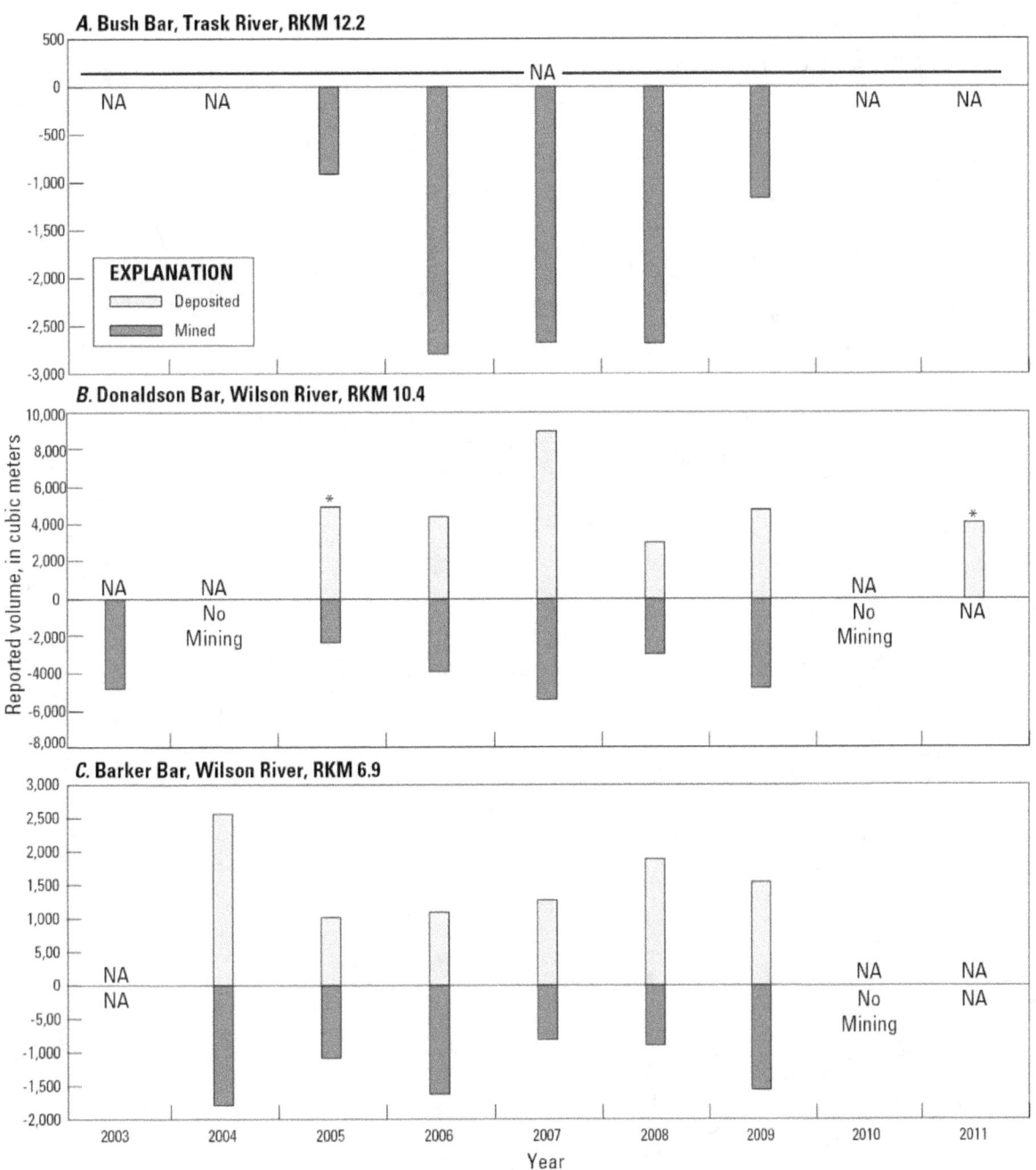

Figure 16. Graphs showing reported estimates of deposited and mined gravel from 1999 to 2011 for instream mining sites along the Trask, Wilson, Kilchis, Miami, and Nehalem Rivers, northwestern Oregon. Data compiled from permit files housed at Oregon Department of State Lands (accessed August 2011). [RKM, river kilometer; NA, data not available]

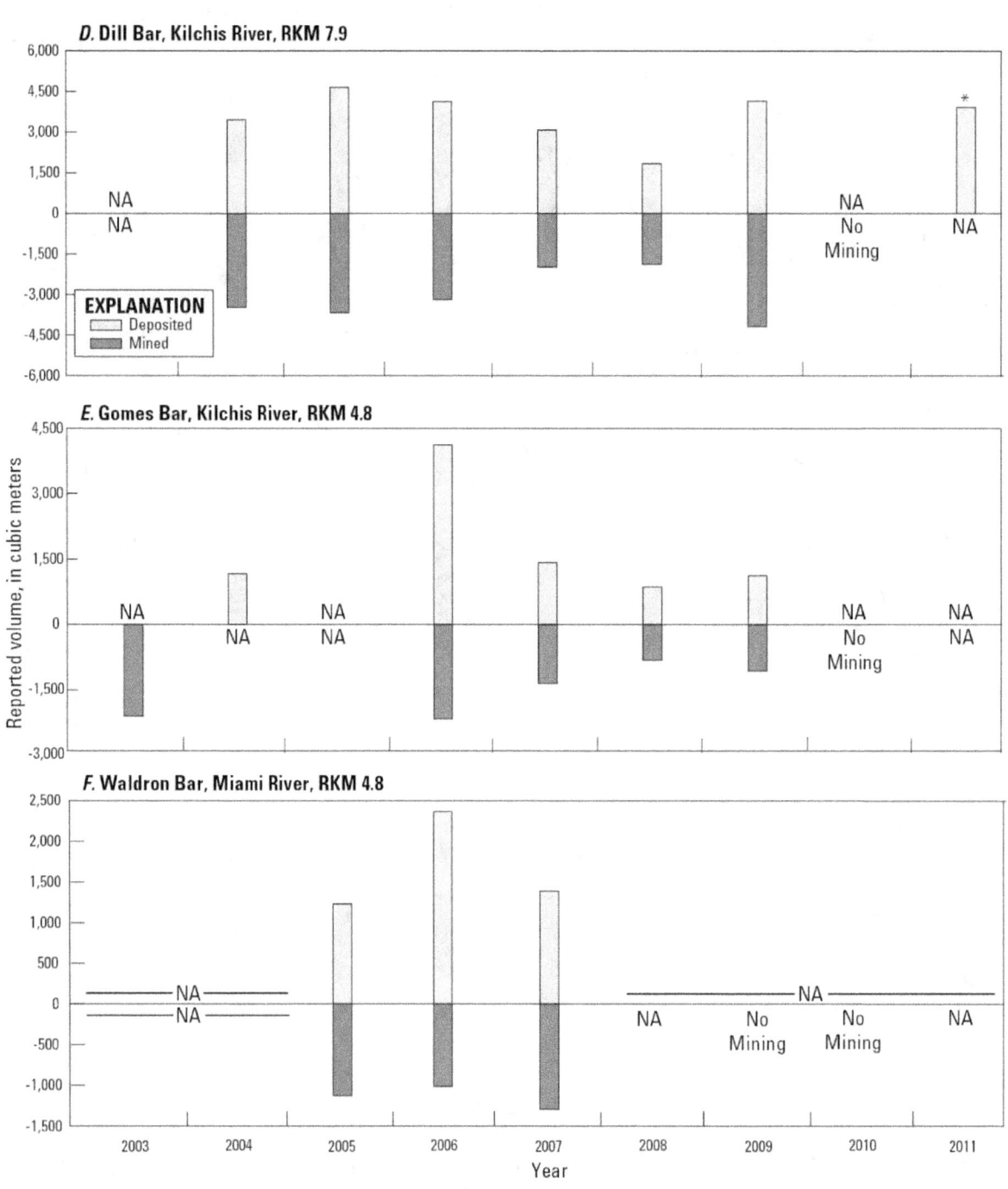

Figure 16 (continued). Graphs showing reported estimates of deposited and mined gravel from 1999 to 2011 for instream mining sites along the Trask, Wilson, Kilchis, Miami, and Nehalem Rivers, northwestern Oregon. Data compiled from permit files housed at Oregon Department of State Lands (accessed August 2011). [RKM, river kilometer; NA, data not available]—continued

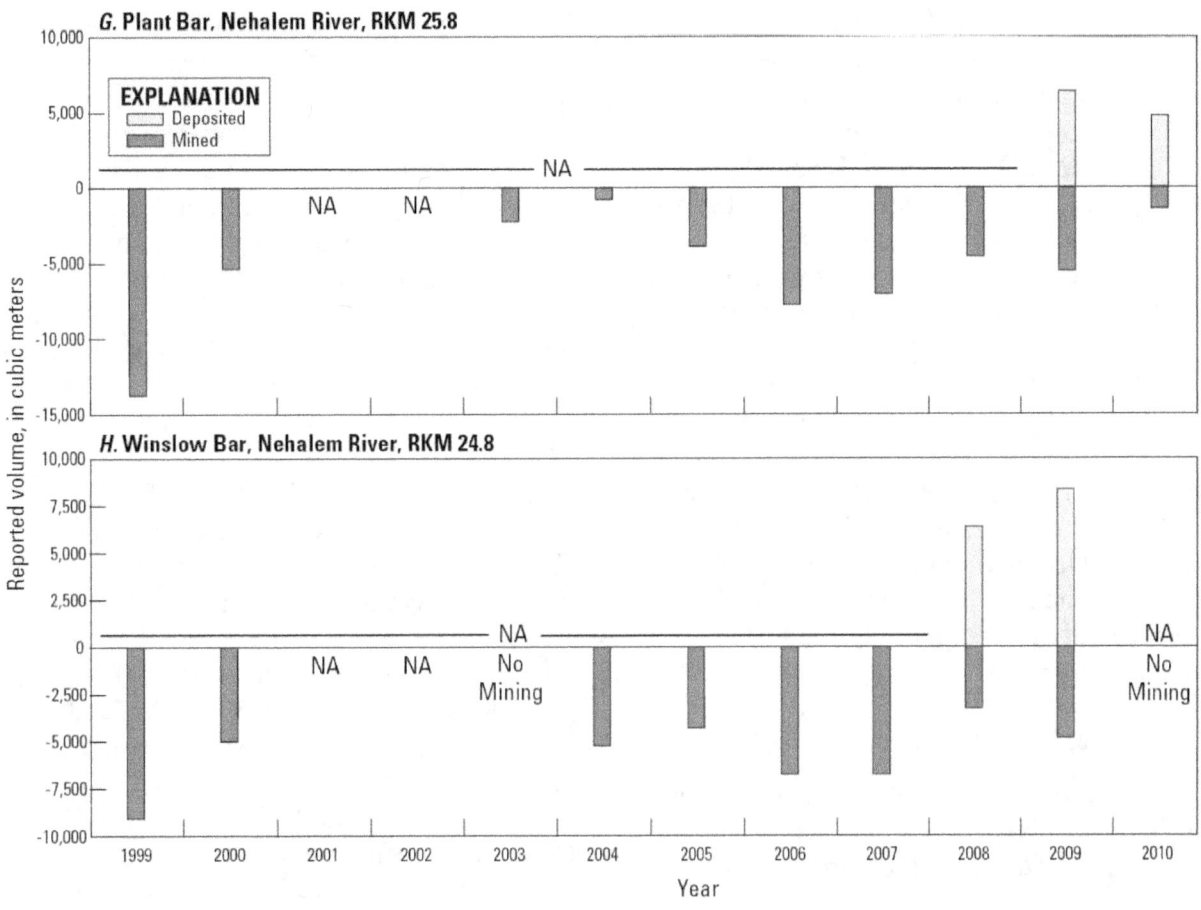

Figure 16 (continued). Graphs showing reported estimates of deposited and mined gravel from 1999 to 2011 for instream mining sites along the Trask, Wilson, Kilchis, Miami, and Nehalem Rivers, northwestern Oregon. Data compiled from permit files housed at Oregon Department of State Lands (accessed August 2011). [RKM, river kilometer; NA, data not available.

Despite little evidence of systematic change in bar volume or particle-size distribution (Stinson and Stinson, 1998) at mined sites, repeat bar and channel delineations show that several mined bars have changed in size, shape, or position relative to the main channel from 1939 to 2009 (see the "Delineation of Bar and Channel Features, 1939–2009" section). Detailed analyses of bed-material flux and morphological changes along the Trask, Wilson, Kilchis, Miami, and Nehalem Rivers would enable more quantitative assessments of changes in bar replenishment and morphology in relation to peak flows as well as support the evaluation of the possible effects of gravel mining on overall bed-material flux and downstream channel conditions. Photographs, such as those taken in 1994, 2000, 2005, 2009, and 2011 of the Trask, Wilson, Kilchis, and Miami Rivers (table 9) and in 1994, 2000, 2001, 2005, 2009, and 2011 of the Nehalem River (table 10), would likely support detailed geomorphic assessments.

Bridge-Inspection Reports

The Oregon Department of Transportation (ODOT) conducts routine bridge inspections to assess overall bridge condition, footing stability, and scour. ODOT's bridge inspection database contains reports for 21 bridges in the six study areas (Oregon Department of Transportation, written commun., 2011; table 14). ODOT has resurveyed channel cross sections at 18 bridges, with at least two survey locations within each study area and at least one survey in a fluvial reach in four of the six study areas (repeat cross sections were unavailable for the fluvial reaches on the Trask and Nehalem Rivers). The surveys span 1926–2010 and include as many as four surveys at some locations (table 14). We also examined the supplemental data accompanying the survey reports, including inspection and underwater reports, photographs, and scour assessments that may assist in assessing channel and bed-material conditions adjacent to the bridges.

The most recent inspection surveys and underwater reports include some descriptions of bed material, wood accumulation, and bridge infrastructure scour (table 14). The streambeds were described as soft silt on the Tillamook River (RKM 6.4), sandy silt on the Trask River (RKM 2.1), gravel and silt bordered by a bedrock outcrop to the south on the Wilson River (RKM 14.1), gravel and sand on the Kilchis River (RKM 4.2), cobble and gravel and then sand and gravel at RKM 8.5 and 0, respectively, on the Miami River, and sand and silt on the Nehalem River (RKM 18.8 and 10.6). Several inspection reports document the accumulation of large wood near bridges on the Tillamook (RKM 11.5), Trask (RKM 7.0 and 2.1), Wilson (RKM 2.8), Kilchis (RKM 4.2), Miami (RKM 0), and Nehalem (RKM 22.4, 18.8, and 10.6) Rivers. These reports also note bank slumping, erosion of bank protection, undermining of channel protection, or "minor channel damage" (as stated in ODOT reports) on the Tillamook (RKM 11.5 and 8.8), Trask (RKM 11.6, 7.0, 3.8, and 2.1), Wilson (RKM 14.1 and 6.3), Kilchis (RKM 6.0, 4.2, 1.5, and 1.0), Miami (RKM 8.5, 2.7, and 0), and Nehalem Rivers (RKM 22.4 and 18.8). ODOT documented scour of bridge infrastructure at six of these locations (Trask RKM 7.0, Wilson RKM 14.1 and 6.3, Kilchis RKM 1.0, Miami RKM 8.5, and Nehalem RKM 22.4) plus one other location (Tillamook RKM 6.4).

The repeat cross sections show that channels near bridge crossings in all study areas are dynamic with many subject to incision and aggradation as well as lateral shifts in channel position (table 14). Thalweg elevation changes included a mixture of incision and aggradation on the Tillamook and Trask Rivers (figs. 17A–D and 18A–B). The thalweg of the Tillamook River incised a net 0.5 to 2.6 m at three locations (RKM 11.5, 8.8, and 1.3) over different survey periods, but aggraded 3.1 m near RKM 6.4 from 1996 to 2004. Likewise, the Trask River thalweg incised a net 2.3 m at RKM 7.0 primarily from 1998 to 2004, but aggraded 0.5 m downstream at RKM 2.1 from 2003 to 2004. Thalweg position

Table 14. Summary of net changes measured from channel cross sections collected by the Oregon Department of Transportation (ODOT, written commun., 2011) in the six study areas in the Tillamook Bay subbasins and Nehalem River basin, northwestern Oregon.

[RKM, river kilometer; USGS, U.S. Geological Survey; Rd. Road; NA, unavailable; Hwy, highway]

Study area	Bridge	Reach	RKM	ODOT bridge ID	Survey years	Net thalweg elevation change (meters)	Maximum net erosion (meters)		Maximum net deposition (meters)		ODOT notes	(USGS notes)
							Left bank	Right bank	Left bank	Right bank		
Tillamook	Bewley Creek Rd	Fluvial	11.5	18538	1999, 2004	-0.6	-1.0	-1.3	+0.7	0.0	Eroded bank protection; wood in span	
	Tillamook River Rd	Tidal	8.8	19625	2004a, 2004b[1]	-0.5	-1.0	-0.3	0	+0.4	Minor channel damage	
	Burton	Tidal	6.4	01594A	1996, 2004	+3.1	0	-0.1	+2.7	+2.1	Unstable scour of infrastructure; channel over soft silt bed and protected (*secondary thalweg aggrades 1.8 m from 1996 to2004*)	
	Hwy 131	Tidal	1.3	01345C	1961, 1998, 2004	-2.6	-2.1	-2.2	+1.7	0	Channel protected (*net changes likely greater owing to limited data in 1961 survey*)	
Trask	Long Prairie Rd	Fluvial	11.6	20306	NA	--	--	--	--	--	23 m of bank slumping downstream of bent and minor bank erosion	
	Hwy 9	Tidal	7.0	07147	1948, 1998, 2004, 2008	-2.3	-1.9	-0.7	+1.3	+3.7	Unstable scour of infrastructure; bank protection and north and south stream banks eroded; drift in bent	
	Tillamook River Rd	Tidal	3.8	17929	2004	--	--	--	--	--	Minor channel damage	
	Stillwell	Tidal	2.1	05640A	2003, 2004	+0.5	0	0	+1.5	+0.4	Bank slumping; some erosion around piles after 1996 flood; sandy silt streambed; old trees lodged in channel	

61

Table 14. Summary of net changes measured from channel cross sections collected by the Oregon Department of Transportation (ODOT, written commun., 2011) in the six study areas in the Tillamook Bay subbasins and Nehalem River basin, northwestern Oregon.—continued

[RKM, river kilometer; USGS, U.S. Geological Survey; Rd, Road; NA, unavailable; Hwy, highway]

Study area	Bridge	Reach	RKM	ODOT bridge ID	Survey years	Net thalweg elevation change (meters)	Maximum net erosion (meters)		Maximum net deposition (meters)		ODOT notes (USGS notes)
							Left bank	Right bank	Left bank	Right bank	
Wilson	Mills	Upper Fluvial	14.1	01868	1939, 1996, 2004, 2008	+0.4	-1.4	-1.9	+0.6	0	Unstable scour of bridge infrastructure; minor channel damage; gravel and silt streambed; pier on bedrock outcrop on south bank
	Sollie Smith	Lower Fluvial	6.3	57C23	1996, 2004	+2.1	0	-0.7	+2.0	+1.5	Unstable scour of bridge infrastructure; minor channel damage
	Hwy 9	Tidal	2.8	01499	1930, 1998, 2004, 2008	+0.4	-2.9	-1.2	+1.3	0	Bank slumping; wood build-up causing scour
Kilchis	Kilchis River Rd	Fluvial	6.0	20999	2008, 2010	-0.4	-1.2	-1.0	+2.5	0	Bank slumping
	Curl Rd	Fluvial	4.2	57C20	1996, 2004	0	-0.1	-0.7	+0.6	+0.6	Minor channel damage; gravel and sand streambed; some wood build-up
	Alderbrook Loop	Tidal	1.5	00455A	1996, 2004	-0.2	-0.5	-0.3	0	+0.3	Bank slumping
	Kilchis River and Possetti Rd[2]	Tidal	1.0	07424	1951, 1998, 2004, 2008	-0.5	-0.7	-0.2	+1.9	+0.9	Unstable scour of bridge infrastructure; erosion of bank protection and south bank

Table 14. Summary of net changes measured from channel cross sections collected by the Oregon Department of Transportation (ODOT, written commun., 2011) in the six study areas in the Tillamook Bay subbasins and Nehalem River basin, northwestern Oregon.—continued

[RKM, river kilometer; USGS, U.S. Geological Survey; Rd, Road; NA, unavailable; Hwy, highway]

Study area	Bridge	Reach	RKM	ODOT bridge ID	Survey years	Net thalweg elevation change (meters)	Maximum net erosion (meters)		Maximum net deposition (meters)		ODOT notes	(USGS notes)
							Left bank	Right bank	Left bank	Right bank		
Miami	New Miami River Rd	Lower Fluvial	8.5	57C59	1996, 2004	-0.6	-0.6	-0.2	+0.3	+0.7	Extensive scour of bridge infrastructure; channel protection undermined; cobble and gravel streambed	
	Moss Creek Rd	Lower Fluvial	2.7	57C12	1996, 2004	-0.6	-0.5	-0.4	0	+0.3	Minor channel damage; some bank erosion under span	
	Hwy 9/101	Tidal	0	01226A	1990, 1997, 2005	-0.5	-3.1	-0.1	+0.8	+1.5	Minor channel damage; large debris in channel; sand and gravel bed	
Nehalem	Miami Foley Rd	Tidal	22.4	01362A	NA	--	--	--	--	--	Extensive scour of bridge infrastructure; bank slumping and erosion; large build-up of drift at bents	
	Hwy 463	Tidal	18.8	01217	1926, 1997, 2003, 2007	+1.2	-1.5	0	+2.4	+0.9	Bank slumping; sand and silt streambed; large debris in channel and surrounding piers; some scour at toe of embankments; wood in channel	
	Hwy 9	Tidal	10.6	00574F	1980, 2001, 2005, 2009	+2.2	0	-0.2	+1.2	+0.8	Channel protected; large wood and debris in channel; sand and silt streambed	

[1] 2004a surveyed on 3/11/04; 2004b surveyed on 9/10/04

[2] 1951 cross section derived from bridge plans

[3] ODOT report indicates the 1926 survey may be derived from bridge plans or cross section survey.

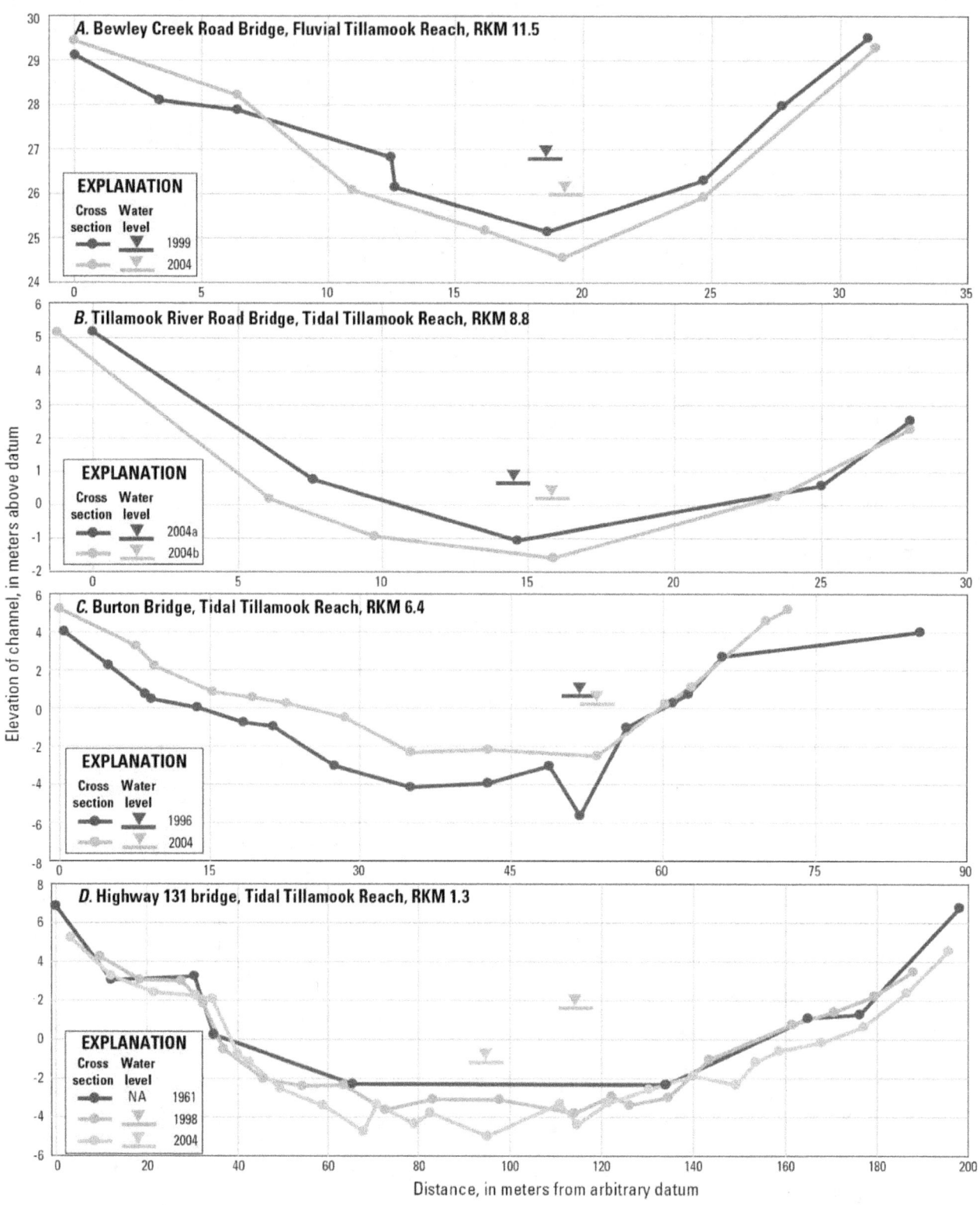

Figure 17. Diagrams showing channel cross sections surveyed at RKM 11.5, 8.8, 6.4, and 1.3 along the Tillamook River, northwestern Oregon. Data provided by the Oregon Department of Transportation (written commun., 2011). [RKM, river kilometer]

64

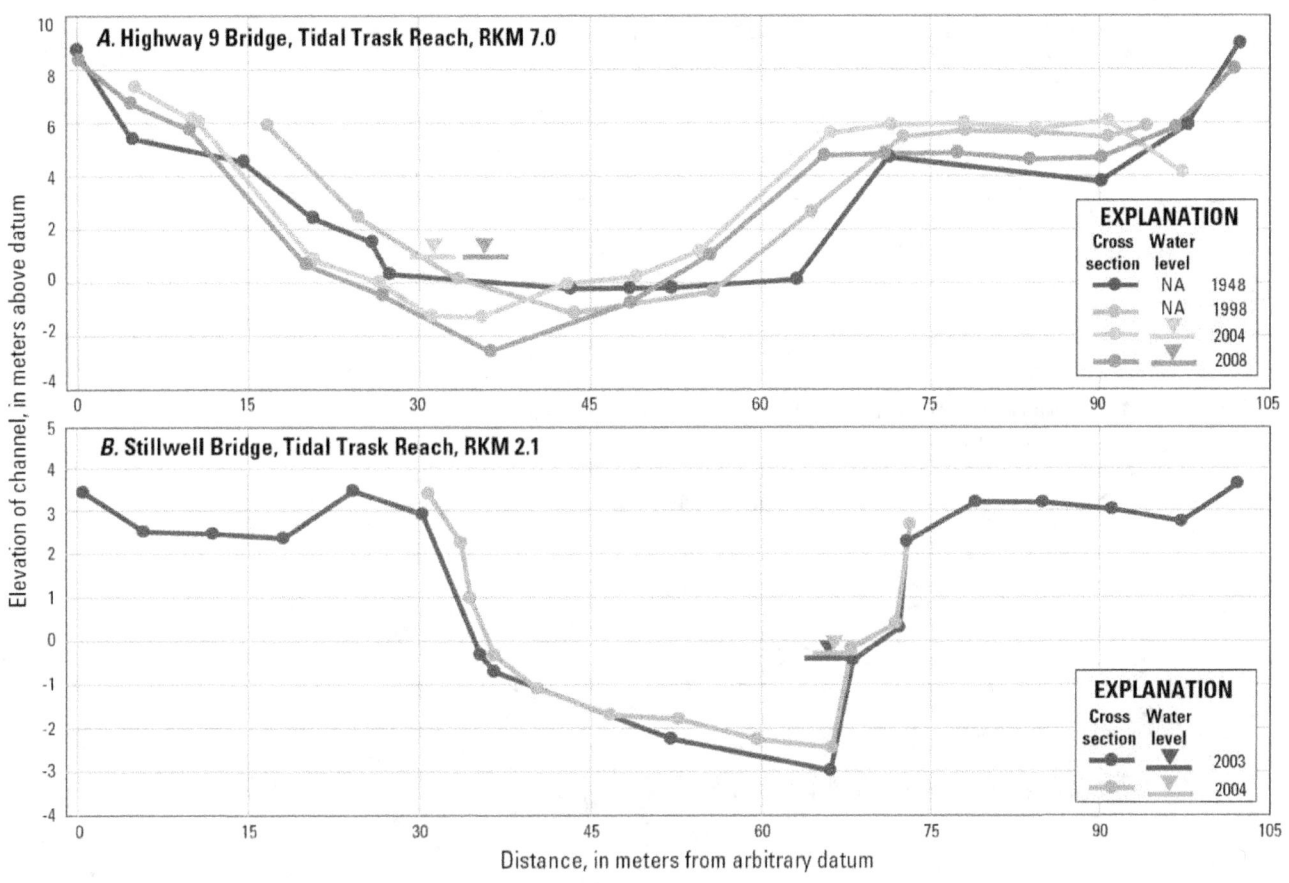

Figure 18. Diagrams showing channel cross sections surveyed at RKM 7.0 and 2.1 on the Trask River, north-western Oregon. Data provided by the Oregon Department of Transportation (written commun., 2011). [RKM, river kilometer]

was relatively stable between surveys except where the thalweg shifted laterally 19.0 and 8.1 m toward the left banks at Tillamook RKM 1.3 and Trask RKM 7.0, respectively, from 1998 to 2004. In addition to aggradation, incision, and some lateral shifting of channel position, banks at all cross sections on the Tillamook and Trask Rivers experienced 1 m or more of lateral deposition and/or erosion.

Along the Wilson River, the thalweg episodically aggraded and incised, resulting in net elevation increases of 0.4 m at RKM 14.1 and 2.8 from the 1930s to 2008 (table 14; fig. 19A, C). The thalweg also aggraded 2.1 m at RKM 6.0 from 1996 to 2004 (fig. 19B). All three cross sections exhibited almost 2 m or more of local

bank deposition and erosion as well as lateral changes in thalweg position. For example, the thalweg shifted towards the right bank approximately 23.0 m at RKM 14.1 from 1939 to 1996, and 11.0 m at RKM 2.8 from 1930 to 1998 (fig. 19A,C), but later returned to its earliest surveyed location at both sites.

Along the Kilchis River, cross sections at RKM 4.2 and 1.5 show either minimal (0.2 m) incision or no detectable change in thalweg elevation and less than 1 m of bank deposition and erosion (table 14; fig. 20A–D). Meanwhile, the upstream cross section at RKM 6.0 experienced more than 2 m of deposition along the left bank

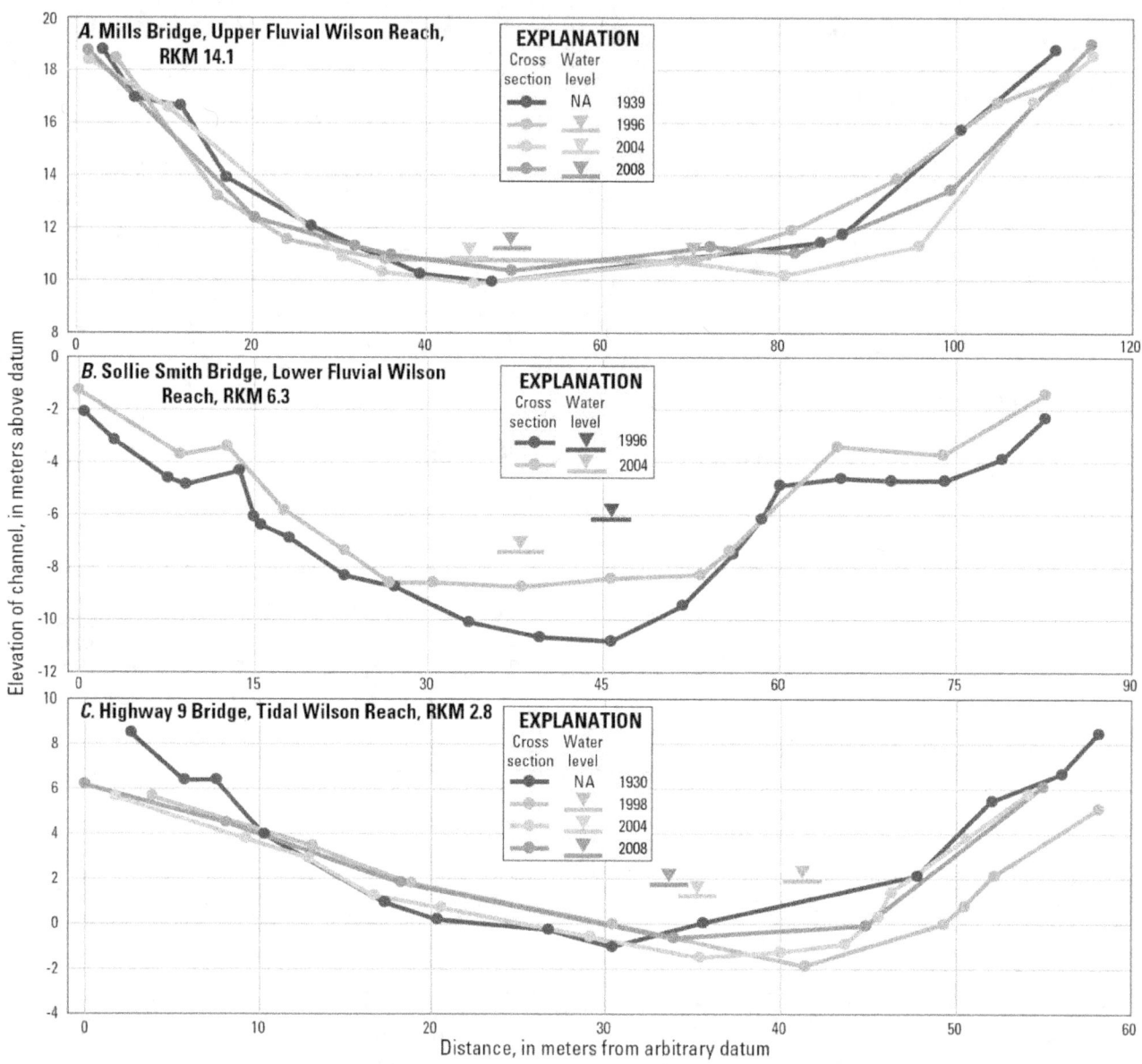

Figure 19. Diagrams showing channel cross sections surveyed at RKM 14.1, 6.3, and 2.8 on the Wilson River, northwestern Oregon. Data provided by the Oregon Department of Transportation (written commun., 2011). [RKM, river kilometer]

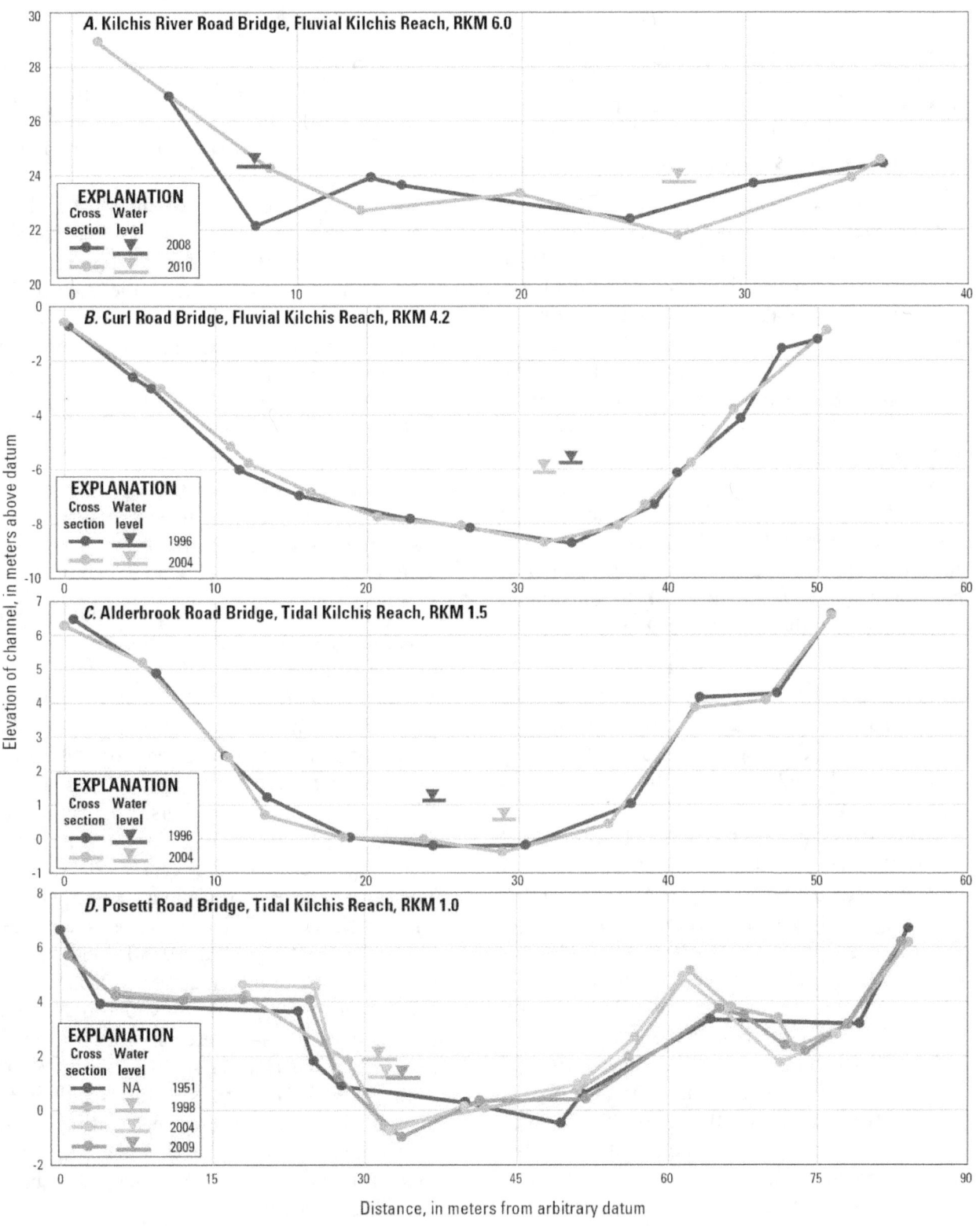

Figure 20. Diagrams showing channel cross sections surveyed at RKM 6.0, 4.2, 1.5, and 1.0 on the Kilchis River, northwestern Oregon. Data provided by the Oregon Department of Transportation (written commun., 2011). [RKM, river kilometer]

as the thalweg shifted towards the right bank and lowered 0.4 m from 2008 to 2010 (fig. 20A). At RKM 1.0, the channel switched from flowing against the right to the left bank from 1951 to 1988, incised a net 0.5 m, and had some bank deposition and erosion (fig. 20D).

The thalweg of the Miami River generally incised over the survey periods (table 14; fig. 21A–C). At RKM 8.5, the thalweg incised 0.6 m, but remained in approximately the same location from 1996 to 2004 (fig. 21A). Over the same period, the thalweg incised 0.6 m and shifted toward the left bank at RKM 2.7 (fig. 21B). The banks at RKM 8.5 and 2.7 experienced some erosion and deposition from 1996 to 2004. Downstream at RKM 0, the channel shifted leftward and aggraded 0.2 m from 1990 to 1997, but then shifted further towards the left bank and incised 0.6 m from 1997 to 2005, resulting in a net incision of approximately 0.5 m (fig. 21C). The banks at RKM 0 experienced greater erosion and deposition than those at the upstream sites.

The thalweg of the Nehalem River aggraded over the survey period at two bridge crossings (RKM 18.8 and 10.6; table 14; fig. 22A–B). At RKM 18.8, the thalweg aggraded a net 1.2 m primarily from 1926 to 1997 while the banks experienced a net 1.5 m of erosion on the left and 2.4 m of deposition on the right. The thalweg at RKM 18.8 has also shifted laterally, sometimes exceeding 15 m between surveys from 1926 to 2007 (fig. 22A). At RKM 10.6, the thalweg aggraded a net 2.2 m between 1980 and 2009 with the greatest elevation increase (approximately 1.5 m) occurring from 2005 to 2009 (fig. 22B). The thalweg shifted towards the left bank from 1980 to 2001, but then remained in a similar overall position in subsequent surveys. The channel banks at RKM 10.6 reflect the overall pattern of channel shifting and aggradation, as they experienced less than 0.2 m of erosion from 1980 to 2009, but nearly 1 m of deposition from 2005 to 2009 (table 14; fig. 22B).

Specific Gage Analysis

Another approach to evaluating vertical adjustments in channel elevation are specific gage analyses (Klingeman, 1973), which enable detection of changes in streambed elevation by assessing variations in water elevation (stage) over time for specific discharge values. At each USGS streamflow-gaging station, discharge is related to stage by a stage–discharge rating curve, which is based on multiple, paired stage and discharge measurements made at a range of streamflows. New rating curves are developed if the channel conditions change substantially (as shown by consistent offsets of newer measurements from established rating curves) or if a station is relocated. The specific gage analysis evaluates trends in downstream hydraulic control as indicated by the sequence of rating curves; hydraulic control is in turn a function of bed elevation.

We conducted specific gage analyses for the streamflow-gaging stations on the Wilson River near Tillamook (14301500; approximately 0.1 km upstream of Wilson River study area; table 3; fig. 1) and Nehalem River near Foss (14301000; approximately 0.4 km upstream of Nehalem River study area; table 3; fig. 2). We selected the Wilson and Nehalem stations for specific gage analyses because they have long-term periods of record and were operational as of 2011 (table 3). The Wilson River gage is in a section where the channel flows over alluvial deposits and intermittent bedrock. The Nehalem River gage is situated near where the channel transitions from flowing primarily on bedrock to alluvial deposits. Changes in stage were assessed for low to moderate flows (2.0–124.6 m^3/s on the Wilson River and 2.8–283.1 m^3/s on the Nehalem River) because these flows are more sensitive to minor adjustments in bed elevation and are less likely to be influenced by temporal changes in bank vegetation or bank shape.

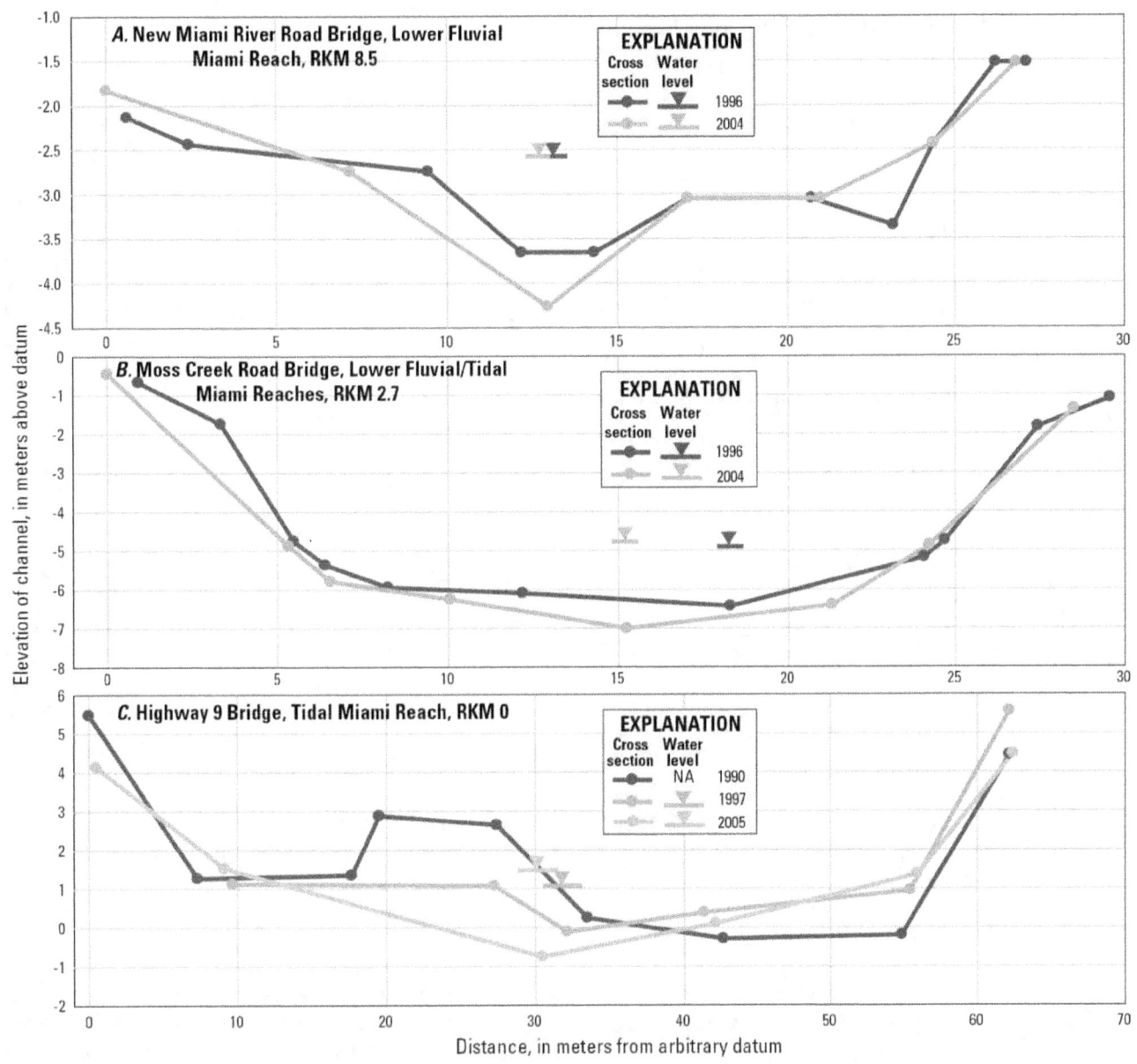

Figure 21. Diagrams showing channel cross sections surveyed at RKM 8.5, 2.7, and 0 on the Miami River, northwestern Oregon. Data provided by the Oregon Department of Transportation (written commun., 2011). [RKM, river kilometer]

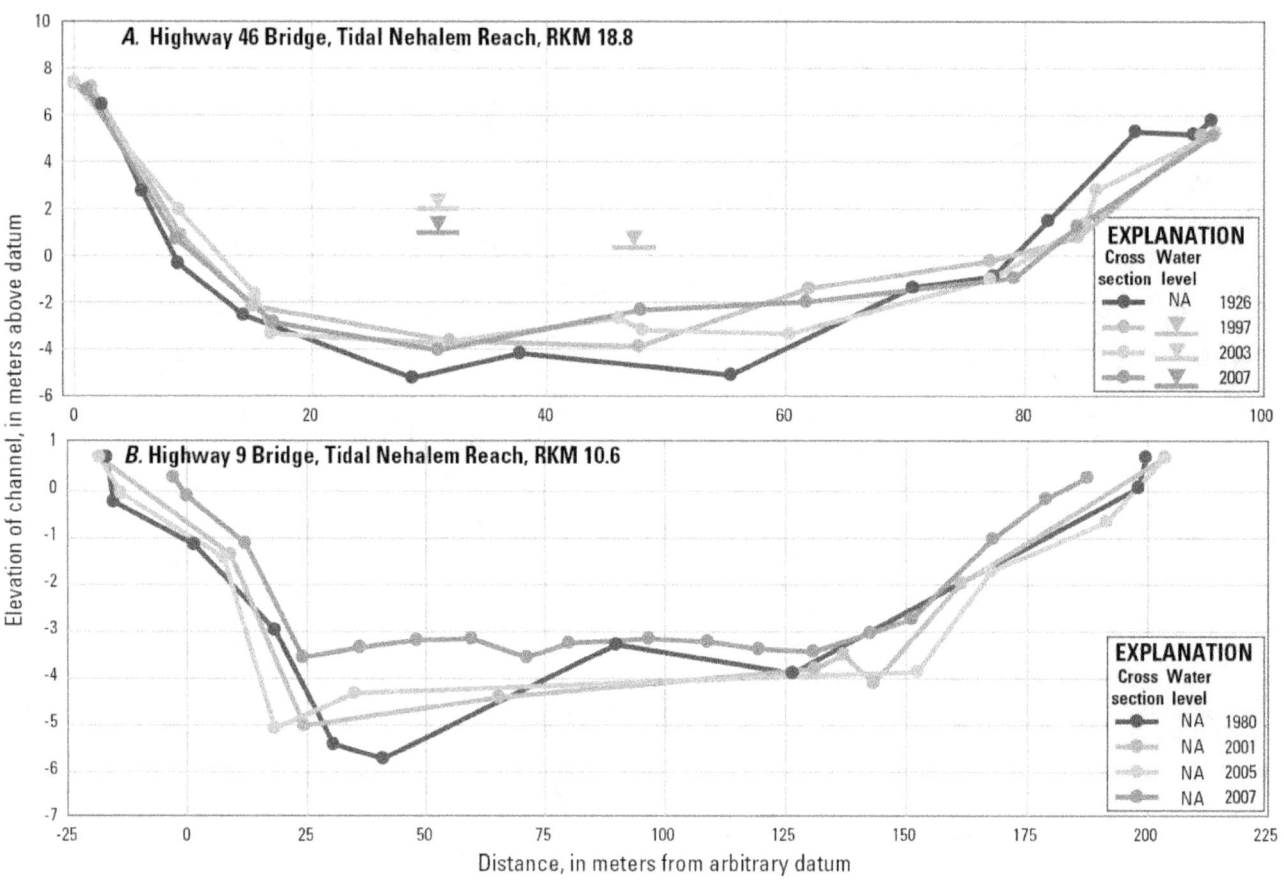

Figure 22. Diagrams showing channel cross sections surveyed at RKM 18.8 and 10.6 on the Nehalem River, northwestern Oregon. Data provided by the Oregon Department of Transportation (written commun., 2011). [RKM, river kilometer]

Although the gaging record for the Wilson River station begins in 1914, the specific gage analysis for this station uses data from July 1931 to January 2010 because the datum for stage measurements made from 1914 to 1916 is unknown and measurements were not made from 1916 to 1931. During the analysis period, the gage was moved four times (resulting in essentially five analysis "windows"), with datum shifts made in 1937 and 2003 (fig. 23A). Stage decreased a net 0.02–0.08 m over 1931–1937, 0.10–0.27 m over 1937–1967, and 0.06–0.26 m over 1973–2003. Net increases in stage, however, ranged from 0.47 to 0.63 m over 1976–1973 and 0.03 to 0.12 m over 2003–2010. This analysis indicates that the channel experiences episod-ic periods of aggradation followed by incision, particularly following some floods, such as those exceeding a 10-year return period (December 21, 1933; December 22, 1964) and a 25-year return period (January 20, 1972; February 8, 1996; fig. 5B). However, some larger floods like those exceeding a 50-year event (November 6, 2006) and almost a 25-year event (December 3, 2007) do not appear to trigger stage changes; this lack of response in the stage-discharge relation may be attributable to differences in flood duration and deposition dynamics at the gage. The small (0.03–0.12 m) increase in stage from 2009 to 2010 does not correspond with a flood event and may indicate changes in cross section controls

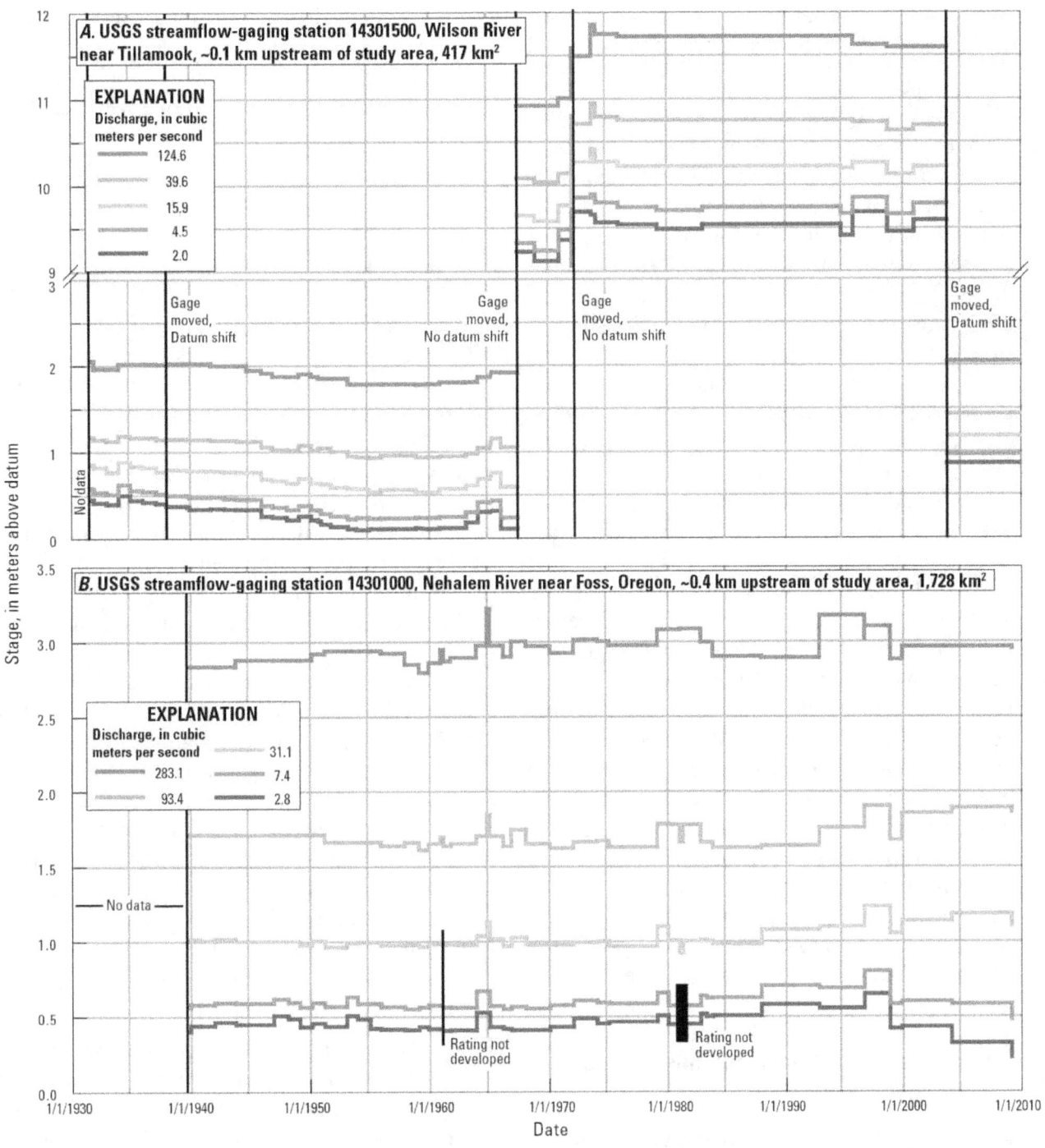

Figure 23. Diagrams showing the stage-discharge rating curves for specific discharges for the U.S. Geological Survey streamflow-gaging stations on the Wilson River near Tillamook, Oregon (14301500) and Nehalem River near Foss, Oregon (14301000), northwestern Oregon. The source data are station records housed at the Oregon Water Science Center, U.S. Geological Survey, Portland, Oregon. [km, kilometer]

(Klingeman, 1973) or sediment delivery to the section following the 2006 and 2007 floods.

On the Nehalem River, the stage-discharge relations for the five analyzed discharges show stage changes spanning as much as 0.92 m between ratings from October 1939 to January 2010 (fig. 23B). Stage decreased a net 0.18 and 0.09 m for the two lowest discharges, but increased a net 0.09 to 0.15 m for three highest discharges. These differences may be attributable to changes in the geometry of the high and low flow portions of the cross section, causing water levels to increase during elevated discharges and decrease at low discharges. For all analysis discharges, stage exhibited short, periodic rises (that increase in magnitude and duration with discharge), particularly over 1963–1964, 1979–1983, and 1992–1999. These episodes coincide with multiple flood events (such as those on January 25, 1964, December 23, 1964, and February 8, 1996; fig. 5D), and perhaps indicate increases in bed-material transport and channel aggradation following relatively large flows and bed-material erosion in other years. Counter to this, however, the December 3, 2007 flood event was greater in magnitude than the 25-year event, but does not appear to have affected the stage-discharge relation, indicating variation in local channel responses to flooding. Future review and analysis of station notes, historical cableway surveys, and individual discharge measurements could provide additional data on channel geometry and bed-material trends at both streamflow-gaging stations.

Delineation of Bars and Channel Features, 1939–2009

For this reconnaissance-level study, we mapped:

1. Channel centerlines for the six study areas using orthophotographs taken in 2009 (tables 9 and 10) to develop the linear reference system for this study, and

2. Bars, channel centerlines, and wetted channel edges for the six study areas using aerial and orthophotographs taken in 1939, 1967, 2005, and 2009 (tables 9 and 10) to assess temporal changes in the location and areal coverage of bars as well as the length and wetted width of the channel.

For both efforts, we delineated lateral and medial bars greater than 200 m^2 in area from aerial and orthophotographs at a scale of 1:2,000 for Tillamook Bay study areas and upstream of RKM 19.0 on the Nehalem River and at 1:10,000 downstream of RKM 19.0 on the Nehalem River. Bar and channel delineations were done using the Geographic Information System (GIS) program ESRI ArcMap 9.3.1 and 10.0.3. Although bars were not classified by grain size, field observations made in October 2010 indicated that most bars in the fluvial reaches were composed of gravel and finer particles. Most bars in the tidal reaches were composed of sand and mud. Fine sediment deposits that flank the channel in the Tidal Tillamook Reach are apparent in the 1969, 2005, and 2009 photographs, but because these surfaces are not obvious bars, they were not mapped in this study. Most mapped bars had little to no vegetation, although some had areas that were partly or wholly covered by grasses, shrubs, and (to a lesser extent) mature trees; however, vegetation or habitat types were not specifically mapped by this effort. Delineation of bars, channel centerlines, and wetted channel edges was repeatedly verified to ensure consistent delineation of features among years and throughout the study area following the protocol of Wallick and others (2011).

The quality of underlying photographs and errors introduced by georeferencing and digitizing processes are three of many potential sources of uncertainty in digital channel maps (Gurnell, 1997; Mount and Louis, 2005; Hughes and others, 2006; Walter and Tullos, 2009). As described above, we selected photographs taken in 1939, 1967, 2005, and 2009 for mapping bars, channel centerlines, and wetted channel edges in the six study areas (tables 9 and 10). Scanned copies of the black and white photographs taken in 1939 and 1967 were acquired from the Corp of Engineers aerial photograph library and University of Oregon Map and Aerial Photography Library, respectively. These photographs were generally of adequate resolution and free of glare and shadow to facilitate detailed mapping of bars and channel features with the exception of some glare and shadow or low resolution along the upper portions of the Tillamook Bay Rivers, particularly in the 1967 photographs of the Upper Fluvial Wilson and Miami Reaches and Fluvial Trask Reach.

The 1939 and 1967 photographs of the six study areas were georectified (table 15) using methods similar to Wallick and others (2011). The total Root Mean Square Error (RMSE) of rectified photographs, an indicator of the horizontal position uncertainties owing to the georectification process, was less than 4.9 m for all study areas. Generally, ground-control points for georectification were located near the mainstem channels so that positional errors for channel features should be less than the RMSE reported for individual photographs. Although land use and land cover change limited the number of ground-control points for the 1939 photographs of the Nehalem River study area, RMSE values for

these rectified photographs are similar to those reported for rectified 1939 and 1967 photographs of the Coquille River (Jones and others, 2012b) and 1967 photographs of the Rogue River (Jones and others, 2012a) on the southwestern Oregon coast.

Streamflow during photograph acquisition may affect bar exposure, influencing the mapped bar and wetted channel areas (table 16). Streamflow data from the long-term Wilson River gage (14301500) was used to assess relative flow conditions for the ungaged Tillamook Bay rivers. From these records, streamflows were generally lowest during the collection of the 2009 photographs (1.3–9.5 m^3/s), and slightly greater in the 1939 (4.6–5.9 m^3/s) and 2005 (5.0–10.0 m^3/s) photographs. Streamflow during the collection of the 1967 photographs was substantially greater than during the other collections, and ranged from 65.7 to 199.3 m^3/s at the Wilson and Nehalem gages, respectively. The higher streamflows in the 1967 photographs likely reduced the area of mapped bars and increased the mapped area of wetted channel width in 1967 relative to the other years.

Table 15. Photograph rectification data for the Tillamook and Nehalem study areas, northwestern Oregon.

| Study areas | Year of photograph coverage | Polynomial transformation applied to photographs | | | | | |
| | | First order transformation | | | Second order transformation | | |
		Study area coverage (percent)	Average number of ground control points	Root Mean Square Error (meters)	Study area coverage (percent)	Average number of ground control points	Root Mean Square Error (meters)
Tillamook (all)	1939	0	--	--	100	11	1.2–4.4
	1967	0	--	--	100	12	2.0–4.9
Nehalem	1939	18	6	3.0–4.5	82	12	0.9–4.4
	1967	0	--	--	100	11	1.7–4.7

Table 16. Streamflow during the acquisition of the aerial photographs used for repeat bar and channel feature delineation on the Tillamook, Trask, Wilson, Kilchis, Miami, and Nehalem Rivers, northwestern Oregon.

[m^3/s, cubic meter per second; --, same as main streamflow; NA, gage inactive; USACE, U.S. Army Corps of Engineers; USGS, U.S. Geological Survey]

Year	River	Flight dates[1]	Mean daily discharge (m^3/s)[2]		
			Minimum	Maximum	Main
1939	Tillamook	5/8; 5/12; 7/20	4.6	5.9	5.9
	Trask	5/8; 5/12	5.2	5.9	5.2
	Wilson	5/8; 5/12	5.2	5.9	5.2
	Kilchis	5/8; 5/12	5.2	5.9	5.2
	Miami	5/12	--	--	5.2
	Nehalem	5/8; 5/12	NA	--	--
1967	Tillamook	2/19	--	--	65.7
	Trask	2/19	--	--	65.7
	Wilson	2/19	--	--	65.7
	Kilchis	2/19	--	--	65.7
	Miami	2/19	--	--	65.7
	Nehalem	2/19	--	--	199.3
2005	Tillamook	7/17; 7/19	5.3	6.1	5.3
	Trask	7/19–20	4.9	5.0	[3]5.0
	Wilson	7/19–20	5.1	5.3	[4]5.1, 5.3
	Kilchis	7/19	5.3	5.3	5.3
	Miami	7/17; 7/19	5.3	6.1	5.3
	Nehalem	7/17; 8/3	5.6	10.0	[4]5.6, 10.0
2009	Tillamook	6/23; 6/27	5.1	5.5	5.1
	Trask	6/27	--	--	[3]5.0
	Wilson	6/27	--	--	5.1
	Kilchis	6/27	--	--	5.1
	Miami	6/27	--	--	[5]1.3
	Nehalem	6/27	--	--	9.5

[1] 1939 dates derived from photographs at USACE library

[2] Discharge from USGS streamflow-gaging station 14301500 Wilson River near Tillamook, Oregon for the Miami, Kilchis, Wilson, Trask, and Tillamook Rivers; discharge from USGS streamflow-gaging station 14301000 Nehalem River near Foss, Oregon for the Nehalem River. Main discharge is the streamflow when most of the reach was photographed. Two discharge values are provided when areal coverages were approximately equal for photograph collection dates.

[3] Discharge from USGS streamflow-gaging station 14302480 Trask River above Cedar Creek

[4] Areal coverage is approximately equal for both dates

[5] Data from OWRD streamflow-gaging station Miami River near Garibaldi, Oregon

Distribution and Area of Bars, 2009

In 2009, unit bar area, or the total area of bars per meter of channel length (m^2/m), ranged from 7.1 to 27.9 m^2/m in the fluvial reaches and 0.7 to 262.0 m^2/m in the tidal reaches (table 17). Of the fluvial reaches, the Upper Fluvial Miami Reach had the greatest unit bar area (27.9 m^2/m). Of the tidal reaches, the Nehalem Tidal Reach had the greatest unit bar area (262.0 m^2/m), owing to extensive mud flats and tidal wetlands between RKM 9.6 and 3.0 where the floodplain widens to 2.9 km (fig. 15). The unit bar values on the Wilson, Miami, and Nehalem Rivers are similar to rivers along the southwestern Oregon coast, such as Hunter Creek and the Chetco River that drain the gravel-rich Klamath Mountains (table 18).

In fluvial reaches, bar area was generally greatest where declining gradients and widening channels promoted the deposition of sediment received from the contributing watersheds or where channels were relatively unconfined throughout the fluvial reaches (fig. 24A–F). For instance, bar area peaked on the Tillamook River near RKM 12.0 and Trask River near RKM 14.0 where the floodplains and active channels begin to widen, permitting sediment storage, and then generally diminished downstream (figs. 8, 10, and 24A–B). Similarly, bar area fluctuated longitudinally, but still increased considerably in relatively unconfined sections near RKM 10.0 on the Wilson River and RKM 10.0 and 4.0 on the Miami River. In contrast, bar area on the Kilchis and Nehalem Rivers peaked near or at the downstream boundary of the fluvial reaches, coinciding with the head of tide and channel gradient reductions. These distributions of bar area relate to the relation between transport capacity and sediment supply (as discussed below) and background drivers, such as valley confinement and channel gradient.

Results for Repeat Bar and Channel Delineation, 1939–2009

Mapping of bars from aerial and orthophotographs dating from 1939 to 2009 shows that unit bar area decreased during this time period for all reaches except for tidal reaches on the Tillamook (98.0 percent increase) and Nehalem (14.7 percent increase) Rivers (table 17; fig. 25). In all other reaches, reductions in unit bar area ranged from 5.3 to 83.6 percent in fluvial reaches and 24.2 to 83.1 percent in tidal reaches.

From 1939 to 2009, net changes in the number (fig. 25) and average area of mapped bars (table 17) varied by reach. Overall, bars became less numerous and smaller in average area in six reaches (Fluvial Tillamook, Fluvial and Tidal Trask, Tidal Wilson, and Lower Fluvial and Tidal Miami Reaches), less numerous but larger in average area in three reaches (Upper Fluvial Wilson, Tidal Kilchis, and Tidal Nehalem Reaches), and more numerous but smaller in average area in four reaches (Tidal Tillamook, Lower Fluvial Wilson, Lower Fluvial Miami, Fluvial Nehalem Reaches). The Fluvial Kilchis Reach was the only reach to maintain the same number of bars even though average area decreased from 1939 to 2009.

Channel centerline length changed 1 percent or less in the Tidal Trask, Wilson, and Miami Reaches, Fluvial Kilchis Reach, and Nehalem River study area from 1939 to 2009 (table 19; fig. 25). Channel length decreased in the Fluvial Trask (4 percent; 390 m), Lower Fluvial Wilson (1.9 percent; 150 m), and Lower Fluvial Miami (1.4 percent; 110 m) Reaches and increased on the Tillamook River (2.3 percent or 90 m in the fluvial reach; 1.4 percent or 140 m in the tidal reach) and in the Upper Fluvial Wilson (1.2 percent; 30 m), Tidal Kilchis (1.1 percent; 30 m), and Upper Fluvial Miami (4.8 percent; 110 m) Reaches. Sections with substantial channel planform changes are discussed below.

Table 17. Repeat bar attribute data as delineated from photographs taken in 1939, 1967, 2005, and 2009 for the Tillamook, Trask, Wilson, Kilchis, Miami, and Nehalem Rivers, northwestern Oregon.

[m²/m, square meter of bar area per meter of channel length; m, meter; %, percent]

River	Reach	Unit bar area (m²/m)					Number of bars					Average bar area (m²)				
		1939	1967	2005	2009	Net % change	1939	1967	2005	2009	Net % change	1939	1967	2005	2009	Net % change
Tillamook	Fluvial	21.1	7.2	7.3	7.1	-66.4	21	14	25	17	-19.0	3,800	1,940	1,140	1,650	-56.6
	Tidal	7.3	11.2	14.1	14.5	98.0	3	11	10	11	266.7	24,450	10,140	14,290	13,370	-45.3
Trask	Fluvial	58.9	38.8	9.9	9.7	-83.6	46	22	44	41	-10.9	11,660	16,070	2,090	2,190	-81.2
	Tidal	7.7	2.7	2.1	2.3	-70.4	17	8	5	7	-58.8	3,140	2,380	2,910	2,260	-28.0
Wilson	Upper Fluvial	19.7	11.7	16.0	18.6	-5.3	15	8	14	12	-20.0	3,330	3,710	3,040	4,060	21.9
	Lower Fluvial	52.2	27.3	12.6	12.6	-75.8	27	15	34	33	22.2	14,310	13,450	2,810	2,910	-79.7
	Tidal	4.3	1.8	1.9	0.7	-83.1	11	4	10	7	-36.4	1,940	2,280	940	520	-73.2
Kilchis	Fluvial	34.6	13.5	10.0	9.2	-73.4	28	15	31	28	0.0	6,170	4,500	1,650	1,680	-72.8
	Tidal	13.0	7.4	8.2	9.9	-24.2	11	6	8	7	-36.4	3,130	3,260	2,730	3,780	20.8
Miami	Upper Fluvial	54.6	9.0	18.9	27.9	-48.9	15	14	23	16	6.7	8,720	1,540	1,970	4,200	-51.8
	Lower Fluvial	24.7	7.9	7.0	8.1	-67.3	69	34	45	50	-27.5	2,750	1,780	1,220	1,270	-53.8
	Tidal	6.7	0.8	2.2	2.1	-69.5	10	2	6	4	-60.0	890	560	510	690	-22.5
Nehalem	Fluvial	36.3	19.8	23.0	18.3	-49.8	29	14	38	39	34.5	8,690	9,470	4,240	3,220	-62.9
	Tidal	228.3	195.8	203.9	262.0	14.7	53	34	43	44	-17.0	105,550	141,070	115,950	146,450	38.7

Table 18. Unit bar area data for predominantly fluvial reaches from this study and prior studies in select Oregon coastal rivers (Wallick and others, 2011; Jones and others, 2011, 2012a, 2012b).

[km^2, square kilometer; m^2/m, square meter of bar area per meter of channel length]

River/Creek	Basin area (km^2)	Unit bar area for predominantly fluvial reaches (m^2/m)	Source
Nehalem	2,207	18.3	This study
Miami	94	8.1 and 27.9	This study
Kilchis	169	9.2	This study
Wilson	500	12.6 and 18.6	This study
Trask	451	9.7	This study
Tillamook	156	7.1	This study
Umpqua[1]	12,103	5.0 to 17.6	Wallick and others (2011)
Coquille	2,745	0.4 to 12.6	Jones and others (2012b)
Rogue	13,390	10.6 to 63.1	Jones and others (2012a)
Applegate	1,994	4.3 and 71.5	Jones and others (2012a)
Illinois	2,564	91.8	Jones and others (2012a)
Hunter	44	19.1 and 19.7	Jones and others (2011)
Chetco[1]	914	9.3 to 77.5	Wallick and others (2010)

[1]Bar area and channel length mapped from 2005 orthophotographs; all others mapped from 2009 orthophotographs

Fitzhugh Bar on the Chetco River, Upper Reach.

Jones Bar on the Umpqua River, Coast Range Reach.

Orchard Bar on the Rogue River, Lobster Creek Reach.

Elliot Bar on the Coquille River, Broadbent Reach.

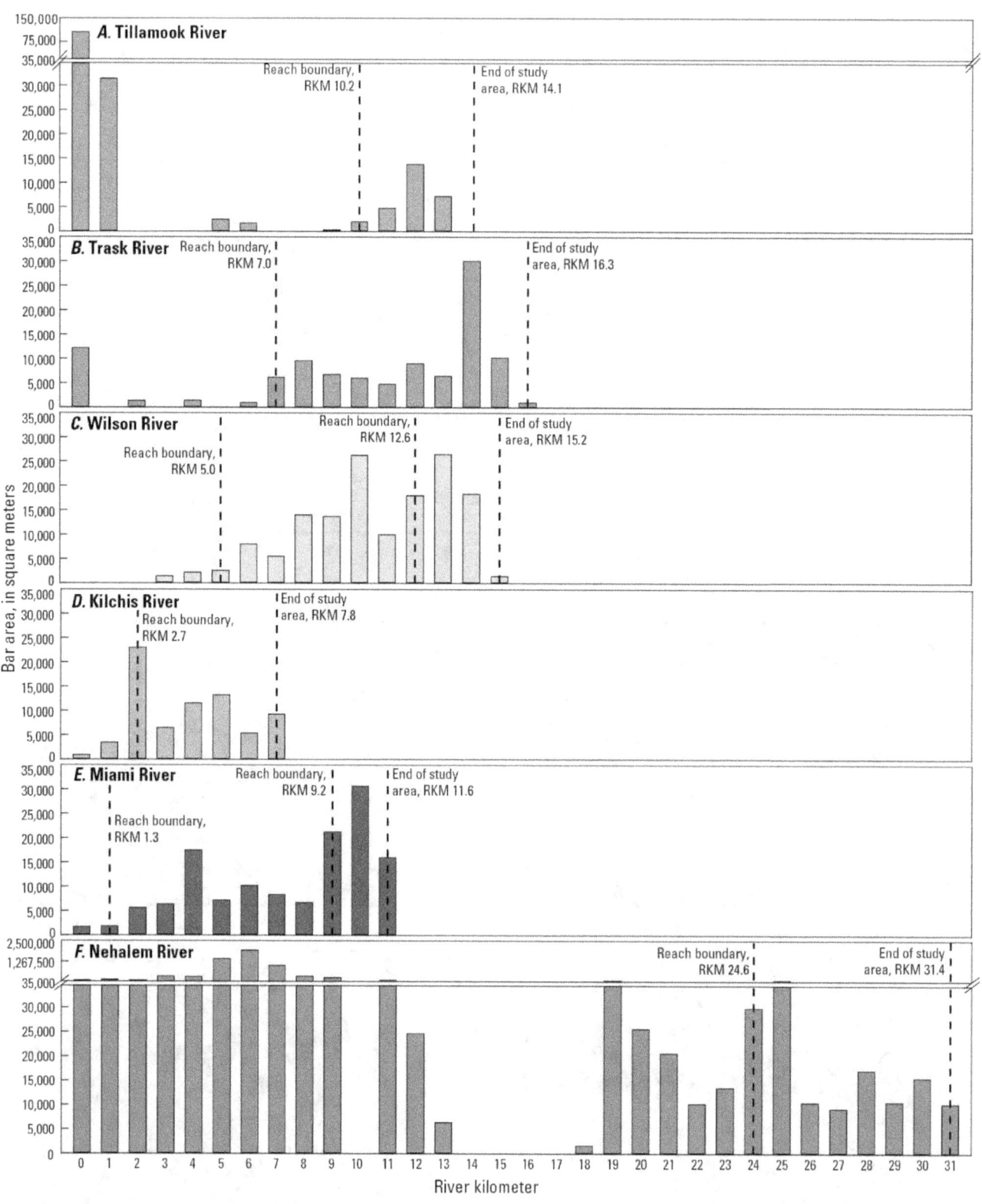

Figure 24. Graphs showing bar area by river kilometer as delineated from orthophotographs taken in 2009 for study areas on the Tillamook, Trask, Wilson, Kilchis, Miami, and Nehalem Rivers, northwestern Oregon. [RKM, river kilometer]

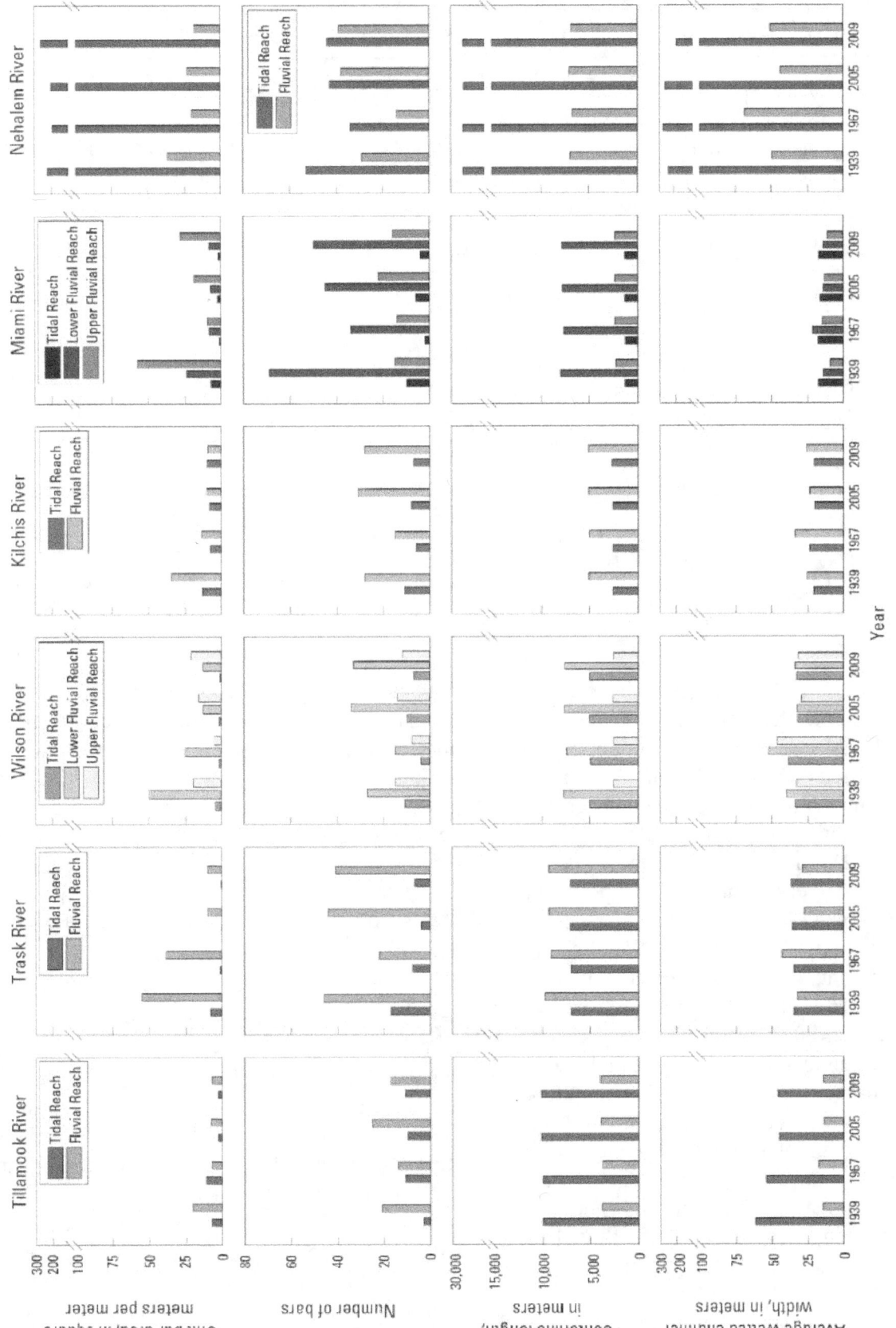

Figure 25. Graphs showing unit bar area, number of bars, channel centerline length, and average wetted channel width as delineated from photographs taken in 1939, 1967, 2005, and 2009 for study areas on the Tillamook, Trask, Wilson, Kilchis, Miami, and Nehalem Rivers, northwestern Oregon.

79

Table 19. Repeat channel feature data as delineated from photographs taken in 1939, 1967, 2005, and 2009 for the Tillamook, Trask, Wilson, Kilchis, Miami, and Nehalem Rivers, northwestern Oregon.

River	Reach	Centerline length (meters)					Average wetted channel width (meters)				
		1939	1967	2005	2009	Net change (percent)	1939	1967	2005	2009	Net change (percent)
Tillamook	Fluvial	3,870	3,790	3,940	3,960	2.3	15	18	13	14	-7.0
	Tidal	9,980	9,990	10,130	10,120	1.4	62	54	46	46	-25.8
Trask	Fluvial	9,700	9,100	9,300	9,310	-4.0	35	43	28	29	-17.1
	Tidal	6,980	6,970	7,000	7,000	0.3	35	35	36	37	5.7
Wilson	Upper Fluvial	2,580	2,540	2,650	2,610	1.2	34	46	30	32	-5.9
	Lower Fluvial	7,740	7,400	7,600	7,590	-1.9	42	52	33	34	-19.0
	Tidal	5,000	4,980	5,000	5,000	0	34	39	33	33	-2.9
Kilchis	Fluvial	5,100	5,000	5,120	5,120	0.4	26	34	24	26	0
	Tidal	2,650	2,640	2,670	2,680	1.1	21	24	20	20	-4.8
Miami	Upper Fluvial	2,290	2,390	2,400	2,400	4.8	9	14	13	11	22.2
	Lower Fluvial	7,970	7,660	7,830	7,860	-1.4	14	22	14	14	0
	Tidal	1,360	1,330	1,350	1,350	-0.7	18	18	16	17	-5.6
Nehalem	Fluvial	6,930	6,710	7,010	6,870	-0.9	50	68	44	51	2.0
	Tidal	24,500	24,500	24,450	24,600	0.4	227	256	246	186	-18.1

From 1939 to 2009, changes in the average wetted width of the channels were less than 7 percent in fluvial reaches on the Tillamook, Wilson (Upper Fluvial), Kilchis, Miami (Lower Fluvial), and Nehalem Rivers and tidal reaches on the Trask, Wilson, Kilchis, and Miami Rivers (table 19; fig. 25). In contrast, average wetted channel width decreased more than 17 percent in the Fluvial Trask (17.1 percent; 6 m), Lower Fluvial Wilson (19.0 percent; 8 m), Tidal Nehalem (18.1 percent; 41 m), and Tidal Tillamook (25.8 percent; 16 m) Reaches and increased by 22.2 percent (2 m) in the Upper Fluvial Miami Reach. Although mapped wetted channel width is sensitive to the streamflow and tide conditions at the time photographs were taken, streamflow was comparable in 1939 and 2009 (table 16). Consequently, some of the larger changes in average wetted channel width likely signify actual channel narrowing or widening in the fluvial reaches. A more detailed delineation of active channel width (instead of wetted channel width, which can be affected by small streamflow and

stage differences) and accounting for streamflow and stage differences may help better quantify possible changes in channel width in relation to the area and number of bars for theses study areas. Accounting for possible tide differences may help in assessing channel width changes in tidal reaches.

Discussion of Mapped Changes in Bar and Channel Features, 1939–2009

As outlined above and shown in the figures below, the Tillamook Bay rivers and the Nehalem River generally had extensive bed-material deposits flanking the channels in 1939, but diminished bed-material deposits in 2009 (with the exception of the Tidal Tillamook and Nehalem Reaches). Although any mapped bar and channel datasets inherently have some level of uncertainty and error, the magnitude of the reductions in bar area reported here and visual comparison of the aerial photographs suggest considerable declines in bar area from 1939 to 2009. Comparison of the mapping results and the four sets of photographs indicates that the reduction in bar area may be attributable to several factors, including vegetation establishment on bars that previously lacked apparent vegetation, lateral channel changes and resulting alterations in sediment deposition and erosion patterns, and streamflow and/or tide differences between photographs. Other factors that may be associated with the observed reduction in bar area but not assessed in this reconnaissance level study include changes in the sediment and hydrology regimes of these rivers over the analysis period. The following sections describe the mapped bar and channel changes from 1939 to 2009 by river and reach.

Tillamook River

In the fluvial reach of the Tillamook River, unit bar area declined a net 66.4 percent from 1939 to 2009 with the decline greatest from 1939 to 1967 (table 17; fig. 25). Most of the net reduction in bar area, especially in the large lateral and point bars from RKM 14.1–11.8, owes to vegetation growth and subsequent stabilization of previously apparently unvegetated bars (such as near RKM 13.6 and 12.2; fig. 26A–C) and changes in the channel's position and deposition patterns (such as from RKM 13.4–12.0). Upstream of RKM 11.4, the channel shifted laterally in several locations. For instance, the Tillamook River cut a new channel through a lateral bar, moving 65 m southward between RKM 13.0 and 12.8. At RKM 11.6, the channel straightened and shifted 65 m southwestward. In addition, sinuosity increased from RKM 13.4 to12.0, resulting in a modest increase in channel centerline length (table 19). Downstream of RKM 11.6, the lateral stability of the channel over the analysis period probably results in part from confinement by the valley wall along the left channel bank near RKM 11.0 (fig. 26D–F). Overall, channel length increased modestly (2.3 percent), as did average wetted width (7 percent) over the analysis period (table 19).

In the Tidal Tillamook Reach, unit bar area increased by approximately 4 m^2/m from 1939 to 1967 and 3 m^2/m from 1967 to 2005, and then remained relatively stable from 2005 to 2009 (table 17; fig. 25). The overall net increase of 98.0 percent in unit bar area from 1939 to 2009 is associated with an increase in mapped bar area in the reach's lowermost 1.8 km (fig. 27A–C). Differences in bar area here may owe to possible tidal differences between photographs and the formation and growth of bars behind log booms and piles between 1939 and 1967 (such as from RKM 7.2 to 6.8; fig. 27D–F). During the analysis period, the channel's average wetted width narrowed 25.8 percent or 16 m (table 19). Some of the reduction in average wetted channel width is attributable to a medial bar near the Tillamook River mouth, which had grown in size by 2009. Reductions in wetted width may also owe to deposition behind piles and log booms from 1939 to 1967 and the occurrence of features likely composed of fine sediment flanking the tidal channel apparent in the 1967, 2005, and 2009 photographs (fig. 27A–F). The stability of the channel's position from 1939 to 2009 is attributable to levees and bank protection, which border approximately 77 percent of the banks in this reach (table 6).

Trask River

In 1939, the Fluvial Trask Reach had the highest unit bar area value of the fluvial reaches (58.9 m^2/m; table 17). From 1939 to 2009, however, the net reach unit bar area decreased by 83.6 percent (fig. 25), with substantial reductions in unit bar area from 1939 to 1967 and 1967 to 2005 followed by relatively little change from 2005 to 2009. Most of the apparent changes from 1939 to 1967 were the result of greater streamflows in 1967 (table 16) and glare along the channel, both of which obscure bars in the 1967 photographs (table 16). The reduced unit bar area after 1967 owes to changes in channel position (and thus erosional and depositional spaces) and

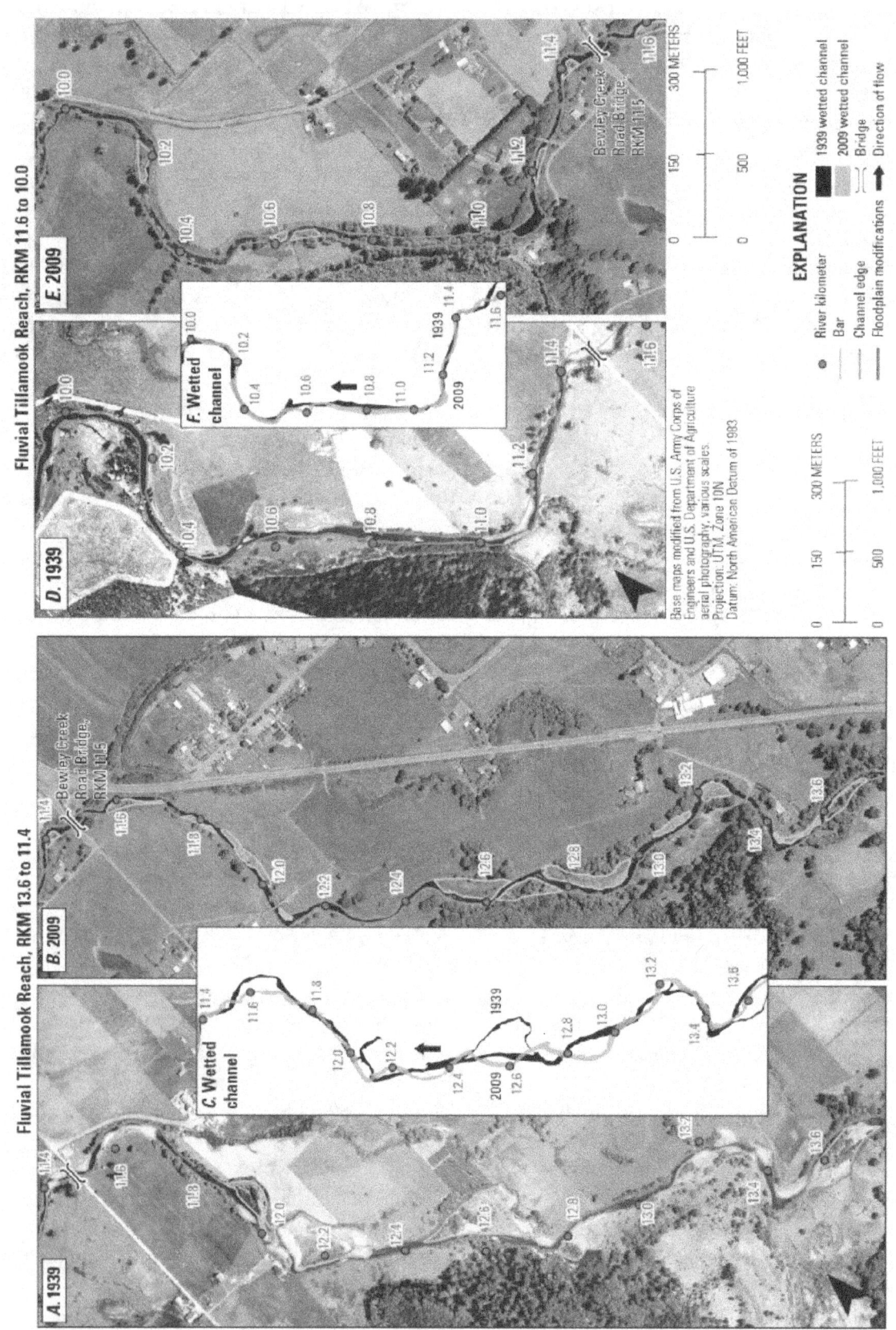

Figure 26. Images showing repeat bar and channel delineations in two sections (river kilometers 13.6–11.4 and 11.6–10.0) of the Fluvial Tillamook Reach, northwestern Oregon. Floodplain modifications identified in the map include dikes, levees, and naturally formed levees reinforced with non-erodible materials (source: Oregon Coastal Management Program, 2011).

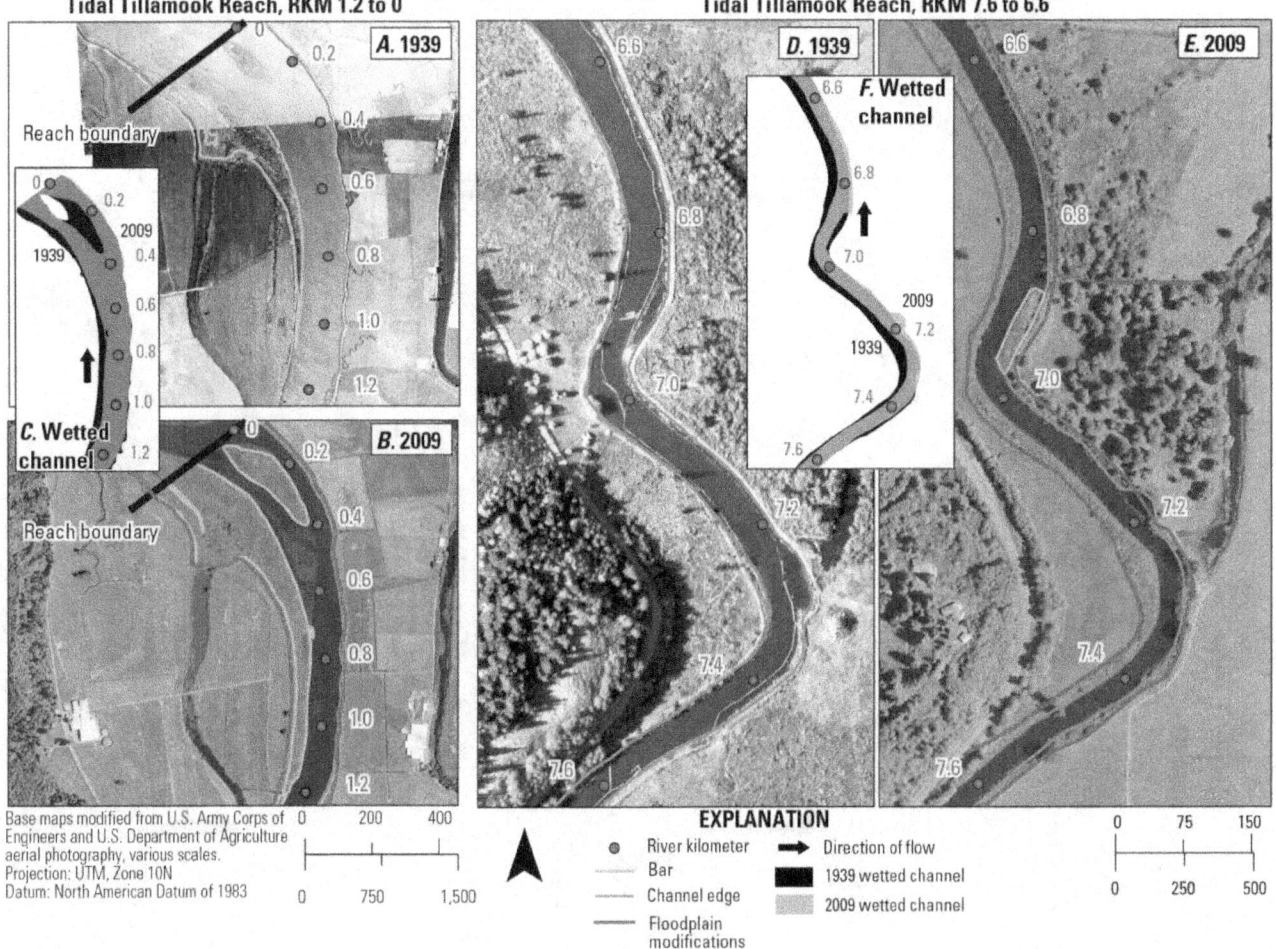

EXPLANATION

- River kilometer
- Bar
- Channel edge
- Floodplain modifications
- Direction of flow
- 1939 wetted channel
- 2009 wetted channel

Figure 27. Images showing repeat bar and channel delineations near the Tillamook River mouth (river kilometer 1.2–0) and pile structures and log booms (river kilometer 7.6–6.6) in the Tidal Tillamook Reach, northwestern Oregon. Floodplain modifications identified in the map include dikes, levees, and naturally formed levees reinforced with nonerodible materials (source: Oregon Coastal Management Program, 2011).

vegetation growth, and stabilization of bar surfaces, such as near RKM 15.2–14.0 (fig. 28A–D) and 13.0–11.8 (fig. 28A–H). Over the analysis period, the lateral position of channel shifted throughout the reach. For instance, the channel moved approximately 100 m southward (measured as the distance between 1939 and 2009 centerlines; fig. 28A–D) from RKM 15.4 to 14.1 and approximately 160 m from RKM 12.8 to 11.8 to cut a straight path through two large bars (fig. 28E–H). The losses of sinuosity at these locations as well as at RKM 10.4–9.2 are partly

responsible for the 4.0 percent (390 m) reduction in channel centerline length (table 19). Over the analysis period, the average wetted width of the channel declined 17.1 percent (6 m; table 19) and is noticeably narrower in locations, such as near RKM 15.6–15.0, in 2009 (fig. 28A–D).

Downstream in the Tidal Trask Reach, unit bar area declined a net 70.4 percent with most of those reductions occurring from 1939 to 1967 (table 17; fig. 25). Overall, the reductions in bar area owe to several factors, including possible tide and streamflow differences between photo

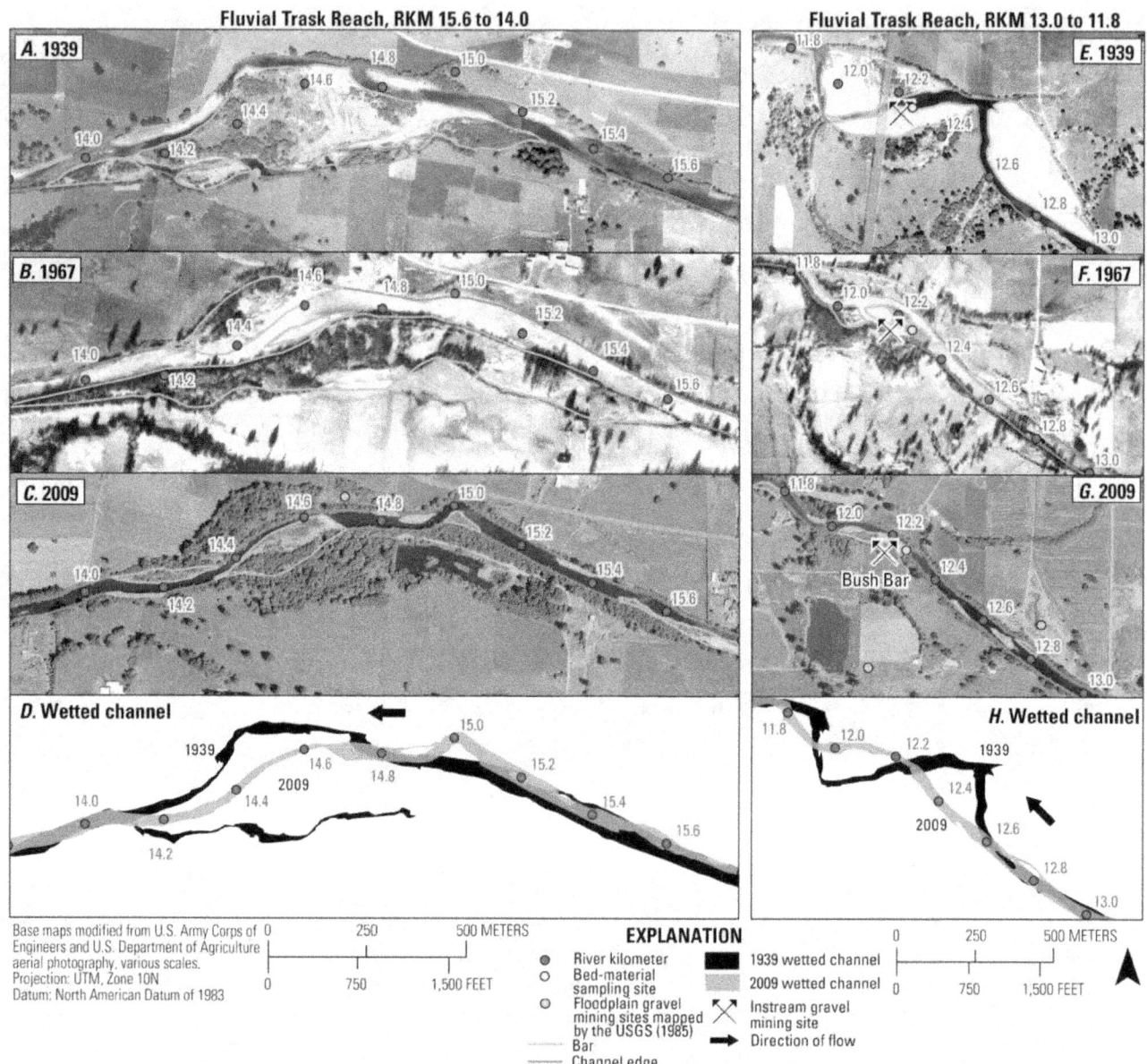

EXPLANATION

Base maps modified from U.S. Army Corps of Engineers and U.S. Department of Agriculture aerial photography, various scales.
Projection: UTM, Zone 10N
Datum: North American Datum of 1983

- River kilometer
- Bed-material sampling site
- Floodplain gravel mining sites mapped by the USGS (1985)
- Bar
- Channel edge

1939 wetted channel
2009 wetted channel
Instream gravel mining site
Direction of flow

Figure 28. Images showing repeat bar and channel delineations, vegetation growth and stabilization of bar surfaces, and lateral channel migrations in two sections (river kilometers 15.6–14.0 and 13.0–11.8) of the Fluvial Trask Reach, northwestern Oregon.

graphs, vegetation growth on previously unvegetated bars (such as near RKM 6.6 in figure 29A–C, and RKM 5.2), and vegetation growth combined with floodplain modifications (such as near RKM 2.8–2.6 in figure 29D–F). The channel changed little in position (less than 18 m) and its length and average wetted width experienced

relatively minor changes from 1939 to 2009 (table 19), likely because approximately 71 percent of banks have some modifications (table 6).

Wilson River

Of all the fluvial reaches, the Upper Fluvial Wilson Reach had the smallest net reduction (5.3

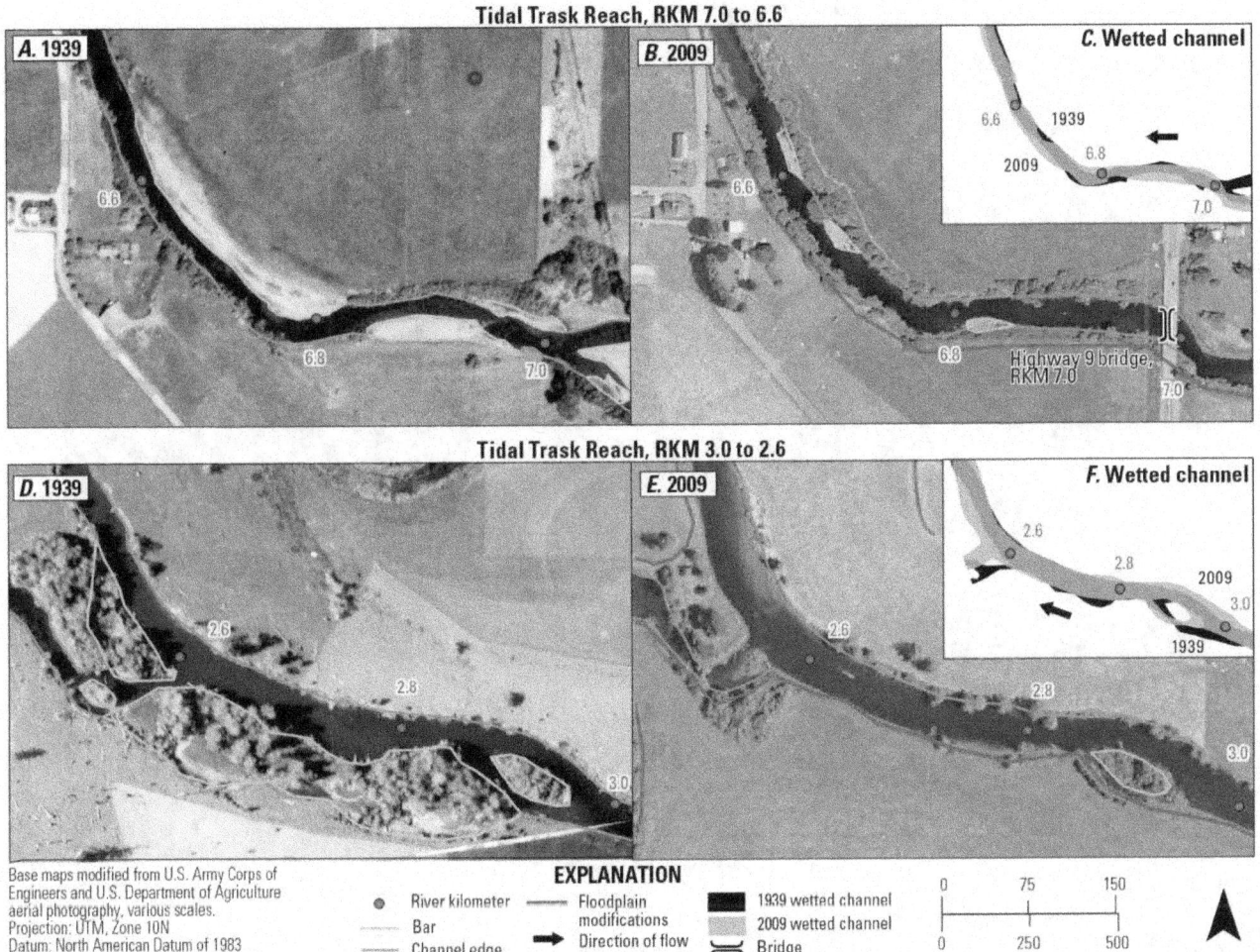

Figure 29. Images showing repeat bar and channel delineations and vegetation growth and stabilization of bar surfaces in two sections (river kilometers 7.0–6.6 and 3.0–2.6) of the Tidal Trask Reach, northwestern Oregon. Floodplain modifications identified in the map include dikes, levees, and naturally formed levees reinforced with nonerodible materials (source: Oregon Coastal Management Program, 2011).

percent) in unit bar area with bar distributions remaining fairly stable from 1939 to 2009 (table 17; fig. 25). Over this period, bar area increased slightly from RKM 14.0–13.8, but declined near RKM 13.4 owing to less apparent bar scour at 1:2,000 (fig. 30A–C). The narrow and confined geometry of the upper reach likely influences sediment deposition at the upstream extent of the Mills Bridge Bar as well as the location and area of bars over time (fig. 30A–C). The photographs indicate that most of the bar loss from 1939 to

1967 resulted from vegetation growth, glare in the 1967 photographs obscuring some of the channel, and higher streamflows in 1967 (table 16). As expected in this confined reach, the channel in the Upper Fluvial Wilson Reach maintained a stable position (with shifts less than 32 m), although it slightly lengthened and narrowed (table 19; fig. 25).

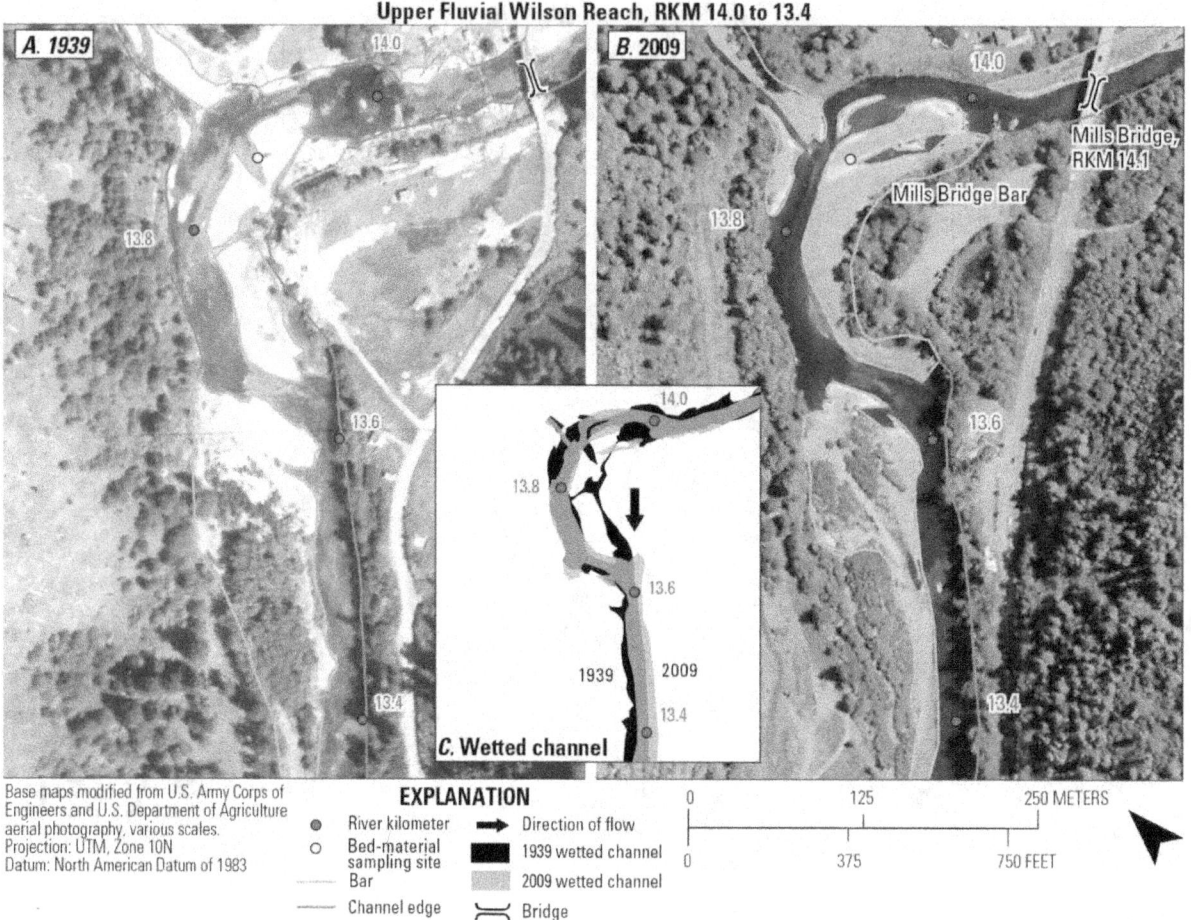

A. 1939

B. 2009

Mills Bridge, RKM 14.1

Mills Bridge Bar

C. Wetted channel

1939   2009

Base maps modified from U.S. Army Corps of
Engineers and U.S. Department of Agriculture
aerial photography, various scales.
Projection: UTM, Zone 10N
Datum: North American Datum of 1983

EXPLANATION

- River kilometer
- Bed-material sampling site
- Bar
- Channel edge

→ Direction of flow
■ 1939 wetted channel
▨ 2009 wetted channel
⋈ Bridge

0   125   250 METERS
0   375   750 FEET

Figure 30. Images showing repeat bar and channel delineations from river kilometer 14.0 to 13.4 in the Upper Fluvial Wilson Reach, northwestern Oregon.

In the Lower Fluvial Wilson Reach, unit bar area declined a net 75.8 percent over 1939–2009, mostly from 1939 to 2005 (table 17; fig. 25). Channel migration (RKM 11.0–8.6 and 8.0–7.0), sediment deposition and erosion changes, and vegetation establishment likely explain most of the net reduction in unit bar area. For example, the channel shifted approximately 225 m northwestward, eroding a lateral bar, to occupy a high flow channel near Upper and Lower Donaldson Bars (RKM 10.6–10.0; fig. 31A–C). The channel also shifted approximately 210 m into a high flow channel on the north side of a lateral bar near RKM 9.4–8.6 (fig. 31A–C). Since 1939, large lateral and point bars in this section have diminished owing to factors like vegetation growth (RKM 10.6–10.0 and 9–8.6) and flood-

plain modifications (RKM 10.0–9.2). Additionally, the channel migrated near RKM 8.2 between the GLO surveys of the 1850s and 1939 aerial photographs (Coulton and others, 1996). At RKM 7.8–7.0, the channel contained large lateral and medial bars in 1939 (fig. 32A–C). In 2009, this same section of the Wilson River has several floodplain modifications, reduced sinuosity, smaller lateral and point bars, and vegetation establishment on formerly active bars. Vegetation establishment explains most of the reduction in bar area where the channel was stable over the analysis period. The channel experienced a 1.9 percent (150 m) reduction in channel length and a 19.0 percent (8 m) reduction in average wetted width (table 19).

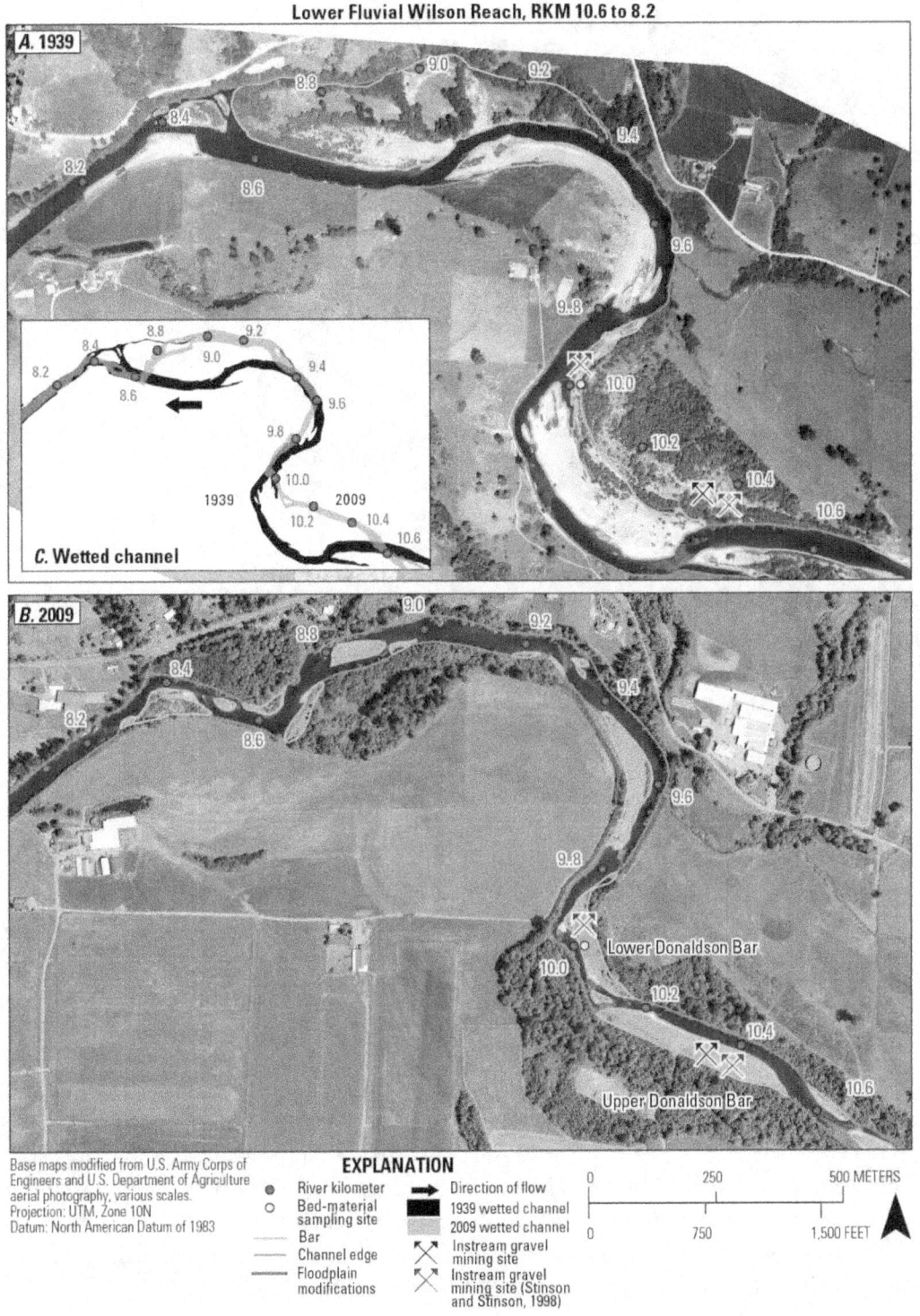

Figure 31. Images showing repeat bar and channel delineations, vegetation growth and stabilization of bar surfaces, and channel migrations from river kilometer 10.6 to 8.2 in the Lower Fluvial Wilson Reach, northwestern Oregon. Floodplain modifications identified in the map include dikes, levees, and naturally formed levees reinforced with nonerodible materials (source: Oregon Coastal Management Program, 2011).

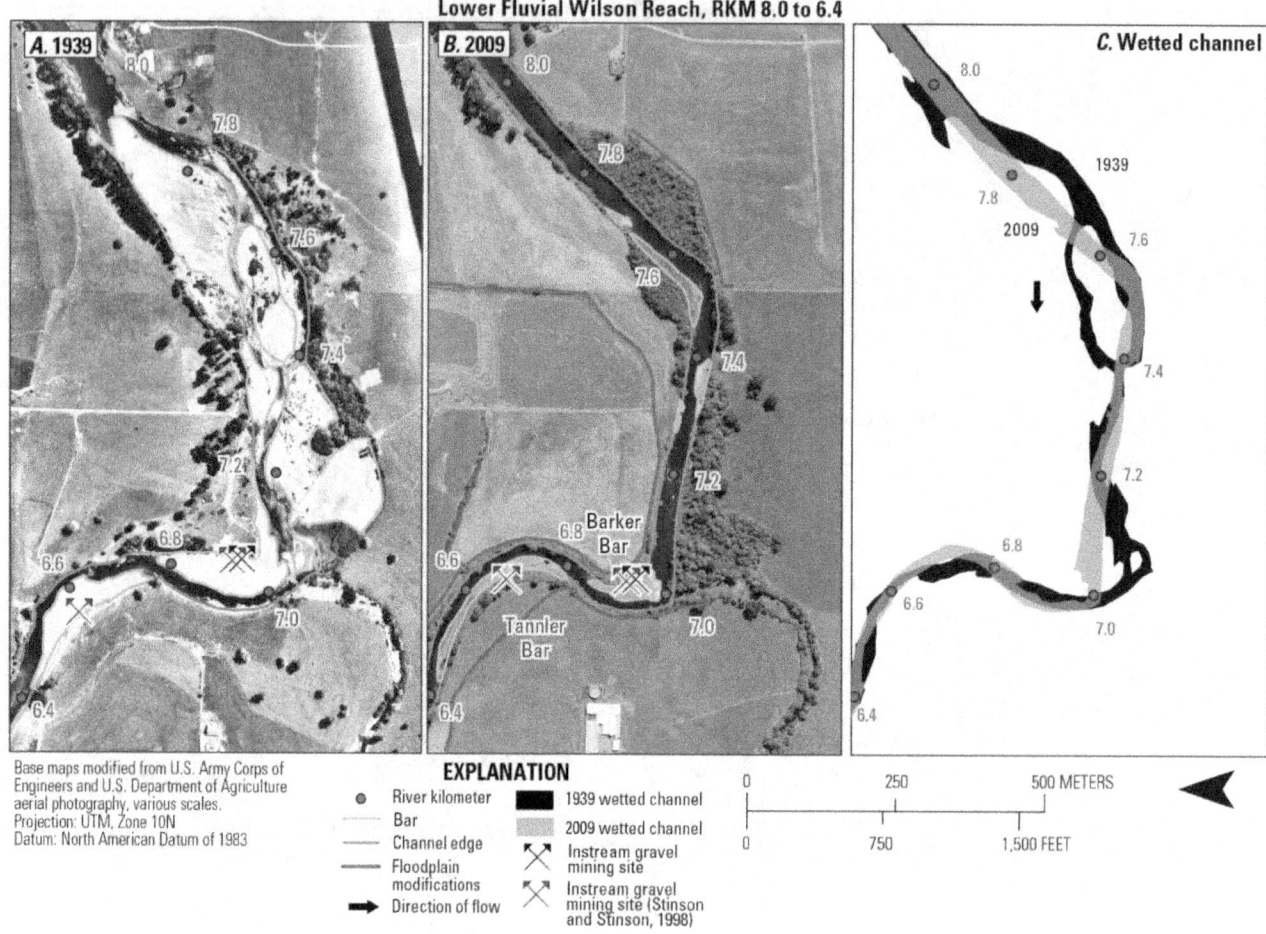

Figure 32. Images showing repeat bar and channel delineations, vegetation growth and stabilization of bar surfaces, and channel simplification from river kilometer 8.0–6.4 in the Lower Fluvial Wilson Reach, northwestern Oregon. Floodplain modifications identified in the map include dikes, levees, and naturally formed levees reinforced with nonerodible materials (source: Oregon Coastal Management Program, 2011).

The Tidal Wilson Reach had the lowest unit bar area in 1939 (4.3 m²/m), which further declined a net 83.1 percent from 1939 to 2009 (table 17; fig. 25). Like the other Wilson River reaches, net reductions in unit bar area are associated with vegetation establishment and subsequent stabilization of bar surfaces (such as near RKM 4.8 and 4.2; fig. 33A–C). Also, some of the bar surfaces delineated from the 1939 photographs were mapped as part of the wetted channel in 2009 (such as near RKM 4.6–3.8; fig. 33A–C), indicating potential erosion of these surfaces as streamflows were similar during pho-

tograph acquisition (table 16). Owing to floodplain modifications that line 77 percent of the tidal channel (table 6), the channel was primarily stable from 1939 to 2009, with lateral changes in position generally less than 40 m, no detectable changes in centerline length, and minor narrowing (table 19).

Kilchis River

The fluvial reach of the Kilchis River experienced a net 73.4 percent loss in unit bar area (table 17; fig. 25). This reduction is attributable to vegetation stabilizing bar surfaces (such as

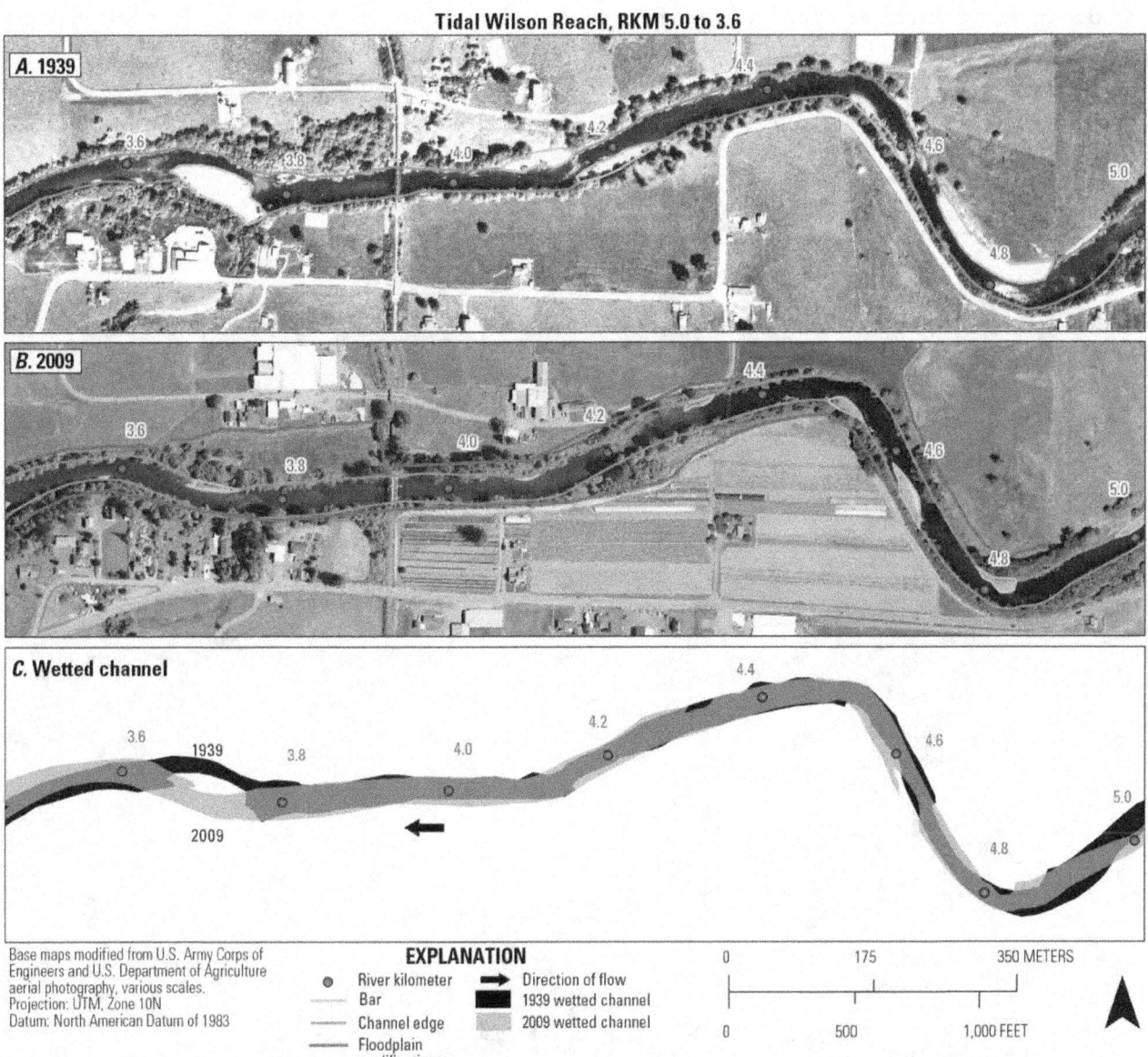

Figure 33. Images showing repeat bar and channel delineations, vegetation growth and stabilization of bar surfaces, and other changes from river kilometer 5.0 to 3.6 in the Tidal Wilson Reach, northwestern Oregon. Floodplain modifications identified in the map include dikes, levees, and naturally formed levees reinforced with nonerodible materials (source: Oregon Coastal Management Program, 2011).

near RKM 7.4–6.8, 6.2–5.0, and 4.0–2.7; figs. 34A–C and 35A–C) and channel planform changes and associated effects on depositional and erosional patterns (such as near RKM 6.4–6.0; RKM 3.4–2.7). A few of the 1939 bars coincide with the wetted channel mapped in 2009 near RKM 7.0, 6.8, and 5.0 (fig. 34A–C), indicating possible erosion of these bars. Over the analysis period, the Kilchis River channel migrated more than 50 m at three places (RKM 6.4–6.0, 5.8–5.2; RKM 3.4–2.7). In particular, the channel moved approximately 120 m south and straightened from RKM 6.4–6.0, resulting in the loss of a large point bar near RKM 6.2. The Kilchis River near RKM 6.2 is slightly downstream of where GLO surveyors noted a change in channel planform from 1857 to 1884 (near RKM 6.5, as described above), indicating that this location has been persistently dynamic. As shown in figures 34A–C and 35A–C, the channel contains smaller and narrower lateral and point bars in 2009 compared to 1939. The Kilchis River channel otherwise maintained a stable position with no detectable change in average wetted width and a minor increase in channel length (table 19).

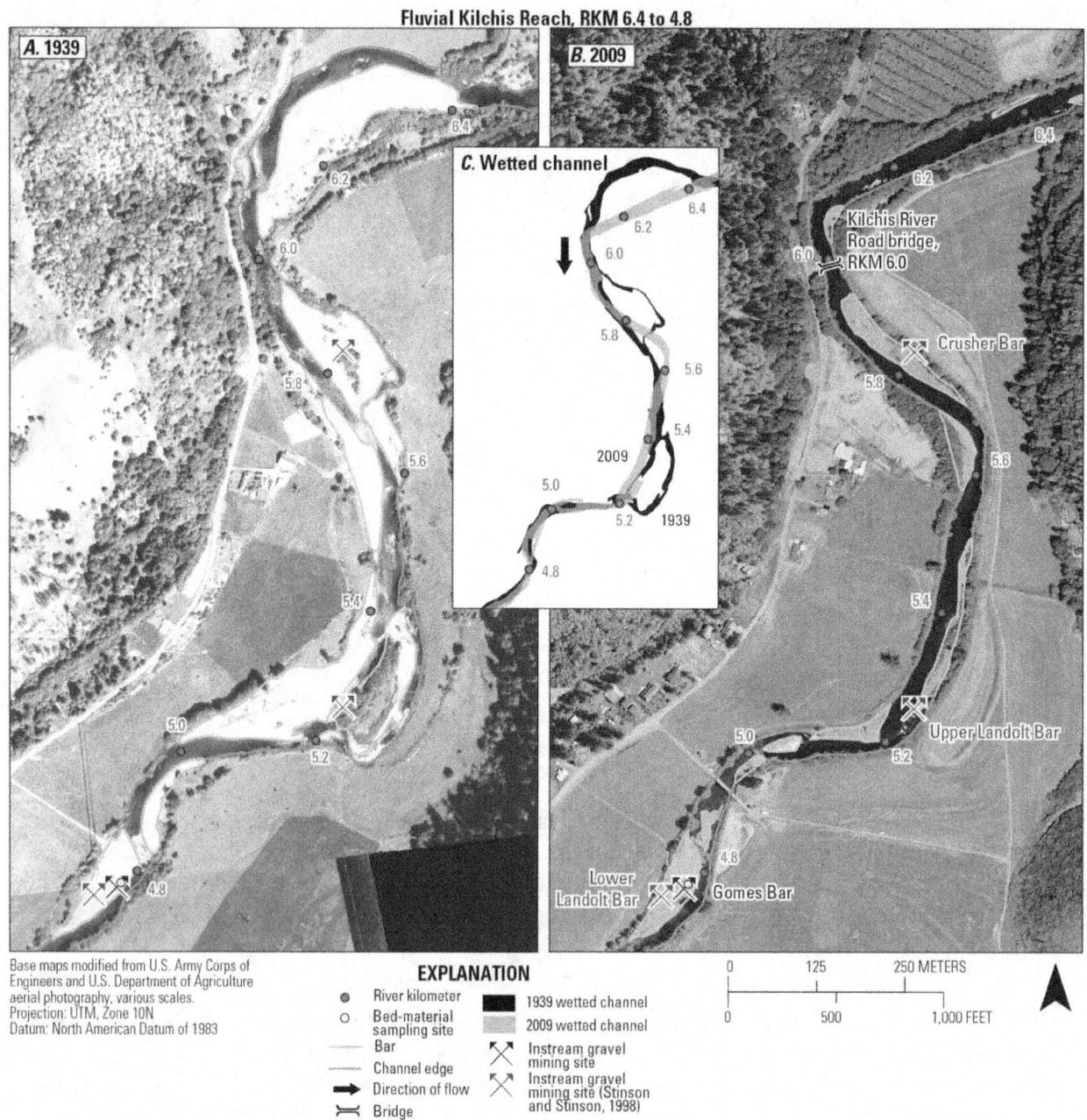

Figure 34. Images showing repeat bar and channel delineations, vegetation growth and stabilization of bar surfaces, and channel migrations from river kilometer 6.4 to 4.8 in the Fluvial Kilchis Reach, northwestern Oregon.

Figure 35. Images showing repeat bar and channel delineations, vegetation growth and stabilization of bar surfaces, and channel migrations from river kilometer 4.0 to 2.8 in the Fluvial Kilchis Reach, northwestern Oregon. Floodplain modifications identified in the map include dikes, levees, and naturally formed levees reinforced with nonerodible materials (source: Oregon Coastal Management Program, 2011).

Of the tidal reaches, the Tidal Kilchis Reach had the second highest unit bar area in 1939 and third highest in 2009 (13.0 and 9.9 m²/m, respectively; table 17). This tidal reach also had the lowest net reduction in unit bar area of the tidal reaches (24.2 percent loss compared to losses of 69.5 to 83.1 percent in other tidal reaches; table 17). In 1939 and 2009, bar area was greatest from RKM 2.9–1.8 near of the head of tide (fig. 36A–C). As shown in figure 36A–C, riparian vegetation was less prominent in 1939 compared to 2009. By 2009, vegetation had established successfully on the large lateral bar on the south bank. Channel sinuosity increased slightly from RKM 2.4–2.0, likely because of sediment deposition on the north bank upstream of RKM 2.2. Otherwise, the Tidal Kilchis Reach had a relatively stable planform, a small increase in chan-

nel length, and some narrowing in the average wetted channel width (table 19).

Miami River

In the Upper Fluvial Miami Reach, unit bar area declined a net 48.9 percent over the analysis period, with the declines primarily occurring from 1939 to 1967 followed by increases from 1967 to 2009 (table 17). The initial reduction in bar area apparently resulted from increased vegetation growth on the bar surfaces that were exposed in 1939 and some channel planform changes (fig. 37A–F). In later years, the area of bars increased throughout the reach, particularly from RKM 11.6–10.2, owing to the erosion of vegetation surfaces and an apparent increase in the area of the active channel area. Over the analysis period, the channel shifted its lateral

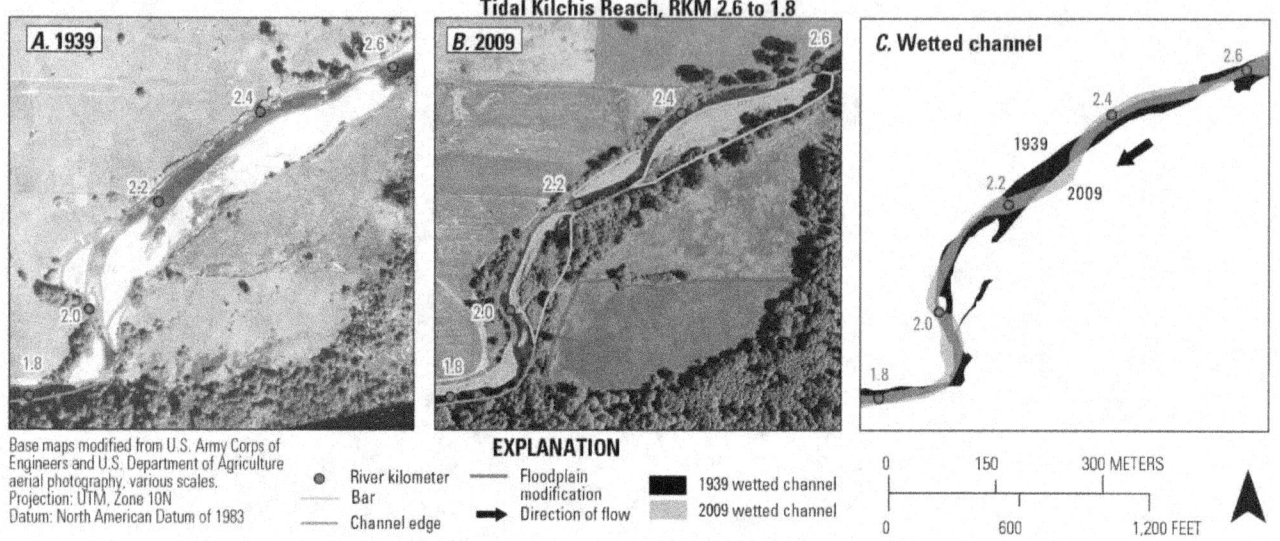

Figure 36. Images showing repeat bar and channel delineations, vegetation growth and stabilization of bar surfaces, and channel migrations from river kilometer 2.6 to 1.8 in the Tidal Kilchis Reach, northwestern Oregon. Floodplain modifications identified in the map include dikes, levees, and naturally formed levees reinforced with nonerodible materials (source: Oregon Coastal Management Program, 2011).

position throughout the reach and increased by 110 m in length (table 19). Average wetted channel width increased 22.2 percent or 2 m from 1939 to 2009, which is probably within the range of uncertainty associated with rectifying and digitizing from historical aerial photographs (table 19).

In the Lower Miami Fluvial Reach, unit bar area declined a net 67.3 percent from 1939 to 2009 with the greatest loss occurring from 1939 to 1967 and minor fluctuations in mapped unit bar area from 1967 to 2009 (table 17). Throughout the reach, bars that were apparently unvegetated in 1939 had established vegetation by 1967, and remained largely vegetated in 2009, resulting in a substantial loss in mapped bar area (figs. 38A–C and 39A–C). Additionally, some of the reductions in bar area owe to channel migration and resulting changes in depositional and erosional patterns, such as at RKM 7.4. Over the analysis period, the channel shifted laterally in the relatively unconfined sections throughout the reach; most shifts were generally less than 170 m

between aerial photographs used in this study. Although some planform changes increased sinuosity, some changes straightened segments, such as near RKM 8.0–7.2 and 2.4–2.2, and may explain the modest reduction (1.4 percent or 110 m) in channel centerline length (table 19). No net changes were detected in average wetted width (table 19).

Like the other reaches on the Miami River, the Tidal Miami Reach exhibited a net reduction (69.5 percent) in unit bar area from 1939 to 2009, primarily from 1939 to 1967 (table 17). Unit bar area increased from 0.8 to 2.2 m^2/m from 1967 to 2005, and then remained relatively stable from 2005 to 2009. The overall reduction in unit bar area from 1939 to 2009 is attributed to vegetation establishment on formerly unvegetated bars like near RKM 1.2, 0.8, and 0.1 and some lateral channel shifts like near RKM 1.1 and 0.7 (fig. 40A–C). Upstream of RKM 0.5 where the Miami River is unconfined by floodplain modifications, the channel shifted (generally less than 40 m) in several locations, but

92

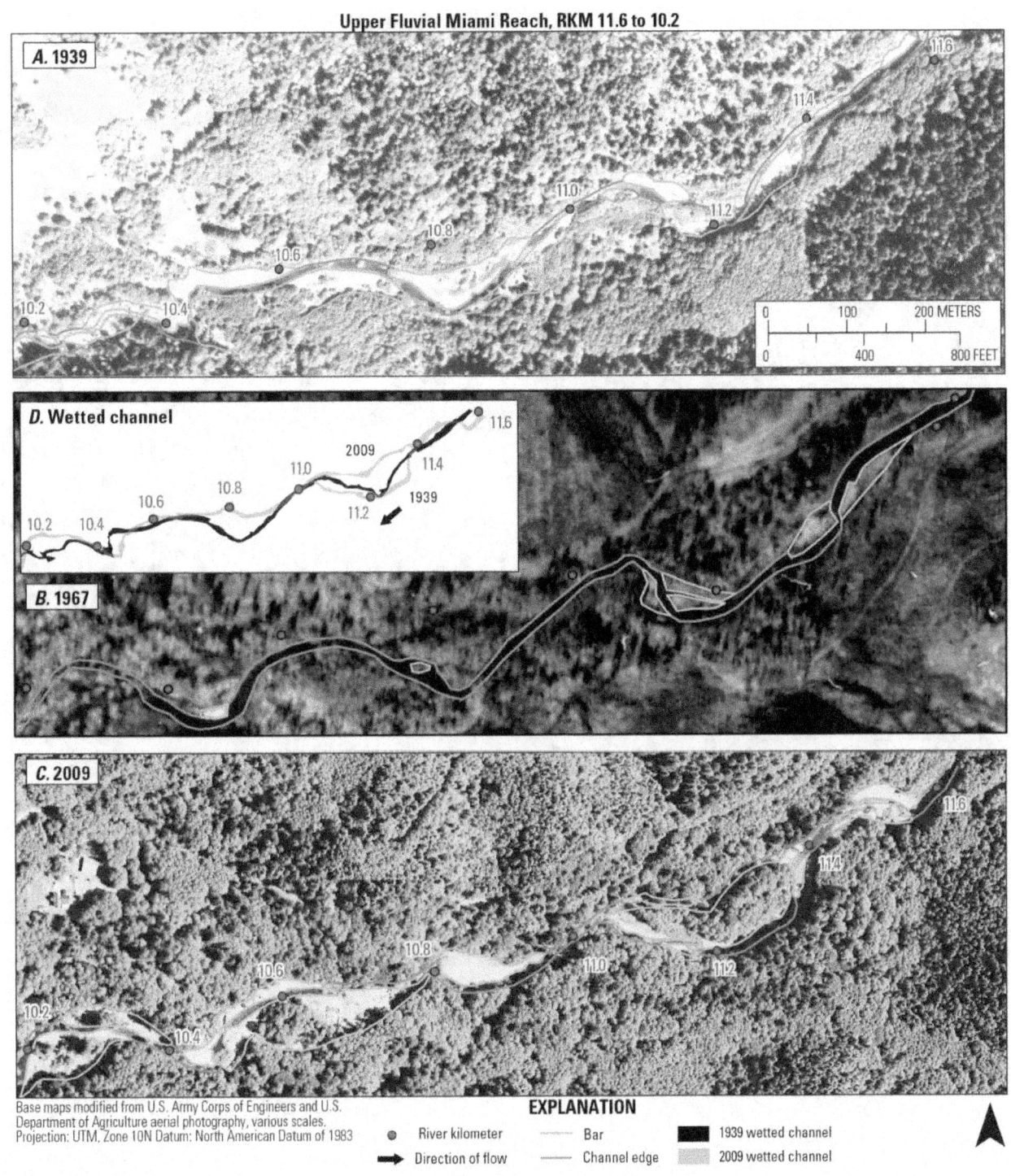

Figure 37. Images showing repeat bar and channel delineations, channel migrations, and vegetation changes from river kilometer 11.6 to 10.2 in the Upper Fluvial Miami Reach, northwestern Oregon.

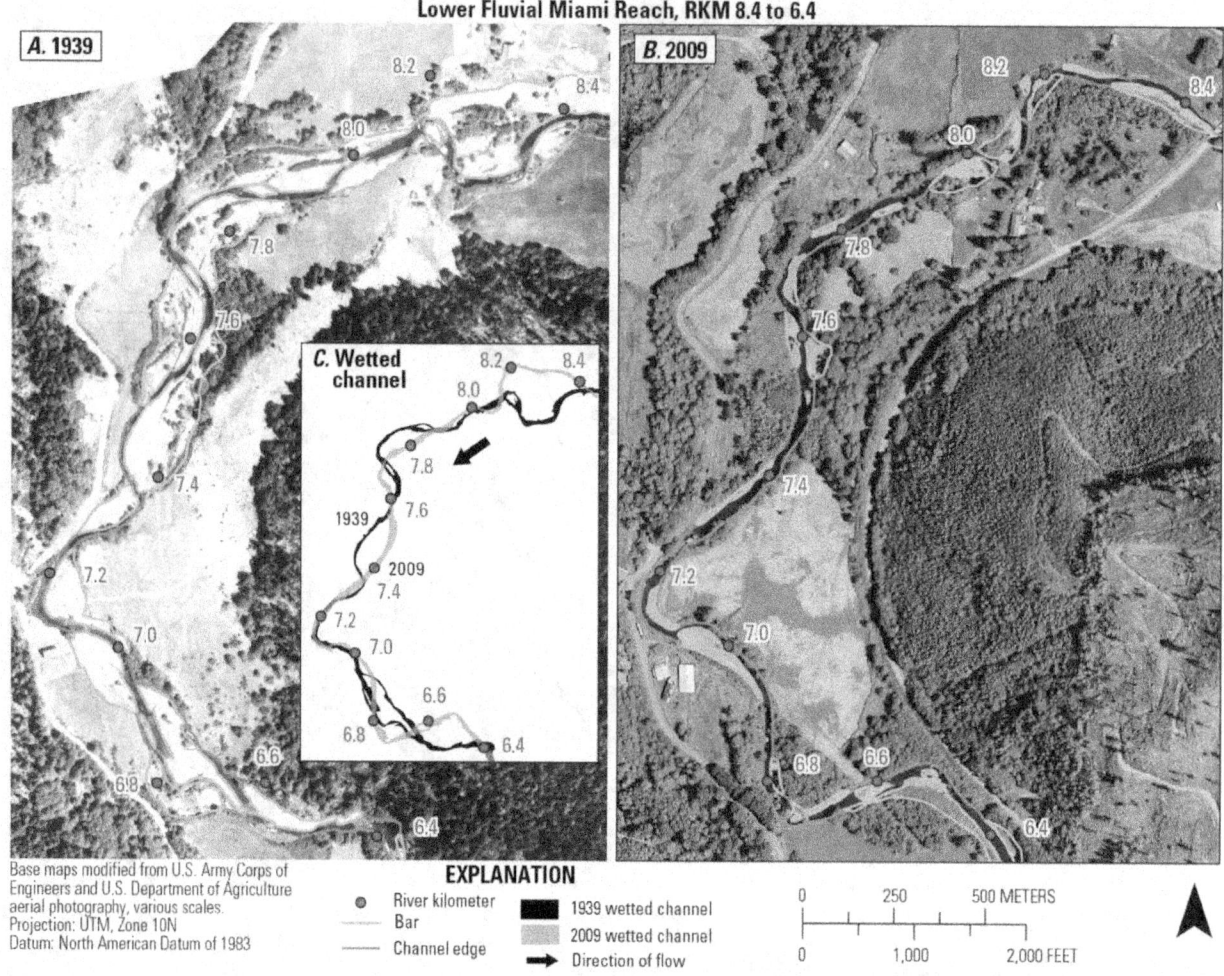

Figure 38. Images showing repeat bar and channel delineations, vegetation growth and stabilization of bar surfaces, and channel migrations from river kilometer 8.4 to 6.4 in the Lower Fluvial Miami Reach, northwestern Oregon.

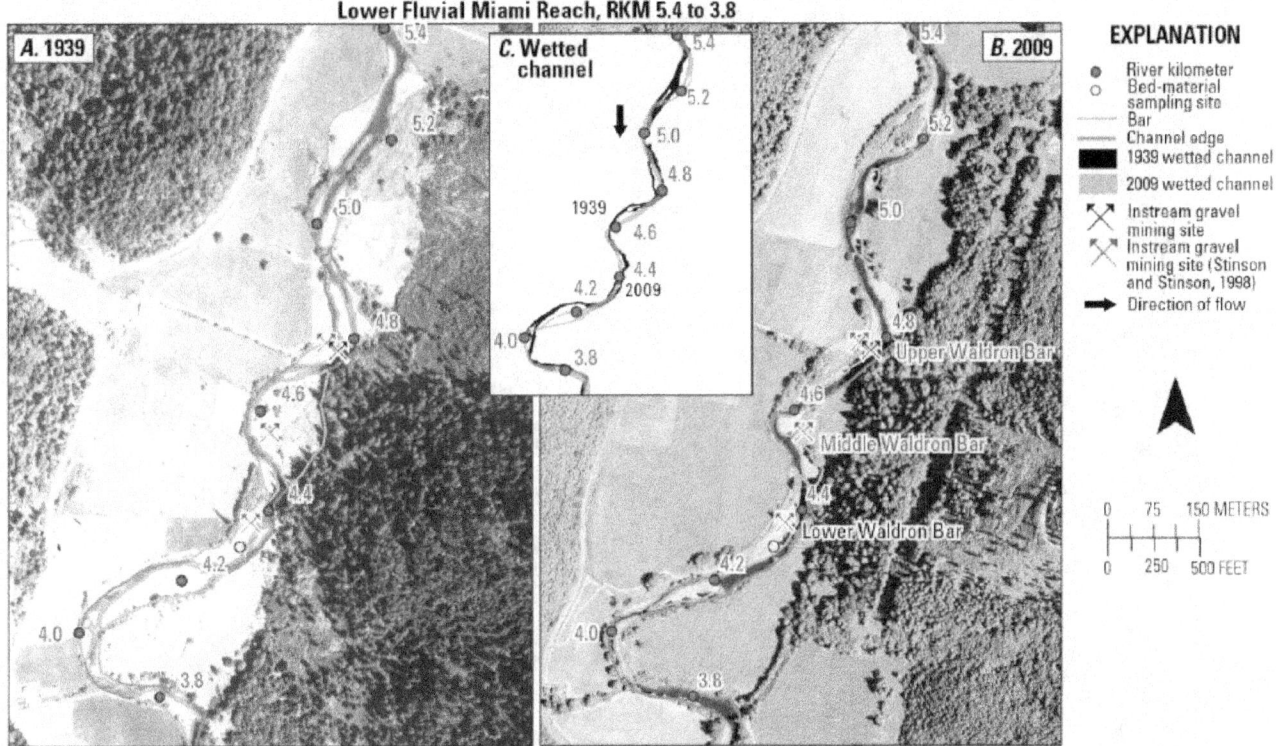

Figure 39. Images showing repeat bar and channel delineations and vegetation growth and stabilization of bar surfaces from river kilometer 5.4 to 3.8 in the Lower Fluvial Miami Reach, northwestern Oregon.

Measurement transect at Lower Waldron Bar

Surface of Lower Waldron Bar within measurement transect

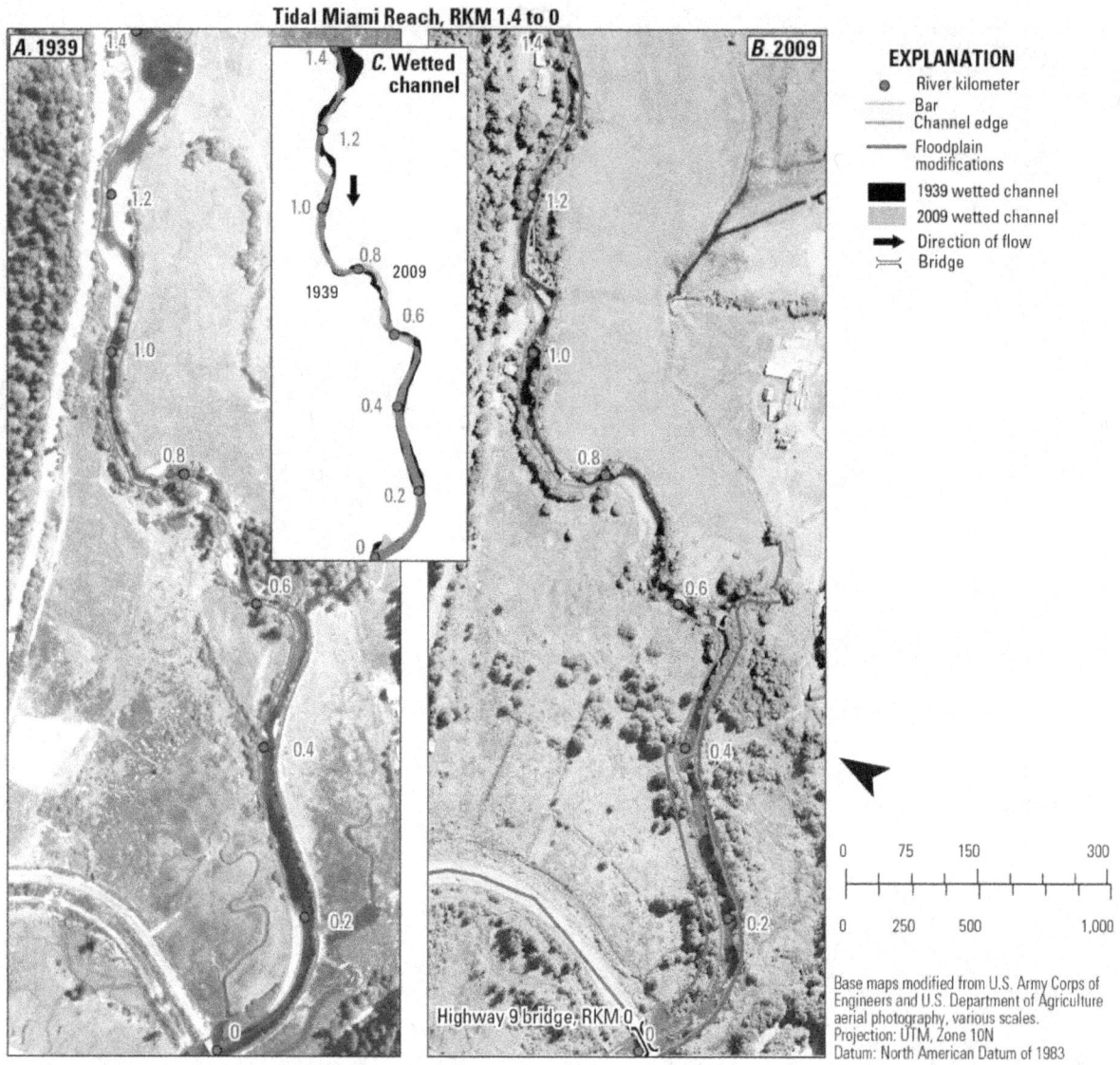

Figure 40. Images showing repeat bar and channel delineations and vegetation growth and stabilization of bar surfaces from RKM 1.4 to 0 in the Tidal Miami Reach, northwestern Oregon. Floodplain modifications identified in the map include dikes, levees, and naturally formed levees reinforced with nonerodible materials based on Oregon Coastal Management Program (2011). [RKM, river kilometer]

changed little in terms of centerline length (net 0.7 percent or 10 m reduction) and average wetted width over the analysis period (net 5.6 percent or 1 m reduction; table 19).

Nehalem River

The mapping results for the Fluvial Nehalem Reach indicated that unit bar area declined 45.6

percent from 1939 to 1967 and then fluctuated from 1967 to 2009, resulting in a net unit bar area reduction of 49.8 percent from 1939 to 2009 (table 17). Nearly two–thirds of the net loss in bar area occurred from RKM 26.6–24.6, which is a broad unconfined segment of the floodplain where the channel transitions from fluvially to tidally influenced (figs. 14, and 41A–C). This

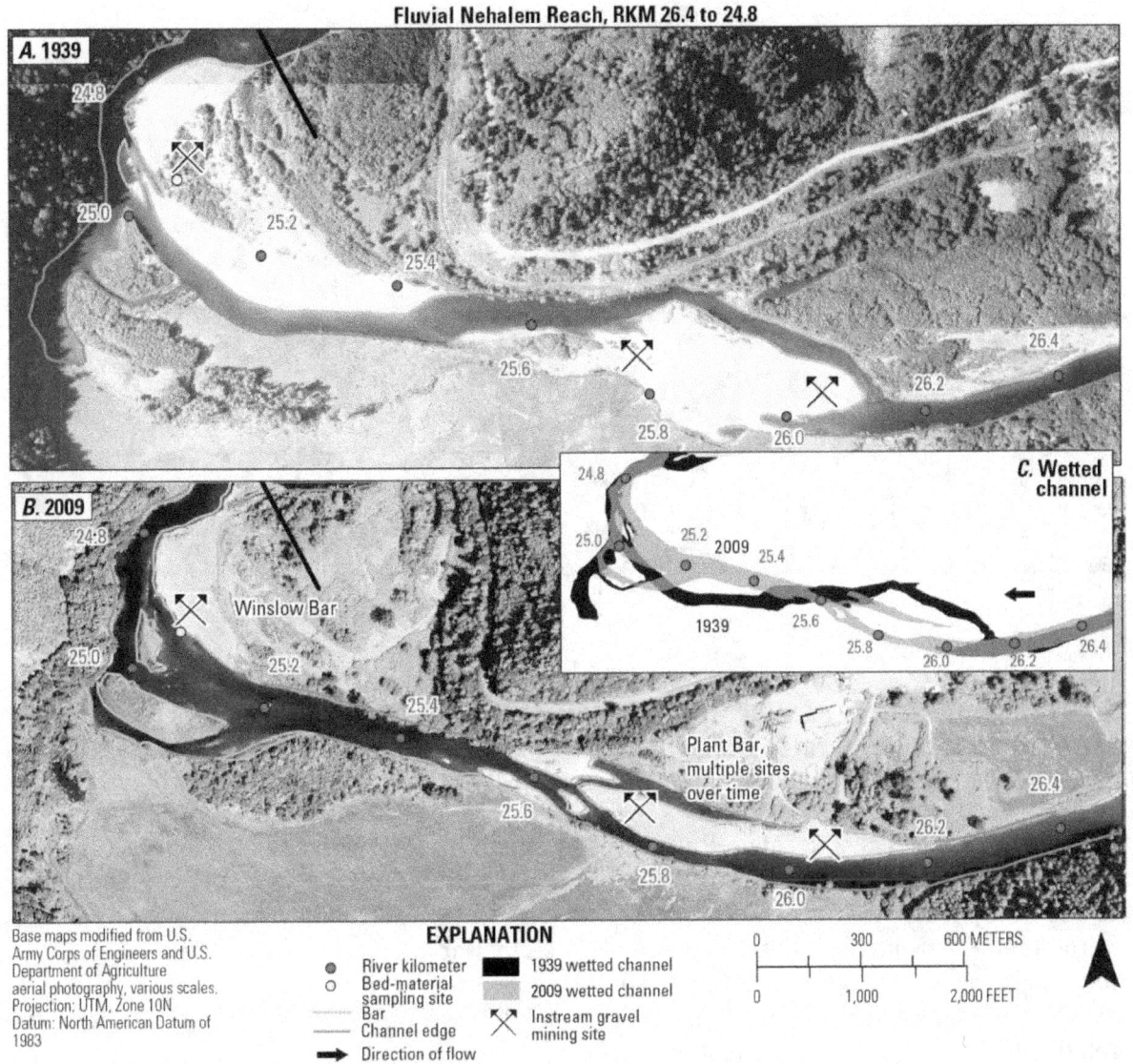

Figure 41. Images showing repeat bar and channel delineations, vegetation growth and stabilization of bar surfaces, and channel migrations from RKM 26.4 to 24.8 in the Fluvial Nehalem Reach, northwestern Oregon. [RKM, river kilometer]

reduction is attributable to the lateral channel migration between 1939 and 1967 and subsequent vegetation establishment. The channel moved over 150 m south from RKM 26.2 to 25.6, eroding into a large lateral bar on the south bank, and about 90 m north from RKM 25.6 to 25.0, eroding into a large point bar on the north bank. Upstream of RKM 26.6, bar area also diminished from 1939 to 2009 as vegetation estab-

lished on bars that were apparently unvegetated in 1939 (such as near RKM 30.2, 28.0, and 27.2–26.6) or bars mapped in 1939 were eroded or underwater in 2009 (such as near RKM 29.8 and 27.6; fig. 42A–C). The position of the channel was relatively stable with lateral changes of less than 35 m in this upper section. Overall, the channel changed little in length or width from 1939 to 2009 in this reach (table 19).

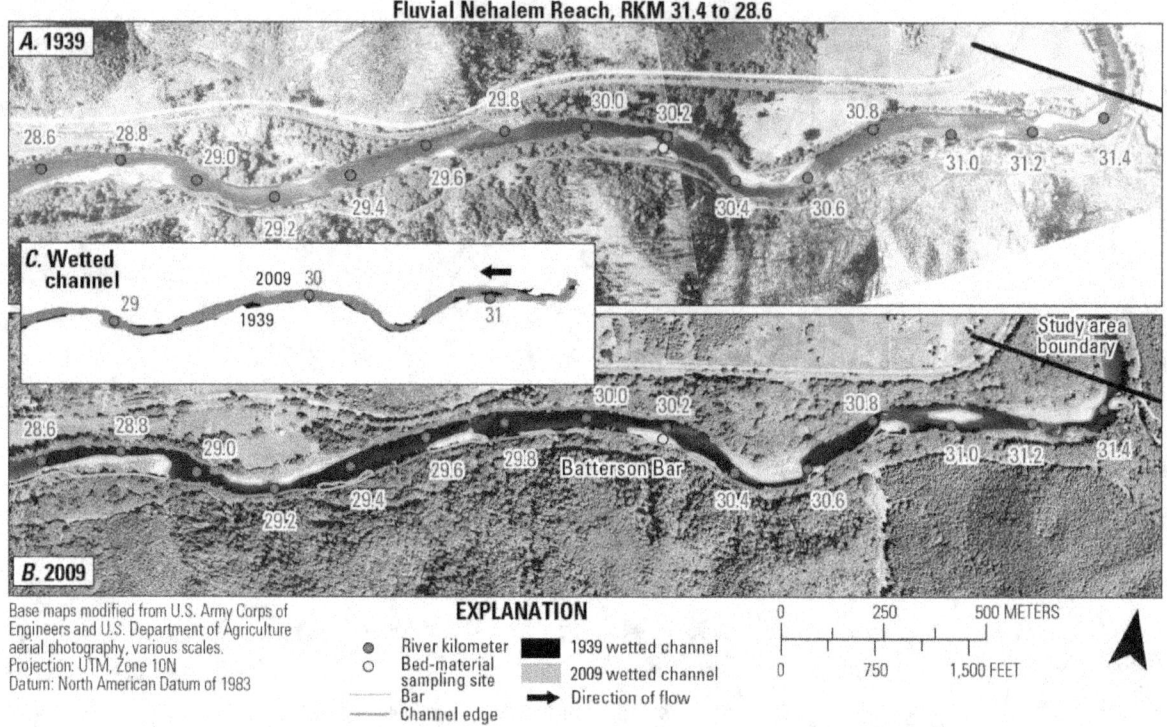

Base maps modified from U.S. Army Corps of Engineers and U.S. Department of Agriculture aerial photography, various scales.
Projection: UTM, Zone 10N
Datum: North American Datum of 1983

EXPLANATION

- ● River kilometer
- ○ Bed-material sampling site
- Bar
- Channel edge

- ■ 1939 wetted channel
- 2009 wetted channel
- → Direction of flow

0   250   500 METERS
0   750   1,500 FEET

Figure 42. Images showing repeat bar and channel delineations and stable channel planform from RKM 31.4 to 28.6 in the Fluvial Nehalem Reach, northwestern Oregon. [RKM, river kilometer]

Downstream in the Tidal Nehalem Reach, unit bar area increased a net 14.7 percent from 1939 to 2009 despite a small decrease from 1939 to 1967 (table 17). This increase in unit bar area occurred within the Nehalem Bay (RKM 9.6–0) as more tidal mud flats and bars were mapped in 2009 relative to 1939 (fig. 43A–C). Most of these mapping differences likely owe to tide differences between photographs because the general outlines of the large mud flats mapped in 2009 are visible but submerged in the 1939. Despite the overall increase in bar area over the analysis period, bar area declined a net 17 percent from RKM 24.6–19.2 (fig. 44A–C). Vegetation establishment on formerly unvegetated bar surfaces (such as near RKM 24.2 and 22.8) and, to a lesser extent, other factors like bar erosion or differences in streamflow and/or tide (such as near RKM 24.8, 22.8, and 22) explain most of this reduction in bar area. Over the analysis period, the position of the channel was relatively stable except for lateral movements as much as

140 m from RKM 21.6–20.4 and 195 m from RKM 6.6–2.2 (fig. 43A–C). Channel width narrowed 18.1 percent (41 m) between 1967 and 2009 (table 19).

River Sections Near Instream Gravel Mining Sites

Bar and channel trends near segments with instream gravel mining are similar to the overall trends for most of the fluvial reaches. Near most sites, lateral migration and vegetation establishment appear to have resulted in decreased bar area and slightly less sinuous channels.

On the Trask River, lateral channel migration resulted in a straighter channel near Bush Bar at RKM 12.2 (fig. 28E–H). This section had three large channel-flanking bars and three smaller lateral bars in 1939, encompassing an area of 48,900 m². By 2009, this section contained five much smaller bars with a total 1,900 m² flanking a much straighter channel.

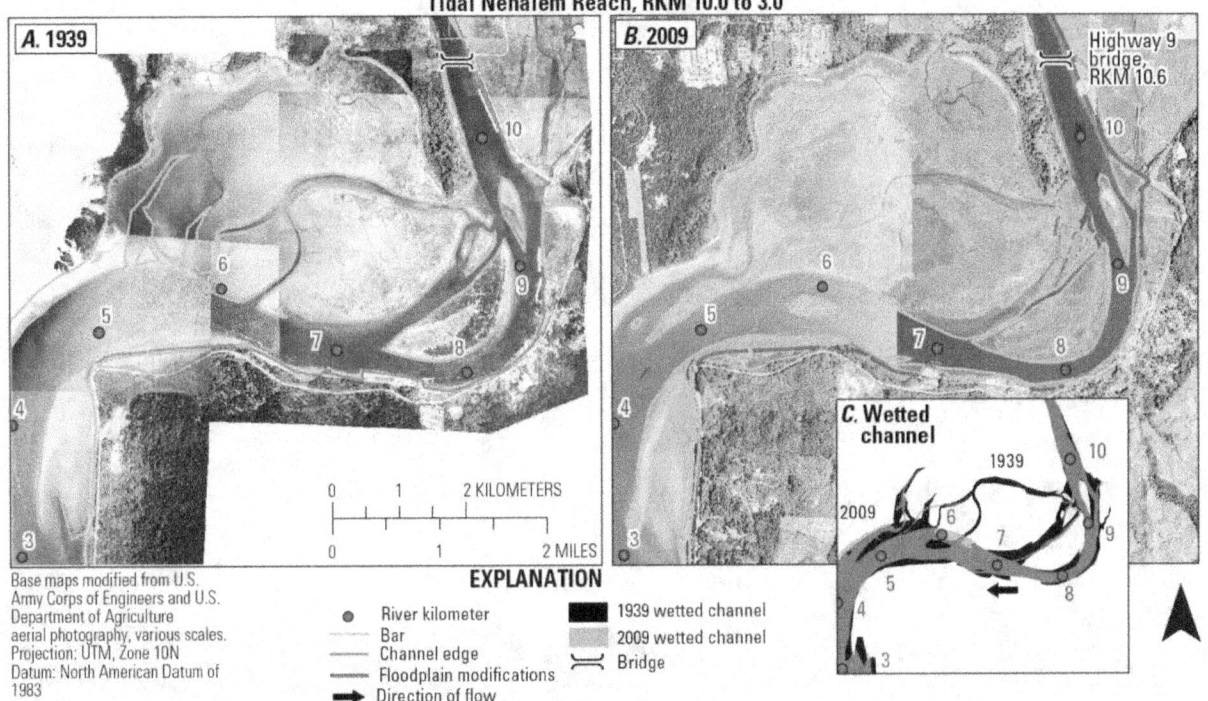

Figure 43. Images showing repeat bar and channel delineations from RKM 10.0 to 3.0 in the Tidal Nehalem Reach, northwestern Oregon. Floodplain modifications identified in the map include dikes, levees, and naturally formed levees reinforced with nonerodible materials based on Oregon Coastal Management Program (2011). [RKM, river kilometer]

On the Wilson River, lateral channel migration has significantly affected the geometry and area of Upper and Lower Donaldson Bars (RKM 10.4 and 10.0, respectively; fig. 31A–C). By 1967, the channel cut a new path through the mapped 1939 bar, splitting this large bar into multiple ones. These multiple bars became increasingly vegetated over the analysis period; the main vegetated surface is now south and west of the current location of Lower Donaldson Bar (fig. 31A–C). The area of bars mapped from RKM 10.5–9.8 declined from approximately 45,670 m[2] in 1939 to 23,970 m[2] in 2009.

Downstream, near Barker and Tannler Bars (RKM 8.0–6.4; fig. 32A–C), the Wilson River had eight bars mapped in 1939 totaling 100,390 m[2] in area, but only six bars mapped in 2009 totaling 12,860 m[2] in area. This reach of the Wilson River is constrained by levees, which have probably inhibited bar growth. Slightly down-

stream at Tannler Bar (RKM 6.6; fig. 32A–C), which was sampled by Stinson and Stinson (1998), the bar remained in the same location, but diminished from approximately 9,000 to 5,000 m[2], owing to apparent vegetation growth.

On the Kilchis River (fig. 34A–C), repeat mapping shows channel planform changes, side channel loss, and vegetation establishment near Crusher (RKM 5.8), Upper Landolt (RKM 5.3) and Averill Bars (RKM 2.9). All of these historical mining were sampled by Stinson and Stinson (1998). From RKM 6.4–5.0, the extensive gravel deposits mapped in 1939 were reduced to much narrower surfaces in 2009, with total mapped bar area declining from 76,700 to 14,600 m[2] over the analysis period. Similarly, near Averill Bar at RKM 2.9, bar area and side channel losses are evident over 1939–2009 (fig. 35A–C). Near Gomes Bar (historically known as Lower Landolt Bar; RKM 4.8), however, the channel has

99

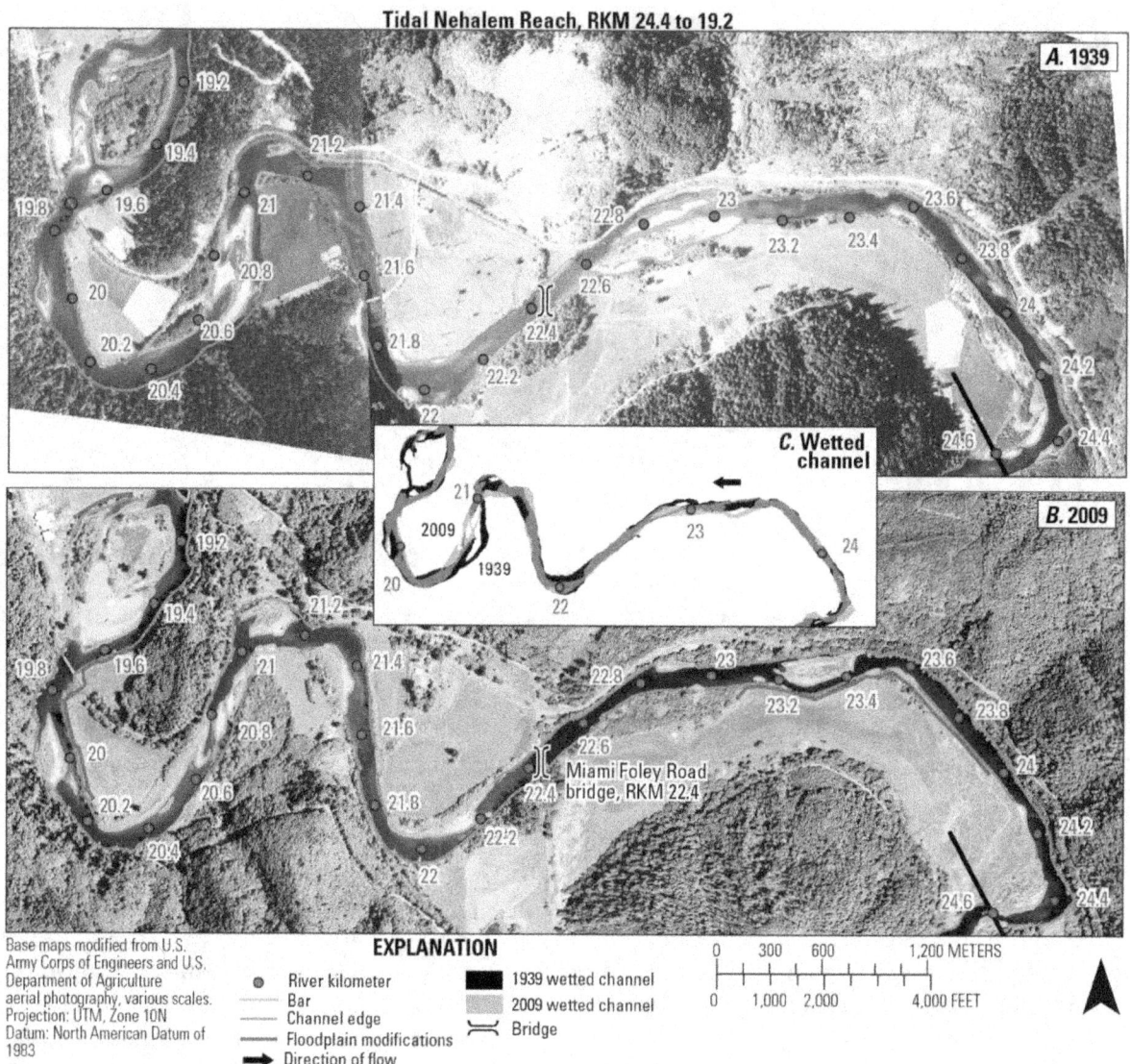

Figure 44. Images showing repeat bar and channel delineations and planform changes from RKM 24.2 to 19.2 in the Tidal Nehalem Reach, northwestern Oregon. Floodplain modifications identified in the map include dikes, levees, and naturally formed levees reinforced with non-erodible materials based on Oregon Coastal Management Program (2011). [RKM, river kilometer]

been stable and bar area has slightly increased from about 5,000 to 6,000 m² (fig. 34A–C).

On the Miami River, sections near active and historical mining sites generally show channel planform changes, vegetation establishment on formerly unvegetated surfaces, and a reduction in bar area. Gravel has been mined from at least two historical sites (Upper and Middle Lower Waldron Bars at RKM 4.8 and 4.6) and one historical and active site (Lower Waldron Bar at RKM 4.8; fig. 39A–C). Bars became smaller in extent and vegetated in some locations while channel planform changed in several locations over the analysis period. In this section, the total area of mapped bars was approximately 26,800 m² in 1939 and 14,200 m² in 2009.

On the Nehalem River, gravel has been mined from Plant and Winslow Bars (RKM 25.8 and 24.8, respectively; fig. 41A–C). Owing to channel migrations, the location of Plant Bar has moved from the south to the north bank of the Nehalem River. Over the analysis period, the area of Plant Bar has declined from approximately 51,600 to 18,600 m². Although Winslow Bar has not changed in location, this bar also diminished from approximately 84,200 to 18,900 m² between 1939 and 2009. Losses in bar area at both sites appear to be related to a combination of bar erosion and vegetation establishment.

Because trends in the number and area of bars and channel planform mirror overall trends, particularly in the overall reduction in bar area, it is unclear how these changes may specifically relate to gravel mining activities. Even in the absence of gravel mining, unconfined fluvial sections of the Trask, Wilson, Kilchis, Miami, and Nehalem Rivers are likely dynamic with active building and erosion of bars in conjunction with lateral channel migration over time. Changes in gravel volumes as a result of mining activities, however, likely have some local effects on channel behavior and bar geometry, although documenting such effects would require more detailed site-specific studies and a comprehensive understanding of the flow and sediment regimes of these rivers and their interactions with human modifications of the floodplain and gravel mining.

Analyses of Bed-Material Particle Sizes

In October 2010, we measured the distributions of surface particle sizes at nine bars, and collected subsurface bulk samples for five of these bars along the Trask, Wilson, Kilchis, Miami, and Nehalem Rivers (table 20). These bars were selected based on bar size, accessibility, and condition (such as little to no vehicle disturbance). To maintain consistency with previous bed-material studies along the Oregon coast (Wallick and others, 2010; 2011; Jones and others, 2011, 2012a, and 2012b), we collected bed-material data at point or lateral bars likely formed by recent deposition events as indicated by the absence or minimal coverage of vegetation.

At these bars, we measured 200 surface particles using a modified grid technique (Kondolf and others, 2003) and gravelometer measurement template (Federal Interagency Sediment Project US SAH–97 Gravelometer), which allows for standardized measurement of sediment clasts greater than 2 mm in diameter. Diameter measurements of surface particles were taken at 0.3-m increments along two parallel 30-m tapes that were placed 1 to 2 m apart and parallel to the long axis of the bar. To support consistent intersite comparisons, measurement transects were located at the bar apex (defined as the topographic high point along the upstream end of the bar) when possible. Measurements at the Bush Bar were collected at the upstream end of the bar in an area relatively undisturbed by recent gravel mining. Measurements at all other active instream mining sites were made before gravel mining activities began for the season.

Subsurface bed material was also sampled at five bars to evaluate differences in particle sizes between surface and subsurface bed material (a measure of bar "armoring"). We removed approximately 1 m² of bar-surface material, and then collected 59 to 67 kg of subsurface material. Bulk samples then were dried and analyzed for ½-phi particle sizes by the U.S. Geological Survey Sediment Laboratory in Vancouver, Washington.

The median diameter (D_{50}) of surface particles was generally coarsest (surface D_{50} greater than 64.0 mm) at Bruck, Bush, and Batterson Bars in the upper fluvial reaches of the Kilchis, Trask, and Nehalem Rivers, respectively (table 20; fig. 45A–H). The Lower Waldron Bar on the Miami River and Mills Bridge and Lower Donaldson Bars on the Wilson River had median surface particles ranging from 37.8 to 48.5 mm in diameter. Median bar surface material was 32.0 mm or less in diameter at Clear Creek and

Table 20. Bed-material data collected at sampling sites along the Trask, Wilson, Kilchis, Miami, and Nehalem Rivers, northwestern Oregon.
[RKM, river kilometer; D_{16}, 16th percentile diameter in millimeters (mm); D_{50}, median diameter in mm; D_{84}, 84th percentile diameter in mm]

River	Reach	Bar[1]	Site Type	Location	Easting (meters)	Northing (meters)	Surface particles			Subsurface particles			Armoring ratio
							D_{16}	D_{50}	D_{84}	D_{16}	D_{50}	D_{84}	
Trask	Fluvial	Bush	Active or recent mining	RKM 12.2	439,721	5,031,982	35.9	68.4	108.7	1.0	12.5	40.2	5.5
Wilson	Upper Fluvial	Mills Bridge	Control	RKM 13.8	442,264	5,035,716	20.7	45.0	85.0	--	--	--	--
	Lower Fluvial	Lower Don-aldson	Historical mining	RKM 10	439,103	5,035,845	14.8	48.5	81.5	0.7	16.8	56.0	2.9
Kilchis	--	Clear Creek	Historical mining	2.8 km upstream of study area	438,682	5,042,560	11.0	32.0	71.7	--	--	--	--
	--	Bruck	Historical mining	0.6 km upstream of study area	437,329	5,041,495	36.5	84.6	146.7	--	--	--	--
	Fluvial	Gomes	Active or recent mining	RKM 4.8	435,078	5,040,118	14.9	29.4	55.5	1.1	10.5	33.6	2.8
Miami	Lower Fluvial	Lower Wal-dron	Active or recent mining	RKM 4.3	432,045	5,048,425	18.7	37.8	78.2	4.4	23.8	53.6	1.6
Nehalem	Fluvial	Batterson	Control	RKM 31.2	440,329	5,060,849	53.0	104.1	167.5	--	--	--	--
	Fluvial	Winslow	Active or recent mining	RKM 24.8	435,481	5,060,392	14.7	23.6	35.5	0.6	9.6	23.9	2.4

[1] Bar names were assigned based on features on USGS quadrangle maps (such as nearby tributaries), mining permits, or nearby locations

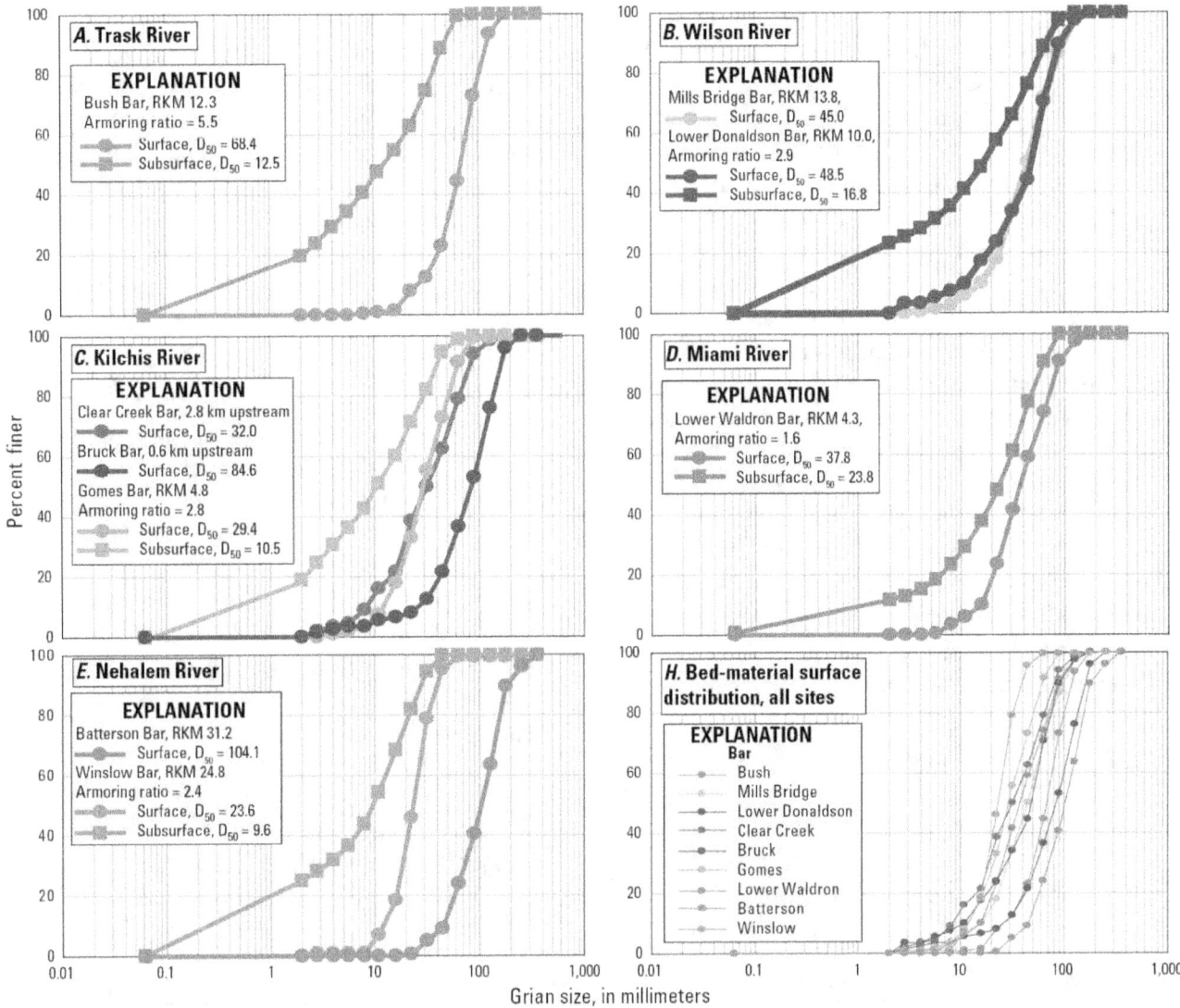

Figure 45. Graphs showing distributions of surface and subsurface particle sizes for bed-material sampling sites along the Trask, Wilson, Kilchis, Miami, and Nehalem Rivers, northwestern Oregon. Surface size distributions were determined by measuring 200 clasts; subsurface size distributions were determined from a bulk sample taken below the armor layer. Locations for Bruck and Clear Creek Bars on the Kilchis River are approximated.

Gomes Bars on the Kilchis River and Winslow Bar on the Nehalem River. For the Kilchis, Wilson, and Nehalem Rivers where surface particle measurements were made at two or more bars, bar surface particles diminished in size along the Nehalem River, increased in size between Mills Bridge and Lower Donaldson Bars on the Wilson River, and fluctuated in size between the three Kilchis River bars. Stinson and Stinson

(1998) reported that sites in the Wilson, Kilchis, and Miami River basins were dominated by particles ranging from 19 to 76 mm in diameter (or pebbles and cobbles), which is comparable to these results (fig. 45C–D).

Differences in surface and subsurface particle sizes can be related to the balance between sediment supply and transport capacity, or the ability of the river to move sediment, which is largely determined by discharge and slope. When a river's transport capacity exceeds its supply of sediment, the surface layer of bars is generally coarser than subsurface layers because finer clasts on the bar surface are selectively transported downstream (Dietrich and others, 1989; Lisle, 1995; Buffington and Montgomery, 1999). The degree of coarsening, or armoring, of the bar surface can be assessed with the armoring ratio, or the ratio of the median grain sizes (D_{50}) for the surface and subsurface layers. This ratio is typically close to 1 (meaning surface and subsurface particles are of similar sizes) for rivers with a high sediment supply, and approaches or exceeds 2 for supply-limited rivers with large transport capacity (Bunte and Abt, 2001). Armoring ratios were lowest at Lower Waldron Bar on the Miami River (1.6) and greatest at Bush Bar on the Trask River (5.5; table 20; fig. 45). The large armoring ratio at Bush Bar may owe to measurement collection at a relatively undisturbed location toward the head of the bar, which may be coarser than the bar apex where measurements were typically taken at other sites. The armoring ratio of 1.6 at Lower Waldron Bar tentatively indicates a relative balance between transport capacity and sediment supply. Armoring ratios ranged from 2.4 to 2.9 at Gomes, Lower Donaldson, and Winslow Bars on the Kilchis, Wilson, and Nehalem Rivers, respectively, and indicate possible sediment supply limitation at these sites.

Armoring ratios reported by this and previous USGS bed-material studies along the Oregon coast vary considerably (table 21). As evident from these previous studies and as summarized by Wilcock and others (2009), bar texture can vary tremendously between sites on gravel-bed rivers. Additional bed-material measurements, especially at unmined bars, would help refine assessments of transport and sediment-supply conditions and longitudinal bed-material trends for these rivers.

Table 21. Armoring ratios reported from this and prior bed-material studies by the U.S. Geological Survey in select Oregon coastal rivers from north to south.

[--, no data collected]

River/Creek	Armoring ratio(s)	number of sites	Source
Nehalem	2.4	1	This study
Miami	1.6	1	This study
Kilchis	2.8	1	This study
Wilson	2.9	1	This study
Trask	5.5	1	This study
Umpqua	0.99–4.73	30	Wallick and others (2011)
South Fork Coquille	3.5	1	Jones and others (2012b)
Rogue	1.2–3.4	7	Jones and others (2012a)
Applegate	1.2	1	Jones and others (2012a)
Hunter	0.97–1.5	2	Jones and others (2011)
Chetco	1.38–2.09	3	Wallick and others (2010)

Discussion and Synthesis

On the basis of a literature review, field observations, topographic analysis and delineation of bars and channels from available photograph coverages, we defined six study areas on the Tillamook, Trask, Wilson, Kilchis, Miami, and Nehalem Rivers that in total make up over 96 km of channel. Within the study areas, the channels flow predominately over alluvial deposits (as well as intermittent bedrock outcrops in the Upper Wilson and Nehalem Fluvial Reaches), and through confined and unconfined segments. Tide affects varying lengths of these rivers, ranging from approximately 1.3 km on the Miami River to 24.6 km on the Nehalem River (table 1). Within these six study areas, our analysis in conjunction with previous studies allow for a broad synthesis of channel and floodplain characteristics as well as overall transport conditions.

Spatial Variation in Bar Conditions

Like other Oregon coastal basins, such as the Umpqua River (Wallick and others, 2011), Rogue River (Jones and others, 2012a), Coquille River (Jones and others, 2012b), and Hunter Creek (Jones and others, 2011), valley and channel confinement and gradient influence channel morphology and bed-material transport in the Tillamook Bay subbasins and Nehalem River basin. In their upper sections, the rivers are confined by their valleys and have relatively steep gradients. As rivers enter the focal areas of this study, channels and valleys widen and their gradients decline, promoting deposition of coarse sediment within the active channels. Subsequent gradient reductions in the tidal reaches further promote the deposition of primarily fine sediment. Valley confinement often exerts some lateral control on channel planform within the fluvial study areas, such as on the Tillamook (RKM 11.6–10.0; fig. 26D–F), Wilson (Upper Fluvial, RKM 14.0–13.4; fig. 30A–C), Miami (Lower Fluvial, RKM 5.4–3.8; fig. 39A–C), and Nehalem (RKM 31.4–28.6; fig. 42A–C) Rivers. Additionally, floodplain modifications restrict the width and position of most of the tidal channels (table 1) that would otherwise probably be considerably wider, have numerous side channels and sloughs, and prone to lateral migration.

Basin geology also exerts considerable control on channel morphology and bed-material transport in these six basins, particularly the varying proportions of Coast Range sedimentary and volcanic rocks (table 2; figs. 1 and 2). The soft rocks of the Coast Range sedimentary subdivision dominates most of the Tillamook River basin, leading to few bars along this river except for between RKM 12.0–13.0 (fig. 24A), which is downstream of several tributaries draining the much harder volcanic rocks. Bar area in the fluvial reaches on the Trask, Wilson, Miami, and Kilchis Rivers is greatest downstream of areas with Coast Range volcanic rocks, and then diminishes as the proportion of tributaries draining Coast Range sedimentary rocks increases, such as downstream of approximately RKM 13.0, 8.0, 2.6, and 8.0 on the Trask, Wilson, Kilchis, and Miami Rivers, respectively (figs. 1 and 24B–E). The abundance of gravel bars within the Fluvial Nehalem Reach (fig. 24F) owes in part to the increased proportion of the Coast Range volcanic rocks within the fluvial reach and in larger tributaries, such as Cronin and Cook Creeks and the Salmonberry River that join the mainstem slightly upstream of the study area (fig. 2). In contrast, channels in the tidal reaches cut through Quaternary deposits and have tributaries that primarily drain Coast Range sedimentary rocks (figs. 1 and 2).

Based on the 2009 mapping for the fluvial reaches, unit bar area was greatest in the upper fluvial reaches of the Wilson and Miami Rivers and the Nehalem Fluvial Reach (table 17; fig. 24C, E, F). For all of these reaches, local valley widening and declines in channel gradient are probably important factors promoting bed material deposition and bar formation. The Fluvial Nehalem Reach has the greatest reported mining volumes (table 12; fig. 16G–H). Other reaches with considerable reported mining include the Lower Fluvial Wilson and Fluvial Kilchis

Reaches (table 12; fig. 16B–C). Unit bar area was lowest in the Fluvial Tillamook and Lower Fluvial Miami Reaches (figs. 17 and 25), owing likely to the large percentage of Coast Range sedimentary rocks in the drainages contributing to these areas (table 8).

In the tidal reaches, however, gradients are generally much lower (0.0001 to 0.0013 m/m; table 8; fig. 9), preventing substantial transport of gravel-sized bed material. Generally, tidal reaches have fewer mapped bars than the fluvial reaches except near the mouths of the Tillamook, Trask, and Nehalem Rivers (fig. 24A, B, F). Bedload, and consequently most bed material, in these reaches is predominately sand and finer-sized particles, much of which was transported as suspended load from upstream, steeper sections. Some large bars like those in the Tidal Tillamook and Nehalem Reaches (fig. 24A,F) are largely composed of this finer material.

Temporal Trends in Bar and Channel Conditions

Channel and valley physiography, hydrology, and geology largely explain the observed spatial patterns in the accumulation and texture of bed material. Interpretations of bar temporal trends, however, are more ambiguous and vary by reach. These interpretations are also influenced by varying climate and hydrologic conditions, natural disturbances like fire and mass wasting that are affected by humans, and complex and locally intense land use practices like floodplain modifications and sand and gravel mining.

In the 1939 photographs, extensive sediment deposits are apparent in the fluvial reaches of all rivers except the Tillamook River (figs. 26A–F, 28A–H, 30A–C, 31A–C, 32A–C, 34A–C, 35A–C, 37A–F, 38A–C, 39A–C, 41A–C, 42A–C). Previous reports, such as those by Coulton and others (1996), Tillamook Bay National Estuary Project (1998), Pearson (2002), Komar and others (2004), and Ferdun (2010), suggested the Tillamook Burn is the likely source of this sedi-

ment. Some sediment in the 1939 photographs was probably associated with the first of the Tillamook Burn fires, which in August 1933 burned the largest area, including portions of the Trask, Wilson, Kilchis, Miami and Nehalem River basins (Oregon State Department of Forestry, 1983; Johnson and Maser, 1999; Tillamook County, 2010). This fire was followed by a flood on December 21, 1933 that exceeded a 10-year event on the Wilson River (14301500; fig. 5B) and likely delivered considerable sediment to downstream channels.

Although these fires almost certainly contributed to the large areas of bars mapped from the 1939 photographs, other factors may also be important. For instance, other Oregon coastal rivers unaffected by the Tillamook Burn or similar fires, such as the Chetco and Umpqua Rivers have reduced bar areas since 1939, owing to long-term decreases in flood magnitude (Wallick and others 2010; 2011). Similarly, reconnaissance level studies have documented reductions in mapped bar area from 1939 to 2009 in the Hunter Creek and Coquille River basins (Jones and others, 2011; Jones and others 2012b). Because of the apparent consistent reduction in bar area for studied Oregon coastal rivers, other factors in addition to the Tillamook Burn may explain the large bar areas mapped by this study from the 1939 photographs.

Bar areas mapped from the 1967, 2005, and 2009 photographs along the fluvial reaches were generally less than those mapped from 1939 photographs, corresponding to net declines in unit bar area for all fluvial reaches (table 17; fig. 25). Similarly, Pearson (2002) reported net reductions in bar area for the Kilchis (51 percent reduction; approximately RKM 7.7 to 0.6 km downstream of RKM 0), Wilson (57 percent reduction; approximately RKM 13.1 to 0.1 km downstream of RKM 0), and Trask (35 percent reduction; approximately RKM 13.4–0) Rivers from 1939 to 1990. In our study, however, two exceptions to this general reduction trend were the Upper Fluvial Wilson and Miami Reaches. In these steeper, more confined reaches, unit bar area substantially declined between 1939 and 1967, but then increased considerably, although not to 1939 values, by 2009.

Although the basin and channel response to the Tillamook Burn may be a key factor affecting temporal trends in sediment supply, other factors are probably also important, including channel planform changes and related alterations in sediment deposition and erosion patterns, vegetation establishment on bars that previously lacked apparent vegetation, and streamflow and/or tide differences between photographs. Other important factors not addressed in this preliminary study may include potential changes in the rivers' hydrologic regimes from 1939 to 2009, which directly affects sediment transport capacity and vegetation establishment on bar surfaces, changes in the occurrence and volume of large wood, debris flows, and mass movements.

Multiple lines of evidence indicate that all fluvial reaches have the potential for some local vertical and lateral channel adjustments in response to changes in streamflow, sediment, and possibly riparian vegetation. Our review of repeat channel cross sections near bridges in the study areas indicates few systematic trends, but evidence of local incision and aggradation up to 2.0 m (table 14; figs. 17–22). For example, the thalweg of the Tillamook and Miami Rivers incised locally 0.5 m or more from 1999 to 2004 and 1996 to 2004, respectively, whereas the thalweg of the Wilson River aggraded locally more than 2.0 m from 1996 to 2004 (table 14). Similarly, the specific gage analyses show channel-elevation fluctuations of as much as 0.3 m on the Wilson and Nehalem Rivers, mainly in conjunction with high flows, but with no apparent systematic long-term trend (fig. 23). Similarly, Pearson (2002) reported general aggradation with localized bed lowering from 1978 to 2000 in the lower fluvial and tidal reaches on the Trask, Wilson, Kilchis, and Miami Rivers.

Likewise, all fluvial reaches have sections with potential for lateral movement and width changes as indicated by the repeat bar and chan-

nel mapping (fig. 24; Tillamook, fig. 26A–C; Trask, fig. 28A–H; Wilson, figs. 31A–C and 32A–C; Kilchis, figs. 34A–C and 35A–C; Miami, figs. 37A–F and 38A–C; Nehalem, fig. 41A–C). Historical accounts noted channel migration on the Wilson and Kilchis Rivers (Coulton and others, 1996). Previous studies have documented localized channel width changes on the Trask, Wilson, and Kilchis Rivers (Follansbee and Stark, 1998a; Snyder and others, 2003; Reckendorf, 2006; Duck Creek Associates, 2008; Reckendorf, 2008a, b). To date, however, determining systematic changes in channel width from previous studies is challenging owing to varying aerial photographs used in analyses, mapped channel attributes (such as active channel width or channel area), and focal areas for analysis (longer or shorter reaches or a mixture of tidal and fluvial sections). Detailed analyses incorporating additional aerial photographs would enable identifying systematic morphologic changes along these rivers.

In the tidal reaches, mapped bar areas also generally declined over 1939–2009 with the exception of net increases on the Tillamook and Nehalem Rivers (fig. 17). The subsequent decline in bar area resulted in part from stabilization by vegetation establishment. Other factors controlling mapped bar area in the tidal reaches include lateral channel changes and resulting alterations in sediment deposition and erosion patterns, and streamflow and/or tide differences between photographs. Net increases in the Tidal Tillamook and Nehalem Reaches are probably attributable to tide differences on both rivers and sediment deposition behind pilings on the Tillamook River.

Over the analysis period, all tidal reaches had relatively stable planforms with lateral channel movements generally less than 40 m from 1939 to 2009 (Tillamook, fig. 27A–F; Trask, fig. 29A–F; Wilson, fig. 33A–C; Kilchis, fig. 36A–C; Miami, fig. 40A–C). The exception is the Tidal Nehalem Reach where the channel migrated laterally approximately 140 m between RKM 21.6–20.4 (fig. 44A–C) and 195 m between

RKM 6.6–2.2 (partially shown in fig. 43A–C). The lateral stability of most of the tidal reaches owes largely to floodplain levees and dikes that stabilize the channel margins in the Tillamook Bay area (table 6; figs. 8 and 10–13) and floodplain modifications and valley confinement in the Tidal Nehalem Reach (fig. 15). As suggested by Pearson (2002), floodplain modifications may prevent the Tillamook Bay rivers from mobilizing sediment stored in streamside areas and the floodplain during high flow events.

Although the tidal reaches are largely stable laterally, repeat channel cross-sections indicate that these reaches have some potential for vertical adjustments (table 14). In some tidal reaches, channels locally aggraded and incised 0.5 m or more on the Tillamook and Trask Rivers (figs. 17B–D and 18A–B), incised 0.5 m or more on the Kilchis and Miami Rivers (figs. 20D and 21C), and aggraded 0.5 m or more on the Nehalem River (fig. 22A–B).

General Bed-Material Transport Conditions

Our observations of the spatial and temporal characteristics of the reaches support preliminary interpretations of current overall bed-material transport conditions. On the basis of mapping results (table 18; fig. 24A–F) and armoring ratios (table 20), fluvial reaches within this study's focal areas on the Tillamook, Trask, Kilchis, and Nehalem Rivers are likely sediment supply-limited in terms of bed material—that is the transport capacity of the channel generally exceeds the supply of bed material. Further studies would be needed to assess the relation between transport capacity and sediment supply outside of the study areas, such as at Bruck Bar, upstream of the study area on the Kilchis River. On the Tillamook and Trask Rivers, sediment is deposited and stored as gravel bars primarily within short sections where the channels transition from relatively confined to unconfined. Elsewhere, however, bar area is comparatively sparse in these reaches (fig. 24A, B). For the Tillamook River, low gravel supply likely owes chiefly to the preponderance of sedimentary rocks in the

basin. For the Trask River, high transport capacity through the fluvial reach owes to the relatively steep channel gradient and narrow valley (table 8). These preliminary observations of sediment supply limitation are consistent with the repeat cross sections measurements indicating bed lowering at two locations in the Fluvial Tillamook Reach (RKM 11.5 and 8.8; table 14) and the high armoring ratio at the Bush Bar in the Fluvial Trask Reach (RKM 5.5; table 20).

In the fluvial reaches of the Kilchis and Nehalem Rivers, bars are most abundant where gradient declines near the head of tide (fig. 24D, F), indicating excess transport capacity in the upstream fluvial reaches. Results suggest the Kilchis River study area is sediment supply-limited, owing to its relatively steep gradient. Similarly, Pearson (2002) reported that the Kilchis River is likely supply-limited in its lower 7.7 km. Above the study area, the relation between transport capacity and sediment supply may vary. For instance, Stinson and Stinson (1998) suggested that the Kilchis River probably has a large sediment supply that may exceed transport capacity, as evidenced by a gravel plug forming at Bruck Bar in 1996. In-channel bedrock outcrops within and along the Nehalem River indicates excess transport capacity. Consistent with these preliminary conclusions of sediment supply limitation for the Fluvial Kilchis and Nehalem Reaches are the armoring ratios that exceed 2.0 at Gomes Bar on the Kilchis River and Winslow Bar on the Nehalem River (table 20).

Preliminary relations between transport capacity and sediment supply are more ambiguous for the fluvial reaches on the Wilson and Miami Rivers. In this study, the Upper Fluvial Wilson Reach had the lowest decline in unit bar area (5.3 percent; table 17) and a modest 0.4 m of net aggradation at RKM 14.1 from 1939 to 2009 (table 14; fig. 19A). Although these changes may indicate that sediment supply balances or slightly exceeds transport capacity in this reach, the presence of bedrock exposures, such as between Mills Bridge and slightly upstream of Mills

Bridge Bar, indicates there are still areas where transport capacity exceeds sediment supply. Additional bed-material data collection and evaluation of armoring ratios would help assess the relation between transport capacity and sediment supply in the Upper Fluvial Wilson Reach. Similarly, the Lower Fluvial Wilson Reach had a relatively high armoring ratio (2.9; table 20), indicating sediment supply limitation at this site. However, the repeat cross sections at RKM 6.3 indicate local deposition of 2.1 m in the thalweg from 1996 to 2004 (table 14; fig. 19B), indicating that sediment supply may locally exceed transport capacity in this reach, such as near RKM 6.3. Although Pearson (2002) suggested that sediment loads on the lower 13.1 km of the Wilson River might be declining to pre-fire levels, extending the streamflow record back to 1900 would be useful to assess the relative effects of the Tillamook Burn and antecedent peak flows on bed-material accumulations on the Wilson River.

On the Miami River, unit bar area increased in 2005 and 2009 despite initial reductions from 1939 to 1967 (table 17). This increase may indicate some level of active sediment supply to the reach in more recent years. Our tentative conclusion regarding bed-material supply is that the reach has a sediment supply that may balance or slightly exceed the transport capacity. Downstream, the Lower Fluvial Miami Reach has an armoring ratio of 1.6 (table 20), which tentatively indicates a relative balance between transport capacity and sediment supply at Lower Waldron Bar. The thalweg, however, incised 0.6 m from 1996 to 2004 at RKM 8.5 and 2.7 (table 14; fig. 21A–B), indicating transport capacity exceeds sediment supply at these locations. Pearson (2002) noted that the lower 3.2 km of the Miami River is transport limited. Future studies that collect additional bed-material measurements at undisturbed sites and collect bedload samples or estimate bed-material fluxes would be useful for understanding the relation between transport capacity and sediment supply in the fluvial reaches of the Miami River.

The tidal reaches on the Tillamook, Trask, Wilson, Kilchis, and Nehalem Rivers are all transport limited because of their exceedingly low gradients (0.0001 to 0.0007 m/m; table 8) and tidal influence. Transport conditions in the Tidal Reach Miami may be less limited owing to its gradient (0.0013 m/m; table 8), which is the greatest of all the tidal reaches. Bed material is primarily sand and finer-grain materials in the tidal reaches. These reaches will be most susceptible to watershed conditions affecting the supply and transport of fine sediment.

The six rivers have likely had substantially varying rates of gravel transport over time. The long tidal reaches on the Tillamook, Trask, and Nehalem Rivers (7.0–24.6 km) reflect Holocene sea-level rise and consequent drowning of the river valleys at rates faster than they are filling with coarse (sand and gravel) bed material. This difference between sea-level rise and coarse sediment flux suggests that these rivers have relatively lower sand and gravel transport rates than other coastal rivers, such as the Rogue River (Jones and others 2012), Chetco River (Wallick and others, 2010), and Hunter Creek (Jones and others, 2011), where the tide affects less than 7 km of channel. By contrast, the shorter tidal reaches of the Wilson, Kilchis, and Miami Rivers (1.3 to 5.0 km; table 1) and the presence of gravel bars to approximately the mouths of Kilchis and Miami Rivers (fig. 24D,E) indicate that coarse bed-material deposition has probably matched rates of Holocene sea-level rise.

Judging from the more abundant, extensive, and largely unvegetated bars evident in the 1939 photographs, most or all of the fluvial reaches were likely transport limited at that time. As described above, this probably resulted from multiple, overlapping factors, such as enhanced sediment supply from fires prior to timber cruises in 1908 (as described in Coulton and others, 1996) and the Tillamook Burn (Coulton and others, 1996; Tillamook Bay National Estuary Project, 1998; Pearson, 2002; Komar and others, 2004; Ferdun, 2010) as well as possibly from more frequent large floods that maintained active bar surfaces and limited vegetation establishment. As these areas have revegetated and sediment supply has diminished with reforestation, transport and supply conditions have possibly balanced about a state of fewer and smaller bars. Some reaches have likely evolved to having transport capacity conditions that at least locally exceed bed-material supply. Such temporal variations in bed-material transport conditions are probably not uncommon in these coastal watersheds where major disturbances like fire and mass wasting events are probably important natural processes introducing sediment into the rivers.

Outstanding Issues and Possible Approaches

This reconnaissance level analysis provides a framework and baseline information for understanding bed-material transport in the Tillamook Bay subbasins and Nehalem River basin. Future analyses could greatly refine the understanding of historical and ongoing bed-material transport processes and their effects on channel morphology. Many of these approaches (as outlined below) could focus on individual reaches of interest. Such information would provide a solid basis for evaluating future hydrologic and geomorphic changes in these basins.

Bed-Material Transport Rates and Sediment Budget

Understanding the possible effects of instream gravel mining on channel condition and longitudinal and temporal changes in bed material requires a thorough accounting of sediment inputs from upstream and lateral sources as well as sediment losses due to particle attrition, transport, and storage. Such information would support an assessment of the volumes of gravel mined from the system by ongoing and past mining activities relative to gravel delivered to the study area. Developing a sediment budget may include the following components:

1. Assess bed-material composition throughout the study areas, focusing on unmined sites. Additional measurements of particle size would be required for calculating bed-material transport and may support assessments of temporal changes in bed-material composition in conjunction with other study components.

2. Assess mass-wasting contributions to bed-material flux. In several of these drainage basins, landslides may be a significant factor in delivering bed material to the channels (Reckendorf, 2008), and their distribution may be strongly related to land use, geology, and natural disturbance processes.

3. Supplement the existing streamflow-gaging network. Modeling and predicting bed-material transport require high quality streamflow information, particularly for peak flows. As of 2011, no streamflow-gaging station is operated on the Kilchis or Tillamook Rivers. Such hydrologic data would be required by most approaches to quantify sediment supplied to the Fluvial Kilchis and Tillamook Reaches. The most accurate approach for obtaining such data would be to expand the gaging station network to include sites on these rivers as well as tributaries probably delivering considerable amounts of gravel like the Little North Fork Wilson River in the Wilson basin and Cook Creek and Salmonberry River in the Nehalem basin. Mean daily flow data measured at new stations could then be used to estimate annual sediment fluxes for the period of record and shorter time periods (such as water years) using methods outlined in Wallick and others (2010) and applied in Wallick and O'Connor (2011). An operational gage would be the optimal location for sampling bedload and later estimating sediment flux in the Kilchis and Tillamook River basins and other tributary basins of interest. An alternative approach, with

lower costs but greater uncertainties, would be to apply regional regression equations to estimate discharge for a range of flow events for specific locations.

4. Estimate sediment flux based upon equations of bedload transport, as conducted by Wallick and others (2010, 2011) on the Chetco and Umpqua Rivers. This approach could be used with most confidence in reaches where bed-material transport is likely transport-limited, such as for the fluvial reaches on the Wilson and Miami Rivers.

5. Estimate sediment flux for a reach of interest by developing a hydraulic model in conjunction with systematic measurements of bed-material size, as conducted in the Chetco River analysis (Wallick and others, 2010). Existing LiDAR coverages available for all study areas and streamflow measurements at the USGS streamflow-gaging stations on the Trask, Wilson, and Nehalem Rivers and OWRD streamflow-gaging station on the Miami River would support the development of such models.

6. Collect direct measurements of bedload transport in order to verify equations for bedload transport and estimate actual bedload fluxes. Possible locations for bedload measurements are Bewley Creek Bridge on the Tillamook River (RKM 11.5), Long Prairie Road Bridge on the Trask River (RKM 11.6), Sollie Smith and Kansas Creek Road Bridges on the Wilson River (RKM 6.3 and approximately 7.8 km above the study area, respectively), Curl Road Bridge on the Kilchis River (RKM 4.2), Moss Creek Road Bridge on the Miami River (RKM 2.7), and Miami Foley Road Bridge on the Nehalem River (RKM 22.4). Ideally, such measurements would be collected at a site of continuous

streamflow measurement, such as the USGS gaging stations on the Trask (Long Prairie Road Bridge, RKM 11.6) and Wilson (Sollie Smith Bridge provided a streamflow recorder was added to the station, RKM 6.3) Rivers and the OWRD streamflow gaging station on the Miami River (Moss Creek Road Bridge, RKM 2.7). Bedload measurements on the Wilson and Nehalem Rivers would be more difficult, where cableways are employed for most streamflow measurements at the existing gages. The nearest bridge to the Wilson River gage is the tall and high traffic load Mills Bridge (RKM 14.1), whereas the nearest bridge to the Nehalem gage is Cook Creek Bridge (about 2.6 km upstream of gage) where the channel flows predominately on bedrock.

7. Estimate sediment flux based on mapped changes in bar area over specific temporal intervals following the morphological approach applied on the Chetco River (Wallick and others, 2010). Ideally, this approach would use LiDAR or other high-resolution topographic data from two periods to calculate volumetric change in sediment storage. This method, however, can also be implemented using a single LiDAR survey and sequential aerial photographs. This approach is best applied in reaches where bed-material transport is likely transport-limited. Despite the inherent uncertainties associated with this type of analysis (Wallick and others, 2010), such data and analyses can also serve as a basis for efficient monitoring of long-term changes in channel and floodplain conditions. This approach would be most feasible for the Wilson and Miami fluvial reaches as well as all tidal reaches.

8. Apply empirical GIS-based sediment yield analyses, factoring in sediment production, delivery to channels, and in-

channel attrition. This approach would be similar to that applied for the Umpqua River basin (Wallick and others, 2011). Although this type of analysis could focus on specific reaches regardless of transport or sediment supply limited conditions, it would require analysis of their entire contributing area. Such analyses would be bolstered by assessments of bed-material composition, thereby confirming the source areas of bed-material delivered to these rivers.

9. Review pre- and post-gravel-mining surveys. The review conducted for this study indicates that these surveys can provide limited quantitative information on bed-material deposition (table 12). Nevertheless, this information, especially if supplemented by additional records, may be helpful for constraining estimated sediment budgets (Wallick and others, 2011).

10. Coordinate bed-material analyses with ongoing suspended sediment and turbidity data collection on the Wilson and Trask Rivers by the USGS Oregon Water Science Center to determine rates of sediment inputs to the Tillamook Bay.

Detailed Channel Morphology Assessment

In this study, we delineated bar surfaces from aerial and orthophotographs spanning 1939 to 2009 for the six study areas and found that unit bar area declined in all fluvial reaches (table 17). These datasets and measurements could serve as the starting point for more detailed and comprehensive analyses of sediment transport processes and morphological trends in these six basins. An approach that would meet these objectives would include the following elements:

1. Detailed mapping of land cover for multiple periods, including delineation of the active floodplain, active channel width, and floodplain features based on vegetation density. Examining changes in bare and vegetated surfaces for smaller time steps would support a quantitative assessment of channel geometry, migration rates, erosion and deposition processes, and vegetation establishment. With this information, we could better describe bed-material processes and associated interactions with factors like floods and vegetation, and identify key temporal changes in bar area patterns. Many aerial photographs are available for such as effort, including those taken in 1951, 1954, 1965, 1970, 1989, 1994, 2000, and 2011 for the Tillamook Bay study areas (table 9) and in 1951, 1954–55, 1960, 1965, 1970, 1980, 1989, 1994, 2000, 2001, and 2011 for the Nehalem study area (table 10). This effort would also support a reliable and consistent assessment of channel changes over time.

2. Detailed mapping of channel features before and after major floods to assess the response of the channel to different magnitude floods and, ultimately, sediment flux and channel evolution in the six study areas. Possible floods for focusing this effort include at least one on the Trask River (1996; fig. 5A), several on the Wilson River (such as those in 1964, 1972, 1975, 1977, 1989, 1996, 1998, 2006, and 2007; fig. 5B), several on the Miami River (such as those in 1977, 1983, 1986, 1990, 1994, and 2008; fig. 5C), and several on the Nehalem River (such as those in 1949, 1955, 1964, 1966, 1972, 1974, 1990, 1996, 2006, and 2007; fig. 5D).

3. Assessment of the potential relationship between channel migration, large wood, vegetation establishment, and peak flows. In the Umpqua and Chetco River basins, historical declines in bar area are associated with long-term decreases in flood magnitude (Wallick and others 2010, 2011). Based on the long-term streamflow records on the Wilson and

Nehalem Rivers, however, decreases in bar area do not appear to be correlated with a reduction in peak flows (fig. 5B, D). Other possible factors, in addition to those likely related to local fire history, include changes in the type and volume of instream large wood as well as changes in riparian vegetation conditions. Further characterization of hydrology patterns in the Tillamook Bay subbasins and Nehalem River basin and possible linkages with climate factors related to flood peaks, such as the Pacific Decadal Oscillation, could support inferences of likely future changes in vegetation establishment and channel planform and profile.

4. Investigation of bed-elevation changes near gages and bridges. Modern channel surveys could be compared to historical surveys, such as cross sections at USGS gages and cableways, flood-study surveys, and more detailed analyses of repeat cross sections near bridges to more systematically document spatial and temporal changes in bed elevation. For instance, USGS collects cross sections at gaging stations near Long Prairie Road and Sollie Smith Bridges on the Trask and Wilson River, respectively, which may be useful for assessing channel changes at the Long Prairie Road Bridge (currently lacks cross section data; table 14) and Sollie Smith Bridge (table 14; fig. 19b). Following Turnipseed and Sauer (2010), more detailed specific gage analyses can also be completed using USGS stage and streamflow data collected from 1984 to 2012. These analyses would be useful for assessing changes in the stage-streamflow relation and channel morphology near USGS gages with a greater temporal frequency (such as a seasonal basis or intermediately following flood events).

5. Investigations of bed-elevation changes using bathymetry. Bathymetric surveys of the tidal and fluvial reaches would be useful for assessing vertical channel stability and assessing possible changes in bed elevation related to sediment deposition and reductions in flood capacity. Such analyses would complement detailed mapping of channel and floodplain characteristics to provide insights on factors controlling observed changes. Properly conducted and archived, such modern surveys could also serve as a basis for long-term monitoring of vertical channel conditions.

Legacy and Ongoing Effects of Land Use Activities

Anthropogenic activities such as historical forestry practices (including log drives and splash damming), dredging and wood removal for navigation, and instream gravel mining and natural disturbances influenced by human activities such as fires and mass wasting have likely affected sediment transport and deposition dynamics in the study areas. Quantitatively assessing the past and present effects of these factors on sediment dynamics would be challenging owing to likely interactions among these factors as well as their interactions with background, physical controls on sediment dynamics, such as basin topography, channel slope, geology, and hydrology. Further investigations of fine and coarse sediment inputs associated with land use activities may provide information on the relative fluxes of different clast sizes delivered to the study area and their temporal and spatial variations. An approach for investigating the relative importance of past activities on overall sediment dynamics would be to:

1. Extend streamflow record to 1900 for the long-term Wilson River gage and other gages of interest (table 3). This information in combination with bedload transport equations may be useful for assessing flow and bed-material transport

prior to the Tillamook Burn fires and the relations between those fires and antecedent streamflows and the large area of bars mapped in 1939.

2. Assess land use and hydrologic conditions and relate to transport capacity and sediment supply in key basins of interest.

3. Determine the distribution of areas of active gravel transport and deposition and analyze temporal trends in channel and floodplain morphology with respect to land use disturbances.

4. Assess changes in bar area and channel position near historical instream gravel mining sites with a detailed geomorphic analysis.

Priority Reaches for Future Analysis

In this study, we mapped and assessed overall patterns in bar and channel conditions for a total of 65 km in the six study basins. Addressing all the data gaps and analyses outlined above is probably not practical in the near future for all six study areas. Specific rivers, however, might particularly warrant additional analysis because of overall geomorphic conditions and ongoing and possible future disturbance activities.

Fluvial study areas on the Wilson, Kilchis, Miami, and Nehalem Rivers may be logical analysis areas thereby providing detailed data on coarse sediment fluxes and channel dynamics for these ecologically important river segments. Additionally, these fluvial study areas have the highest reported deposition and mining volumes for bed material. These study areas are likely responsive to upstream basin disturbances as a result of their relatively low gradients. Although the 1939 photographs do not extend above approximately RKM 7.8 on the Kilchis River, extending the study area further upstream by approximately 1 km would be useful for assessing changes near the historically mined Bruck and Bay City Bars (table 13). Likewise, future efforts may consider extending the Wilson River study

area upstream to include the area near Sylvan Creek.

The tidally affected portions of the study areas may also be logical reaches for in-depth analysis. In these reaches, the issues would pertain more to fine sediment deposition and transport (and associated channel and riparian conditions and processes) rather than coarse bed material. Since the legacy of landuse effects in these basins have probably significantly affected fine sediment transport and deposition, the transport-limited character of these reaches makes them responsive to perturbations in sediment loads and river flow. Additionally, local flood issues and the ecological importance of these tidal reaches may justify additional investigation.

Acknowledgments

The framework for this study was established with the guidance of Judy Linton of the Portland District of the U.S. Army Corps of Engineers. The study was administered by Judy Linton as well as by Bill Ryan, Pamela Konstant, and Cynthia Wickman of the Oregon Department of State Lands. Dennis Johnson of Coastwide Ready-Mix and Brian Mohler of Mohler Sand and Gravel, LLC provided copies of site surveys. These gravel mining operators and other landowners graciously granted access to instream gravel mining sites. Christy Leas, Oregon Department of State Lands, coordinated access to the gravel mining permits files housed at the Oregon Department of State Lands. The University of Oregon Map Library provided a summary of aerial photographs available for the study areas. Paul Pedone, National Resources Conservation Service, assisted with data collection and provided a copy of Stinson and Stinson (1998). Richard Marvin from Oregon Water Resources Department provided data for the Miami gaging station. Frank Reckendorf, Reckendorf and Associates, provided copies of several reports on gravel mining in the Tillamook Bay subbasins.

References Cited

Amaranthus, M.P., Rice, R.M., Barr, N.R., and Ziemer, R.R., 1985, Logging and forest roads related to increased debris slides in southwestern Oregon: Journal of Forestry, v. 83, p. 229–233.

Andrews, Alicia and Kutara, Kristin, 2005, Oregon's timber harvests—1849–2004: Oregon Department of Forestry, 154 p., accessed August 21, 2012, at *http://www.oregon.gov/ODF/STATE_FOREST S/FRP/docs/OregonsTimberHarvests.pdf?ga=t*
.

Atwood, Kay, 2008, Chaining Oregon: Surveying the public lands of the Pacific Northwest, 1851–1855: Granville, Ohio, The McDonald and Woodward Publishing Company, 267 p.

Bancroft, H.H., 1884, The works of Hubert Howe Bancroft, Volume XXVIII, History of the Northwest Coast, Vol II: San Francisco, California, A.L. Bancroft & Company Publishers, 768 p.

Benner, P.A. and Sedell, J.R., 1987, Chronic reduction of large woody debris on beaches at Oregon river mouths, *in* Mutz, K.M., and Lee, L.C., eds, Proceedings of the Society of Wetland Scientists' Eighth Annual Meeting, May 26–29, 1987: p. 335–341.

Benner, Patricia, 1991, Historical reconstruction of the Coquille River and surrounding landscape, *in* Oregon Department of Environmental Quality, ed., Action Plan for Oregon Coastal Watersheds, Estuary, and Ocean Waters 1988–1991: Portland, Oregon, p. 83.

Benoit, C., 1978, Hydrologic Analysis for Forested Lands Tillamook Basin, Tillamook County, Oregon: U.S. Department of Agriculture, Forest Service, 262 p.

Beschta, R.L., 1978, Long-term patterns of sediment production following road construction and logging in the Oregon Coast Range: Water Resources Research, v. 14, no. 6, p. 1011–1016.

Buffington, J.M. and Montgomery, D.R., 1999, Effects of sediment supply on surface textures of gravel-bed rivers: Water Resources Research, v. 35, no. 11, p. 3523–3530.

Bunte, Kristin and Abt, S.R., 2001, Sampling surface and subsurface particle-size distributions in wadeable gravel- and cobble-bed streams for analyses in sediment transport, hydraulics, and streambed monitoring: U.S. Department of Agriculture Forest Service, Rocky Mountain Research Station, General Technical Report RMRS-GTR-74, 428 p.

Burns, S.F., 1998, Landslide Hazards in Oregon, *in* Burns, S.F., ed., Environmental, Groundwater and Engineering Geology, Applications from Oregon: Belmont, California, Star Publishing Company, p. 303–315.

Christy, J.A., 2004, Estimated loss of salt marsh and freshwater wetlands within the Oregon coastal coho ESU: Corvallis, Oregon, Oregon Natural Heritage Information Center, Oregon State University, 7 p., accessed August 20, 2012, at *http://demeterdesign.net/Christy2004_OR%20 coastal%20wetland%20losses2.pdf*

City of Tillamook, 2011, Tillamook City Water Division: accessed August 20, 2012, at *http://www.tillamookor.gov/departments/water .html.*

Cooper, R.M. , 2005, Estimation of peak discharges for rural, unregulated streams in Western Oregon: U.S. Geological Survey Scientific Investigations Report 2005–5116, 134 p.

Coulton, K.G., Williams, P.B., and Benner, P.A., 1996, An environmental history of the Tillamook Bay estuary and watershed: Prepared for the Tillamook Bay National Estuary Project, San Francisco, CA and Corvallis, OR, 58 p., accessed August 20, 2012, at *http://www.tbnep.org/images/stories/document*

s/resource_center_docs/watershed_area_info/
Enivronmental%20History%20Text.pdf.

Dietrich, W.E., Kirchner, J.W., Ikeda, H., and
Iseya, F., 1989, Sediment supply and the
development of the coarse surface layer in
gravel-bedded rivers: Nature, v. 340, no. 6230,
p. 215–217.

Duck Creek Associates, Inc. and associated
consultants, 2008, Wilson River watershed
analysis: Prepared for the Oregon Department
of Forestry, Northwest Oregon Area, Corvallis,
Oregon, 298 p.

Farnell, J.E., 1980, Tillamook Bay rivers
navigability study: Salem, Oregon, Division of
State Lands, 35 p.

Farnell, J.E., 1981, Nehalem, Necanicum,
Nestucca navigability studies: Salem, Oregon,
Division of State Lands, 13 p.

Ferdun, G.S., 2010, Historical time line *in* The
Nehalem estuary and adjacent wetlands,
*http://lnwc.nehalem.org/Estuary/3Historical.p
df*.

Follansbee, Bruce and Stark, Ann, eds., 1998a,
Kilchis watershed analysis: Garibaldi, Oregon,
Tillamook Bay National Estuary Project,
accessed August 20, 2012, at
*http://www.tbnep.org/images/stories/document
s/resource_center_docs/watershed_area_info/
Kilchis/Kilchis-full.zip*.

Follansbee, Bruce and Stark, Ann, 1998b, Trask
watershed analysis: Garibaldi, Oregon,
Tillamook Bay National Estuary Project,
accessed August 20, 2012, at
*http://www.tbnep.org/images/stories/document
s/resource_center_docs/watershed_area_info/
Trask/Trask%20Watershed%20Assessment%2
0for%20web.pdf*.

General Land Office, 1856–57, Original
Township Survey Field Notes for Townships 1
North, and 1 and 2 South, Ranges 9 and 10
West: Portland, Oregon, Bureau of Land
Management.

Gilkey, C.D., 1974, Review report on Nehalem
River and Tillamook Bay stream basins,

Oregon: Portland, Oregon, U.S. Army Corps
of Engineers.

Gurnell, A.M., 1997, Channel change on the
River Dee meanders, 1946–1992, from the
analysis of air photographs: Regulated
Rivers—Research and Management, v. 13, p.
13–26.

Harden, D. R., Colman, S. M., and Nolan, K. M.,
eds., 1995, Mass movement in the Redwood
Creek basin, northwestern California:U.S.
Geological Survey Professional Paper 1454,
G1–G11, available at
http://pubs.er.usgs.gov/publication/pp1454.

Holman, F.V., 1910, Oregon counties—Their
creation and the origins of their names: The
Quarterly of the Oregon Historical Society, v.
11, no. 1, p. 1–81.

Hughes, M.L., McDowell, P.F., and Marcus,
W.A., 2006, Accuracy assessment of
georectified aerial photographs—Implications
for measuring lateral channel movement in
GIS: Geomorphology, v. 74, p. 1–16.

Jenkins, Jeff, Gill, Robert, Reinwald, Todd, and
Vesely, Dave, 2005, Miami River watershed
assessment and analysis of ODF lands:
Beaverton, Oregon, Prepared for the Oregon
Department of Forestry by Atterbury
Consultants, Inc., Upland Environmental, Inc.,
and Pacific Wildlife Research, 151 p.,
accessed August 20, 2012, at
*http://cms.oregon.gov/odf/pages/state_forests/
watershed.aspx#Miami_Watershed_Analysis*.

Johnson, Jill and Maser, Joseph, 1999, Nehalem
River Watershed Assessment: Portland,
Oregon, Prepared by the Environmental
Sciences and Resources Department, Portland
State University for the Upper and Lower
Nehalem River Watershed Councils, accessed
August 20, 2012, at
*http://web.pdx.edu/~maserj/project/project1/1.
htm*.

Jones, K.L., Wallick, J.R., O'Connor, J.E., Keith,
M.K., Mangano, J.F., and Risley, J.C., 2011,
Preliminary assessment of channel stability
and bed-material transport along Hunter Creek,

southwestern Oregon: U.S. Geological Survey Open-File Report 2011–1160, 41 p., available at *http://pubs.usgs.gov/of/2011/1160/.*

Jones, K.L., O'Connor, J.E., Keith, M.K., Mangano, J.F., and Wallick, J.R., 2012a, Preliminary assessment of channel stability and bed-material transport in the Rogue River basin, southwestern Oregon: U.S. Geological Survey Open-File Report 2011–1280, 96 p., available at *http://pubs.usgs.gov/of/2011/1280/.*

Jones, K.L., O'Connor, J.E., Keith, M.K., Mangano, J.F., and Wallick, J.R., 2012b, Preliminary assessment of channel stability and bed-material transport in the Coquille River basin, southwestern Oregon: U.S. Geological Survey Open-File Report 2012–1064, 84 p., available at *http://pubs.usgs.gov/of/2012/1064/.*

Klingeman, P.C., 1973, Indications of streambed degradation in the Willamette Valley: Water Resources Research Institute Report WRRI–21, 99 p.

Komar, P.D., 1997, The Pacific Northwest coast—Living with the shores of Oregon and Washington: Durham, North Carolina, Duke University Press, 195 p.

Komar, P.D., McManus, James, and Styllas, Michael, 2004, Sediment accumulation in Tillamook Bay, Oregon—Natural processes versus human impacts: The Journal of Geology, v. 112, p. 455–469.

Kondolf, G. M., 1994, Geomorphic and environmental effects of instream gravel mining: Landscape and Urban Planning, v. 28, no. 2–3, p. 225–243.

Kondolf, G. M., Smeltzer, Matt, and Kimball, Lisa, 2002, Freshwater gravel mining and dredging issues, Prepared for the Washington Department of Fish and Wildlife, Washington Department of Ecology, and Washington Department of Transportation: Berkeley, California, Center for Environmental Design Research ,122 p., accessed August 21, 2012, at *http://wdfw.wa.gov/publications/00056/.*

Kondolf, G.M., Lisle, T.E., and Wolman, G.M., 2003, Bed sediment measurement, *in* Kondolf, G.M., and Piegay, H., eds., Tools in fluvial geomorphology: Chichester, England, John Wiley and Sons, p. 347–395.

Levesque, P.A., 1980, Principal flood problems of the Tillamook Bay drainage basin, Prepared for the Port of Tillamook Bay: Research Consultant Services, 292 p.

Lisle, T.E., 1995, Particle size variation between bed load and bed material in natural gravel bed channels: Water Resources Research, v. 31, no. 4, p. 1107–1118.

Ma, Lina, Madin, I.P., Olson, K.V., Watzig, R.J., Wells, R.E., Niem, A.R., and Priest, G.R. (compilers), 2009, Oregon geologic data compilation [OGDC], release 5 (statewide), digital data: Accessed August 21, 2012, at *http://www.oregongeology.com/sub/ogdc/.*

Mangano, J.F., O'Connor, J.E., Jones, K.L., and Wallick, J.R., 2011, Abstract—Experimental attrition rates of bed-material sediment from geologic provinces of Western Oregon and their application to regional sediment models, *in* American Geophysical Union, Fall Meeting 2011 program, abstract #EP51A–0826: San Francisco, California,

Miller, R.R., 2010, Is the past present? Historical splash-dam mapping and stream disturbance detection in the Oregon Coastal Province: Corvallis, Oregon, Oregon State University, Master of Science Thesis, 110 p.

Mills, Keith, 1997, Forest roads, drainage, and sediment delivery in the Kilchis River watershed, Tillamook, Oregon, 38 p., accessed August 21, 2012, at *http://www.tbnep.org/images/stories/document s/resource_center_docs/tillamook_bay_river_ mngt/KilchisRoadReport%20for%20web.pdf.*

Morris, W.G., 1934, Forest fires in western Oregon and western Washington: Oregon Historical Quarterly, v. 35, no. 4, p. 313–339.

Mount, Nicholas and Louis, John, 2005, Estimation and propagation of error in the measurement of river channel movement from aerial imagery: Earth Surface Processes and Landforms, v. 30, no. 5, p. 635–643.

O'Connor, J.E., Wallick, J.R., Sobieszczyk, Steve, Cannon, Charles, and Anderson, S.W., 2009, Preliminary assessment of vertical stability and gravel transport along the Umpqua River, Oregon: U.S. Geological Survey Open-File Report 2009–1010, 40 p.

Oregon Coastal Management Program, 2011, Oregon estuarine levees inventory, digital data: Accessed August 21, 2012, at *http://www.oregon.gov/DAS/EISPD/GEO/ index.shtml.*

Oregon Natural Heritage Program, 1999, Oregon land ownership and land stewardship, Oregon Geospatial Enterprise Office, digital data: Accessed August 21, 2012, at *http://cms.oregon.gov/DAS/CIO/GEO/docs/me tadata/land_management.htm.*

Oregon State Department of Forestry, 1983, From Tillamook Burn to Tillamook State Forest: Salem, Oregon, 16 p.

Oregon Water Resources Department, 2011, Mean daily flow and peak flow data for the Miami Station 14301300: Accessed August 21, 2012, at *http://apps.wrd.state.or.us/apps/sw/hydro_nea r_real_time/.*

Pearson, M.L., 2002, Fluvial geomorphic analysis of the Tillamook Bay Basin Rivers, Prepared for the U.S. Army Corps of Engineers, Portland District: Monmouth, Oregon, 71 p., accessed August 21, 2012, at *http://www.tbnep.org/images/stories/document s/resource_center_docs/tillamook_bay_river_ mngt/Fluvial%20Geomorphology%20of%20T B%20Rivers%20-%20Bohica.pdf.*

Phelps, J.D., 2011, The geomorphic legacy of splash dams in the Southern Oregon Coast Range: Eugene, Oregon, University of Oregon, Master of Science Theses, 38 p.

Phillip Williams & Associates, Ltd., Clearwater Biostudies, Inc., Michael P. Williams Consulting, GeoEngineers, Green Point Consulting with assistance from Antonius

Laenen and Patrica Benner, 2002, Tillamook Bay integrated river management strategy, Prepared for the U.S. Fish and Wildlife Service, U.S. Environmental Protection Agency, and U.S. Army Corps of Engineers: Accessed August 21, 2012, at *http://yosemite.epa.gov/R10/ecocomm.nsf/web page/Tillamook+Bay+Integrated+River+Man agement+Strategy.*

Preiffer, Tim, D'Agnese, Sue, and Preiffer, Amy, 1998, Wilson River rockslide mile post 31, Highway #6 Wilson River highway, Tillamook County, *in* Burns, S.F., ed., Environmental, groundwater, and engineering geology, Applications from Oregon: Belmont, California, Star Publishing Company, p. 249– 266.

R2 Resource Consultants, Inc., in association with Lee Benda and Associates, Inc., 2005, Upper Nehalem watershed assessment, Part I—Assessment: Accessed August 21, 2012, at, *https://nrimp.dfw.state.or.us/web%20stores/da ta%20libraries/files/OWEB/OWEB_932_2_Up per%20Nehalem%20Watershed%20Assessmen t%20pt1of4.pdf.*

Reckendorf, Frank, 2006, Environmentally sensitive gravel bar scalping, *in* Eighth federal interagency sedimentation conference, Session 4B–3, Las Vegas, Nevada: Available at *http://pubs.usgs.gov/misc/FISC_1947- 2006/pdf/1st-7thFISCs- CD/8thFISC/Session%204B-3_Reckendorf.pdf.*

Reckendorf, Frank, 2008a, Evaluation of the stream corridor management plan for Tillamook County rivers, Prepared for Coast Wide Ready Mix: Salem, Oregon, 26 p.

Reckendorf, Frank, 2008b, Bar scalping of Donaldson, Barker, Dill, Gomes, and Waldron gravel bars in Tillamook County, Prepared for Coast Wide Ready Mix:Salem, Oregon, 77 p.

Snyder, K.U., Sullivan, T.J., Raymond, R.B., Bischoff, J.M., White, Shawn, and Binder, S.K., 2001, Miami River Watershed Assessment, Report prepared by E&S

Environmental Chemistry for the Tillamook County Performance Partnership: Accessed August 21, 2012, at *http://www.tbnep.org/images/stories/documents/resource_center_docs/watershed_area_info/Miami/Miami-full.zip.*

Snyder, K.U., Sullivan, T.J., Moore, D.L., Raymond, R.B., and Gilbert, E.H., 2003, Trask River Watershed Analysis, Report prepared by E&S Environmental Chemistry for the Oregon Department of Forestry and the U.S. Department of Interior, Bureau of Land Management: Accessed August 21, 2012, at *http://www.oregon.gov/ODF/STATE_FORESTS/Trask_River_Watershed_Analysis.shtml.*

Stinson, Randy and Stinson, Sheila, 1998, Effect of gravel bar harvesting, on gravel bar armour layer and substrate material in four watersheds on the north Oregon coast: Tillamook, Oregon, Tillamook County Soil and Water Conservation District in cooperation with U.S. Deparment of Agriculture, Natural Resource Conservation Service, 42 p.

Swanson, F.J. and Dyrness, C.T., 1975, Impact of clear-cutting and road construction on soil erosion by landslides in the western Cascade Range, Oregon: Geology, v. 3, p. 339–396.

Tillamook Bay National Estuary Project, 1998, Tillamook Bay environmental characterization: a scientific and techincal summary, Garibaldi, Oregon, [307 p.], *http://www.tbnep.org/resource-center/tep-reports/watershed-and-area-information,*

Tillamook Bay Taskforce, The Oregon State Water Resources Department, and U.S. Department of Agriculture Soil Conservation Service, 1978, Tillamook Bay Drainage Basin erosion and sediment study: Portland, Oregon, U.S. Department of Agriculture Soil Conservation Service, [variously paged].

Tillamook County, 2000, Stream corridor management plan for the lower Trask, Wilson, Kilchis, Miami and Nestucca Rivers, Tillamook, Oregon, 36 p., *http://www.co.tillamook.or.us/gov/Bocc/STRE AM%20CORRIDOR%20MANAGEMENT%20PLAN.htm*

Tillamook County, 2010, Community wildfire protection plan, Tillamook, Oregon, 42 p.

Turnipseed, D.P. and Sauer, V.B., 2010, Discharge measurements at gaging stations: U.S. Geological Survey Techniques and Methods book 3, chapter A8, 87 p., available at *http://pubs.usgs.gov/tm/tm3–a8/.*

U.S. Army Corps of Engineers, 1895, Annual report of the Chief of Engineers, U.S. Army, to the Secretary of War for the year, Part V: Washington, D.C., General Publishing Office, 3615 p.

U.S. Army Corps of Engineers, 1896, Annual report of the Chief of Enginners, United States Army, to the Secretary of War for the Year 1896: Part V: Government Printing Office, Washington DC, 3401 p., accessed August 21, 2012, at *http://books.google.com/books?id=bZNTAAAA YAAJ.*

U.S. Army Corps of Engineers, 1897, Report of the Chief of Engineers, U.S. Army, to the War Department, Part IV: Washington, D.C., General Publishing Office, 3503 p.

U.S. Army Corps of Engineers, 1975, Final environmental impact statement, operation and maintenance of jetties and dredging projects in Tillamook Estuary, Oregon: Portland, Oregon, [variously paged].

U.S. Army Corps of Engineers, Portland District, 2005, Tillamook Bay and Estuary, Oregon, General Investigation Feasibility report: Portland, Oregon, 45 p., accessed August 21, 2012, at *http://www.tbnep.org/images/stories/documents/resource_center_docs/tillamook_bay_river_mngt/TillamookFeasibilityStudy.pdf.*

U.S. Congress, 1889, The executive documents of the House of Representatives for the first session of the Fiftieth Congress, 1887–88: U.S. Government Printing Office, Washington D.C., accessed August 21, 2012, at *http://books.google.com/books?id=0UdHAQA AIAAJ.*

U.S. Congress, 1890, The executive documents of the House of Representatives for the first session of the Fifty-first Congress, 1889–90: U.S. Government Printing Office Washington DC, accessed August 21, 2012, at *http://books.google.com/books?id=iXc3AQAAI AAJ.*

U.S. Geological Survey, 2011, Water-data reports for stations 14301500, 14302480, and 14301000: Available at *http://wdr.water.usgs.gov/*

Walker, G.W., MacLeod, N.S., 1991, Geologic map of Oregon: U.S. Geological Survey, scale 1:500,000, accessed August 21, 2012, at *http://geopubs.wr.usgs.gov/docs/geologic/or/o regon.html.*

Wallick, J.R., Anderson, S.W., Cannon, Charles, and O'Connor, J.E., 2010, Channel change and bed-material transport in the lower Chetco River, Oregon: U.S. Geological Survey Scientific Investigations Report 2010–5065, 68 p., available at *http://pubs.usgs.gov/sir/2010/5065/.*

Wallick, J.R. and O'Connor, J.E., 2011, Estimation of bed-material transport in the lower Chetco River, Oregon, water years 2009–2010: U.S. Geological Survey Open-File Report 2011–1123, 12 p., available at *http://pubs.usgs.gov/of/2011/1123/*

Wallick, J.R., O'Connor, J.E., Anderson, Scott, Keith, Mackenzie, Cannon, Charles, and Risley, J.C., 2011, Channel change and bed-material transport in the Umpqua River basin, Oregon: U.S. Geological Survey Scientific Investigations Report 2011–5041, 112 p., available at *http://pubs.usgs.gov/sir/2011/5041/*

Walter, Cara and Tullos, D.D., 2009, Downstream channel changes after a small dam removal—Using aerial photos and measurement error for context; Calapooia River, Oregon: River Research and Applications, v. 26, no. 10, p. 1220–1245.

Wells, Gail, 1999, The Tillamook: a created forest comes of age: Corvallis, Oregon, Oregon State University Press, 184 p.

Wilcock, P.R., Pitlick, John, and Cui, Y.T., 2009, Sediment transport primer—Estimating bed-material transport in gravel-bed rivers: U.S. Deparment of Agriculture Forest Service, Rocky Mountain Research Station, General Technical Report RMRS–GTR–226, Fort Collins, Colorado, 78 p.

Willingham, W.F., 1983, Army Engineers and the development of Oregon: a history of the Portland District U.S. Army Corps of Engineers: U.S. Army Corps of Engineers, Portland, Oregon, UN 24, 258 p., accessed August 21, 2012, at *http://140.194.76.129/publications/misc/un24/t oc.htm.*